Christopher Milne

Christopher Robin Milne was the son of author A. A. (Alan Alexander) Milne and Dorothy de Selincourt. As a young child, he was the basis of the character Christopher Robin in his father's Winnie-the-Pooh stories and in two books of poems.

Christopher Milne was a shy boy and did not like the attention that he received from the public because of his father's success with the Pooh books. In 1974, Milne decided to publish the first of three autobiographical books. *The Enchanted Places* gave an account of his childhood and of the problems that he had encountered because of the Pooh books.

Christopher Milne

THE PATH
THROUGH
THE TREES

BELL

First published in 1979 by Methuen

This edition published 2014 by Bello
an imprint of Pan Macmillan, a division of Macmillan Publishers Limited
Pan Macmillan, 20 New Wharf Road, London N1 9RR
Basingstoke and Oxford
Associated companies throughout the world

www.panmacmillan.co.uk/bello

ISBN 978-1-4472-6986-1 EPUB
ISBN 978-1-4472-7133-8 HB
ISBN 978-1-4472-6985-4 PB

Copyright © Christopher Milne, 1979

Visit www.panmacmillan.com to read more about all our books
and to buy them. You will also find features, author interviews and
news of any author events, and you can sign up for e-newsletters
so that you're always first to hear about our new releases.

To Lesley and Clare and to the memory of my Father

Acknowledgements

Acknowledgements and thanks are due to the estate of Robert Frost for permission to reproduce *The Road Not Taken* from *The Poetry of Robert Frost*, edited by Edward Connery Lathem and published by Jonathan Cape Ltd.

Preface

In my first book, *The Enchanted Places*, I was writing about my childhood, saying what I needed to say about Pooh and Christopher Robin. The present book is in a way a sequel, starting where the other left off. But, rather more than that, it is a complement. It is about the non-Pooh part of my life. It is an escape from Christopher Robin.

It is the story of a young man who left home, and in one of his pockets he had a handful of talents given him by his mother and in the other a handful given him by his father. What did he do with them? Where did they take him?

If you can divide humanity into two groups, those who are better with their head than their hands and those who are better with their hands than their head, then my father was in the first and my mother in the second. I, inheriting from both of them, have in consequence spent much of my time hopping from the one group to the other, uncertain which was the more likely to lead me to fame and fortune. This is not the best way of achieving either. Nor does it produce an autobiography in which each chapter follows the last in a steady progression towards an ultimate goal

The result, therefore, is a disjointed story – but a happy life.

The Road Not Taken

Two roads diverged in a yellow wood,
And sorry I could not travel both
And be one traveler, long I stood
And looked down one as far as I could
To where it bent in the undergrowth;

Then took the other, as just as fair.
And having perhaps the better claim.
Because it was grassy and wanted wear;
Though as for that the passing there
Had worn them really about the same.

And both that morning equally lay
In leaves no step had trodden black.
Oh, I kept the first for another day!
Yet knowing how way leads on to way,
I doubted if I should ever come back.

I shall be telling this with a sigh
Somewhere ages and ages hence:
Two roads diverged in a wood, and I –
I took the one less travelled by.
And that has made all the difference.

Robert Frost

Prologue. *The Path Through the Trees*

The road runs up the valley and a little stream keeps it company. It is a narrow road – if two cars meet unexpectedly one will almost certainly have to reverse – and the hills rise steeply on either side. After about a mile there is a gap in the hills on the left and here another valley, another road and another stream join the first. There is a bridge and a giant plane tree and then, twenty yards up this second road, a pink-walled, slate-roofed house. The house is at the foot of a slope, the land rising steeply behind it so that on the ground floor there is a door in the front onto the road and on the first floor there is a door at the back into the garden; and if your shoes are not too muddy this is often the best way from the one to the other.

At the back the ground goes on rising until it reaches the top. The top of what? Not really the top of the garden because it is no longer garden up there. Not the top of the orchard, because the apple trees are lower down. The top of the estate? The top of the wood? The top of the copse? The top of the wilderness? None of these sounds quite right; so we just call it 'the Top', because that's what it feels like when you reach it. But it isn't really even that, as you discover to your surprise if you cross the road and climb the hill on the other side. From here you can see that our Top is only about a third of the way up. You can also see why there are two quite separate ways there; for it lies at the junction of two slopes. There is the slope that faces the first valley. This is a gradual one and the path on this side climbs between fruit trees and hazels, through daffodils, primroses, bluebells, campions and knee-high grass according to season. The other slope faces the second valley and is steeper and rockier. Here the path climbs in a succession of steps and terraces, between oaks and blackthorns, through bracken and bramble.

All told it is a tiny area, no more than a quarter of an acre, but as you do the round, going up one path and down the other, pausing here and there (if you are unaccustomed to Devon hills) and spending a moment or two on each of the seats you find on the way, you will notice that at each point the view of your surrounding world is different. At one point you look down the first valley, at another you look up it, at a third you look across it, while at a fourth you look across the second valley. Nowhere can you see more than half a mile, and in places scarcely a hundred yards. It is a small world. But with such variety does one need a larger one? I sometimes wonder about this. What is the advantage of size, of distance? Does the astronomer with his telescope see more than the biologist with his microscope? Does the man who travels see more than the man who stays at home? Is the distant view of a bank of primroses more beautiful than a single primrose held in the hand? I don't think so. To the eye a beautiful view is no more than a pattern of light and shade, of this colour and that. Distance and closeness are calculated by the brain, then judged by the heart. Each heart has its own preference and mine has always been for the small and near, with the large and far-away providing the contrast.

So I live at the bottom of a valley. I have a small bookshop in a small town; and I seldom venture far afield.

There is a level terrace just below the Top and here one day I am going to build a hut. Clare and I have already been to the sawmills to buy some of the wood, she in her wheelchair watching, while I picked out the 3 by 3 oak that I will need for the frame. And we have been up to the site to do some preliminary levelling – clearing away brambles and bracken and tidying up the rock face at the back. That was as far as we got last spring, and now it is summer and too hot for that sort of work, and besides there are too many flies. So we'll wait until the cool of autumn and then hope to finish it so that on winter afternoons we can go there and sit there protected from wind and rain and for an hour or so I can dream that I am Thoreau at Walden.

While I was clearing away loose stones from the rock I came upon several little caches of empty hazelnut shells – the larders of a bank vole. And sometimes under a stone I found a slow worm and picked it up and let it twine itself around my fingers and then around Clare's. When I move in the bank voles and slow-worms will have to move out. This is always the way of it. But they needn't move far and many other creatures will not need to move at all.

Willow warbler, chiff-chaff and blackcap will still come in the spring to sing to me. Longhorn moths will still be there in their scores to dance over the bracken on sunny summer mornings; and dor beetles will make aeroplane noises on summer nights. Up there I shall be one of many. For our different reasons we have all chosen this particular hillside. Some of us live here all the year round; others pay annual visits; others come one year but not the next. Why for instance are there so many common blue butterflies here this summer? I have left a patch of grass unscythed for them. It is only a dozen paces across and I have counted up to fifteen resting on the grass stems, and there are seldom fewer than six. Have they come here from further afield because my grass is best? Or was it because some years ago their food plant, birdsfoot trefoil, suddenly blazed into flower below Clare's swing? Was it the trefoil that brought the blues? And what, then, brought the trefoil?

It is as if a multitude of invisible lines all converge on my hillside, and along these lines have come the creatures who now live here. There are the annual lines that bring the migrant birds, short in time but long in distance. Then there are the lines that stretch back through generations and that have brought the residents; the buzzards that circle overhead, the voles, the slow-worms, the blues, the trefoil, the dor beetles. And among all these converging lines is my own. Was my coming as natural and inevitable as theirs? Could a scientist explain it as confidently as he explains the return of the swallow? My line twists and turns, sets off in one direction then seems to change its mind. And along its course are many points where the way appears to diverge, many points where I might have chosen differently and gone somewhere else. Or was the choice only illusory?

> Two roads diverged in a yellow wood,
> And sorry I could not travel both
> And be one traveler, long I stood
> And looked down one as far as I could
> To where it bent in the undergrowth;
> Then took the other. . . .

But was there really a choice even then, even for Robert Frost walking through a Vermont wood? He thought there was. The two roads were so alike, it was just that one of them seemed a little grassier, a little less worn. That was the road he took. But would he have been Robert Frost if he had taken the other?

> Two roads diverged in a wood, and I –
> I took the one less traveled by,
> And that has made all the difference.

This then is the story of the road I took on my journey from Cotchford Farm in Sussex to my hillside at Embridge. When one is a child one has little say in the matter: one's parents decide. Mine chose Cotchford and they chose the various schools I was sent to as I grew up. It seems appropriate, therefore, to begin my story at the point in time when the choice stopped being theirs and became mine. And if I were asked to pick on an actual date when this happened, as good a one as any – and with the advantage that it is also a memorable one – would be September 3rd, 1939.

PART ONE

The Road to War

1. *The Distant War*

I was just nineteen. I had left Stowe and was about to go to Cambridge. My father and I had been spending the last fortnight of August on Dartmoor, near the village of Harford on the Erme. But while we were watching buzzards circling in the blue sky, elsewhere the clouds had been gathering, and in the end the news had brought us hurrying home. On September 1st Germany had invaded Poland. It was now September 3rd and we were awaiting – indeed all the world was awaiting – Great Britain's reply. He and I, side by side on the sofa in the sitting-room at Cotchford, hunched over the wireless. . . .

Four years earlier my father had published a book called *Peace With Honour*. In it he had written: 'I think that war is the ultimate expression of man's wickedness and man's silliness.' He had now just finished his autobiography. In it he had written: '. . . it makes me almost physically sick to think of that nightmare of mental and moral degradation, war.' He had been a pacifist before 1914; he was a pacifist again from 1919 until 1939. And he was now, it might seem, about to betray the cause of which he was one of the more eloquent champions. He who had written: 'A nation has no honour' was now about to thrill with pride that Britain was doing the honourable thing. He had served with an Infantry Battalion in France in 1916, and it needed little imagination to see me following in his muddy, bloody footprints.

And I? Of course I shared his views on this as I shared his views on almost everything. I was too young ever to have labelled myself a pacifist, but I was certainly pacific enough. My only excursion into militarism had occurred at a Christmas party when I was about seven years old. Luke, who was larger if not older than I, had suddenly and unaccountably announced to those around him: 'I fight with my fists!' Feeling – I don't know why – that this called for some sort of reply from me, I had answered: 'Me, too.' I had approached him, been struck on the nose and been borne off by Nanny in a flood of tears. Since then I had been discreet rather than valorous. I may have spent hours pouring over *The Times' History of the Great War* in the library at my prep school, tingling at the more dramatic pictures, but I kept well clear of the more pugnacious among my schoolfellows, and willingly agreed with anyone who told me that war was a bad thing.

So, for our different reasons, we were both pacifists – and now we were about to renounce our beliefs. Why?

My father gave his reasons in a small book called *War Aims Unlimited*. To put them very briefly, they were that Hitler was different: different from anything he had ever imagined possible; that, terrible though war was, peace under Hitler would have been even more terrible. I am not here going to elaborate on his arguments. Indeed I am doubtful if pacifism versus militarism, either in general or in any particular instance, is a proper subject for argument – any more than one can argue about love. War and love: they have much in common. You can theorize about them, but until you have experienced them you cannot know them, for the emotions that they engender are as complicated and as conflicting, as noble and as ignoble, as any that life has to offer.

So I will merely record that on that September morning he and I felt a flood of relief, a thrill of pride, when the news came through that we were at war. And no doubt thousands of others, hunched over their wirelesses, felt exactly the same.

There were two immediate questions to be answered. Would I be going up to Cambridge? And would my parents be returning to London? The answer to the first came a few weeks later. Yes. The answer to the second was No. Indeed, not only would they not be going to London, but Londoners would be coming to live with us. Evacuees.

Thus it all began, and at first it seemed very remote. On the BBC and in the papers we learned that England was doing this and Germany was doing that and Russia was doing something else. We read about German tanks and Polish cavalry and the cautious manoeuvrings of the Allied Armies in France. From these generalities a few individuals emerged: Chamberlain with his butterfly collar and umbrella, Lord Halifax with his bowler hat, Hitler with his little moustache, Stalin with his big one. As that great cartoonist, Low, drew them so I saw them and thought of them, puppets dancing on a stage, puppets whose activities did not as yet touch me very closely. If one day I might have to become a soldier, it seemed that I was going to have to be an undergraduate first. But I had no very strong feelings one way or the other.

Cambridge in October, 1939. The war had been on for a month; yet although it was front page news in the papers, it had already – with so many other, more exciting things clamouring for my attention – receded to the back pages of my thoughts. As a Trinity scholar I lived in college – in P.1. Whewell's Court, to be precise – and there I found that I had been provided with a sitting-room and a bedroom together with the larger and more essential items of furniture. The smaller items I had to provide myself. I made a list. Table lamp, some pictures, saucepan, kettle, china, cutlery . . . and at the bottom I added cigarette box and ash tray. For I was now grown up.

There are three small things that distinguish the grown up from the boy: he can drive, he can drink and he can smoke. Admittedly these were skills boasted of by many while still at school, and certainly with me nothing had been expressly forbidden. It was just that there had been no encouragement either; and when it came to growing up, encouragement was what I needed. My father drove, safely, unenthusiastically and in total ignorance of what went on under the bonnet. When on one occasion my mother asked if I, sitting next to him, was ever allowed to change gear, he said, 'No' – and the subject was dropped. But he sometimes let me hold the steering wheel while he lit his pipe.

My father drank, in moderation and without much discrimination. He liked a glass of cherry brandy before lunch and a cocktail before dinner, and he celebrated special occasions with a bottle of hock. But none of these were the drinks of undergraduates in 1939. If we drank at all we drank beer. My father did not drink beer. He said he didn't like the taste, and I was prepared to accept that I wouldn't like the taste either. So I stuck to bottled cider. This left smoking.

My father smoked a pipe. In fact he was seldom without a pipe in his mouth. I remember on one occasion he and I went for a swim together while on one of our Dorset holidays. We had just dressed and were preparing to spend an hour or so reclining on the beach, idly throwing stones into the water, when he felt in his pocket. 'My God!' he cried. 'I've left my pipe behind. Quick. We must go home *at once.*' And he set off, *running. . . .*

I had never smoked. So now was the moment to make the experiment. Pipe or cigarette? The trouble with a pipe was that you had to start by buying one, and when you went into a shop it would be obvious to everybody that it was your first pipe you were buying. I doubted, too, if I could ever light it in public without everybody noticing how badly I was doing it. Cigarettes were easier. Provided I said, 'Capstan, please,' with sufficient confidence, no one would know that it was the first packet I had ever bought. I said, 'Capstan, please,' and bore my treasure home. . . . In all I suppose I smoked about six cigarettes, and a friend or two helped me with the rest. That was the end of the experiment and I've never smoked since.

Luckily there were plenty of undergraduates in those days who neither smoked nor drank nor drove a car: so it didn't matter. Instead we rode bicycles and discussed politics and both of these I enjoyed. My political life started when a smallish, darkish, spectacled and rather spotty man came into my room, introduced himself and asked if I would like to join the Cambridge University Socialist Club. Was I a Socialist, he asked. 'No,' I said. Did I know what Socialism was about? Well, not really. 'Then join the Socialist Club and find out!' he said cheerfully. So I did. After all there was nothing to lose. It didn't change anything. I could still be a Liberal like my father if I wanted to. So I joined and met other Socialists and learned a lot of things. I learned, for instance, that the war in which we were engaged was an 'Imperialist' war. 'But we're not fighting to enlarge our Empire,' I said. No, but we were fighting to maintain it. 'No we're not. We're fighting for our freedom against Nazi aggression.' 'We are an Imperialist Power,' they replied, 'and therefore this is an Imperialist War.' I was not convinced, but I continued to listen and to learn, to argue and often to disagree. Stalin and Russia were good, they said. England and Chamberlain, bad. But I didn't think it particularly good when Russia invaded Finland, and I found their explanations far from convincing.

It was, however, their attitude to India that finally disillusioned me with the Socialist Club. We were sitting round a gas fire in somebody's room drinking coffee, about eight of us, planning our next campaign. 'We must put India over *big*,' said one of us; and the moment he said it I realized two things. First, that I was not the sort of person who ever wanted to put anything over 'big'; and secondly, if I had been, India would have been at the bottom of my list, not the top. There was a war on, admittedly not yet a terribly exciting one, but things were happening in Europe that were surely of greater importance. I didn't walk out of the meeting in disgust. I didn't hand in my resignation. I just drifted away and spent my evenings doing other things with other people.

However, it was not to learn about politics that I had gone to Cambridge. I was there as a mathematician, having won a major scholarship to Trinity College the previous year. Perhaps if there had not been quite so many things to distract me, I might have remained a mathematician. Perhaps if I had seen mathematics as leading to some desirable goal I might have remained a mathematician. Perhaps if I had been better taught I might have remained a mathematician. But none of these things happened and so it was at Cambridge that my love of mathematics perished. I left eight months later with a Second Class in the Preliminary to Part Two of the Maths Tripos – and no further interest in the subject. It was a first love that, as so often is the way with first loves, burned fiercely, then died suddenly. But though I lost my ability to solve differential equations, something remained, an attitude to life, a way of thought.

People sometimes confuse mathematics with figures, assuming that a person who likes the one will be good at the other. In my case they have assumed that I would be looking after the bookshop accounts. So I was – but only because I could find no one else to volunteer. And as soon as I was able to, I gave it up. I hated it. I did it abominably. And I detest figures.

I liked them once, of course, because mathematics begins with figures; adding and subtracting, multiplying and dividing. I used to get great pleasure testing my Nanny on the eight-times table. But once you have mastered multiplication you want to get onto something else. You don't want to spend the rest of your life just multiplying things together. It's like asking a mountaineer to spend his life walking round and round the base of a mountain. Mathematics has this in common with mountaineering: the proper direction is upwards. As with mountaineering each step upwards can only be tackled when the previous steps have been achieved, and each step – each traverse, each chimney or whatever it might be – poses its own unique problem, demands its own particular solution and gives, when solved, its own peculiar pleasure. Fractions, decimals, algebra, geometry, trigonometry, calculus, mechanics: these are the steps up the mountain side. How high is one going to get? For me the pinnacle was Projective Geometry. Who today has even *heard* of this branch of mathematics? It came, it flourished for a brief while, and then it died; and I cannot now recall what purpose it served or what problems it solved, just that I loved it for its beauty.

But isn't this enough? Does one ask more of mathematics? Does one demand that it shall serve also some practical purpose? No. Mathematics is like music. Neither needs to be useful. It is enough that each gives delight to those who seek delight from it. And if, quite by chance, a practical man comes along wanting to measure the height of a tree or work out the best way of building a bridge, it is an added bonus, a happy accident, if he finds a theorem or a technique that will help him. So it is no criticism of a branch of mathematics to say that the only problems it seems capable of solving are those of its own creation. It is – to take a familiar example from the nursery slopes – no criticism to say that no one but a fool would attempt to fill a bath by turning on tap A and tap B without first making sure that plug C is firmly in position. The point of the problem is the beauty of its solution.

The first great glory of mathematics, then, is that it is always offering you something new; and its second great glory is that it offers you beauty. It is never enough to solve a problem, to get the right answer. One must find the simplest, neatest, most elegant solution. Elegance: that was a word so often used by one of my maths masters at Stowe. Only the really elegant solution gave any pleasure: this was why I so loved Projective Geometry. Its problems called for no laborious calculations, no pages and pages of figures, merely (if you were clever enough to find them) half a dozen lines of ingenious argument.

Today I am down at the bottom of the mountain again. I can't even remember the binomial theorem. But I have not lost my delight in elegance. Today my problems are more practical – designing a new fitting for the bookshop, for instance. And if months go by and the fitting has still not been made (and if Lesley tells me that it really only needs a couple of nails and a bit of wood: lend her my hammer and she'd do it herself) my answer is that, yes, I agree, but that I cannot do it that way and she must wait a little longer until I have hit on the right way of doing it, the simple, neat and elegant way, the only way that will give lasting pleasure.

'Two roads diverged in a wood . . .' and so they do in the field of mathematics. One road is labelled 'Pure', the other 'Applied'. Applied maths led to such things as engineering, the chance – you might think – of combining the mathematical brain that I had inherited from my father with the practical fingers that I had inherited from my mother. What an obvious road to choose! Pure maths led – if it led anywhere – only to teaching. My Grandfather, despite his shyness, had been a brilliant teacher, but I knew that I could never teach. So surely this was the road to reject. Yet I took it. For

Pure Mathematics lured me with a beauty and elegance that I found totally lacking in Applied Mathematics. Where did it lead? Did it matter? The Piper played and I followed the music. In any case at that particular time all roads led to war.

And then at Cambridge the tune changed, and notes became harsh, the siren song no longer enticed me. Mathematics and music: they have this also in common – each needs skilful interpretation. Music must be well played, mathematics well taught. And just as the great composer is seldom also a great player, so is the great mathematician seldom also a great teacher We took our seats in the lecture hall. Our lecturer swept in, spent forty minutes in private communion with the blackboard, then swept out. Our task was to take notes. It was an exercise in handwriting and nothing more.

So, mathematics having failed me, it was indeed to music that I turned. I hired a wireless and listened to concerts as often as I could. And if today a theme pursues its way through my head and if I can attach a name to it, it will almost certainly be from something I met for the first time in P.1. Whewell's Court.

On May 10th, 1940, Germany invaded the Low Countries, Chamberlain resigned and the Local Defence Volunteers were formed. The war was much closer now. I remember walking down Trinity Street with the captain of the Trinity Cricket Club. He was trying to visualize what he had just read in the papers – dead French troops piled up one on top of the other along the Maginot Line. He was a year older than I, due to enlist very shortly. Was he soon to see dead bodies, piled up? Would he himself end up on one of those piles? The Germans flooded into France. Stukas dive bombed troops and refugees alike. Parachutists floated down from the sky, and Fifth Columnists were on the ground to greet them.

At Cambridge the exams came to an end, the sun shone, and we waited, enjoying to the full our last moments of a world, unreal at any time, but doubly so now. Then, a few days later and a fortnight before the official end of term, we were sent down. Coming back in October? Some were: those in reserved occupations – scientists, engineers. Mathematics had been listed as a semi-reserved occupation, meaning that one was allowed an extra year as a civilian. So – yes – I would be coming back in October.

And so we said our goodbyes and wished each other good luck; and I caught the train to King's Cross and then another to Hartfield and thus back to Cotchford. And with me I brought two very precious, very particular memories.

The first concerns a cricket match.

My father had always hoped that one day I would be a great cricketer, captaining the Stowe Eleven perhaps, or even playing for Cambridge. But at Stowe the tender plant that had been so devotedly nourished hour after hour at the nets during the holidays drooped and faded: I got no further than the Third Eleven. So when I went to Cambridge I might well have given up cricket in disgust. After all there were plenty of other delightful ways of spending a summer afternoon. But I didn't. Some residual keenness made me answer 'Yes' when asked if I played – perhaps because the question was put in January when snow was on the ground and summer was a hundred miles away, or perhaps because I knew my father would have been disappointed if I had said 'No'. So my name was put down, and I duly turned up for net practice.

I must make it clear – before I come on to my particular memory – that a College First Eleven isn't quite the same thing as a Public School First Eleven. The games, which are played against other Colleges, are played in a much more friendly, much more casual manner than were those epic battles with rival schools. It doesn't really matter who wins, and so no one feels that the Great Batsman is letting down the side if he spends his afternoons on the river, preferring to save his energies for more testing bowling. Nevertheless, we fielded a team whose variously coloured blazers told of past glories, and among them was a solitary figure, unblazered, uncapped, modestly clad in a plain white jersey I was invited to play, and among my various innings was one of complete perfection, a late flowering, a final, glorious bloom, before the whole plant withered and died and I gave up cricket altogether. And in this innings, two shots in particular, an off-drive and an on-drive. How trivial it seems written down! How trivial it will seem to most readers! A year at Cambridge and almost all he has to set against his failure as a mathematician is a couple of shots in a cricket match! Quite true. And I will hurry on to my second memory in a moment. But may I just be allowed to say to anyone who understands about these things, that the off-drive was a half volley just outside the off stump and shot to the boundary between mid-off and extra cover. The on-drive came in the same over, a full pitch, quite fast, on the leg stump, and I was only just able to get my weight across in time. And never has a ball hit so gently buried itself in a distant hedge so shortly afterwards.

Onto the second memory: a concert at the Guildhall within a few weeks of the end of term. It was given by the Women's Symphony Orchestra and was the first public concert by a professional orchestra I had ever been to. My seat – I must have booked late or been feeling poor – was at the back of the orchestra, facing the conductor. The programme? Coriolan Overture, memorable chiefly for the conductor's expression so visible to me at each recurrence of the main theme; a Beethoven concerto with Myra Hess at the piano, memorable for the fact that I could hear *her* as well as her piano; and finally, most memorable of all, Beethoven's Eighth Symphony. Today if I hear something new I must listen to it maybe ten times before I can recall any of it, and even then the themes do not always come when they are bidden. Perhaps it is different when you are young. I had never heard the Eighth Symphony before and indeed I have scarcely heard it since; yet in the weeks that followed, as I paced through the Cotchford fields and the German bombers flew overhead on their leisurely way to bomb London, back it all came theme after theme, movement after movement. The music, the Sussex countryside, the German bombers: fitting accompaniment to the arguments and emotions that were turning themselves over and over in my head, and which were awaiting only one tiny incident to crystallize into a decision that I could announce in public.

The incident belongs to the next chapter. The decision can be anticipated in this. 'I'm not going back to Cambridge next year,' I said. 'I want to join the army.'

2. Preparations for War

On May 29th came the evacuation of Dunkirk. On June 14th German troops entered Paris. German bombs were already falling on London. A German invasion across the Channel seemed almost a certainty. So it is not really surprising that I had by this time lost my enthusiasm for Cambridge. Yet, almost inevitable though the decision was, it was not one I could quickly or easily make. It took several days of tramping across fields and through woods to mature, and it needed that final incident to tip the scales. The incident was trivial in the extreme. It was not the destruction of an army, not the corpses that littered the roads of France, but the death in a flying accident of a single airman. Flying Officer E. J. Kain, returning to England on leave, attempted a 'victory roll' before landing – and crashed; and Flying Officer Kain, known to everyone as 'Cobber' Kain, was our first Air Ace. So here was a death that seemed to touch me personally, the death of someone whose photograph I had seen in the papers, someone I felt I almost knew.

It is not abstractions – 'liberty', 'England' – that stir the imagination, but people: not even people in the mass but individuals. It is the drummer boy who leads us into battle. It is to the ensign bearer that we rally. How often in the past, I wonder, has it been the ensign bearer or the drummer boy who has determined the great issues of peace and war?

My father received my announcement as I would have wished. He gave me his fullest support and encouragement both then and in the months that followed. And when I say this I don't just mean that he said, 'Your decision receives my fullest support and encouragement', and then left events to take their course. He never left events to take their course if he could help them on their way; and helping them on their way meant going straight to the top. Sir James Grigg was Under Secretary of State for War. My father wrote him a letter.

We had already decided that I should try to get into the Royal Engineers, and I had joined the Engineers' section of the OTC while at Cambridge. But, even if it had been possible for me to get an immediate commission, it was very firmly my wish now to start in the ranks. My reason for this was simply lack of self-confidence. If I was ever going to be an officer, I needed the assurance that it was because I was a good enough soldier, not because I had been to University.

How did one become a Sapper? That was the question. And you may well think it was not one worth bothering an Under Secretary of State about. Indeed, you might well think that a greater problem might have been how to *avoid* becoming a Sapper. However, this was what I had set my heart on, and we just didn't know whether we could trust the War Office not to post me instead to an Infantry Battalion. In any case there was little enough else that a middle-aged author could do to help win the war, so my father probably welcomed this opportunity to exert himself on behalf of his son.

I can't remember now what was the outcome of his letter. But I do recollect another string he pulled producing a reply from an Engineer Colonel in which he said how much easier it would all have been if I were skilled in some suitable trade. Was I by any chance an amateur bricklayer? And then it was that we suddenly saw that my one great qualification was not mathematics but carpentry. 'So if the Engineers need a keen carpenter,' wrote my father, 'he's your man.' 'And,' he added to me, 'while waiting to see where that gets us, you must jolly well make yourself as expert as you possibly can, so that when Lord Gort wants a bridge over the Rhine, Milne is the Sapper he sends for. I wonder if there is a helpful book we could get. And, going once more to the top, he wrote to Christina Foyle, the bookseller, to find out.

Two books are now sitting on my table beside my typewriter:

large, hefty volumes, both of them. The older, in spite of a new hessian-covered spine, is beginning to look its age, which is seventy. They are both by George Ellis and were published by Batsford. The first, the book Miss Foyle kindly gave me in answer to my father's plea, is called *Modern Practical Carpentry*; the second, which I ordered from Foyles shortly afterwards, is *Modern Practical Joinery*. And as I turn their pages now, so I can see myself turning their pages thirty-six years ago, absorbing every word and every drawing. Did I learn how to bridge the Rhine? Well, I learned that the Mohawk River Railroad Bridge was a fine example of the arch-rib, trussed-frame type of construction much used in America. And on the opposite page I could study the intricate criss-crossings of stringers, strainers, braces, ribs, struts, posts and beams, all made of wood, of course, and each dovetailed, housed, scarfed, halved, cogged or saddled into its neighbour.

Bridges and roof trusses, coffer dams and caissons, splayed, canted and bevelled work, stairs, windows and doors: page by page I learned the elaborate, painstaking way the Victorian carpenter went about his trade. Utterly fascinated I followed him into every mortice, every rabbet, every quirk, round every bullnose, down every birdsmouth, up every spandrel and every scarf. And I have remained a Victorian carpenter at heart ever since, refusing to equip myself with power tools, despising butt joints and skew nails when a stopped lap dovetail was the way Mr Ellis did it.

Thus I set about preparing myself for the day when I would be called up. But meanwhile Hartfield itself was threatened.

It is hard to believe now that we were quite seriously expecting the Germans to land on our Sussex coast, for example somewhere around Bishopstone where our friends, the Darlingtons lived; that we were quite seriously expecting to have Panzer columns roaring down from the Forest, over the bridge and up the hill past our house, with parachutists landing in our meadow to welcome them. But it had happened in France. So what were we going to do about it? The important thing was to do *something*, no matter how futile; for only by doing something could we keep up our morale during the months of waiting. And no doubt most of what we did *was* futile. No doubt the invader, had he come, would have swept past our concrete pillboxes, our dragon's teeth, our barbed wire road blocks, brushing them aside as if they had never existed.

But something would have survived from all our preparations, something which was not so easily destroyed: our determination to resist. So we each of us did our modest bit. My mother and I went out into the fields, gathered a harvest of nettles, gave them to Mrs Wilson to cook and ate them with resolution if without much pleasure. My father and I collected all our Ordnance Survey maps and buried them in the garden. And I, for my part, found a length of wire, tied one end to a tree by the main road, and coiled the other end ready to tie to a tree on the opposite side just before the first German motorcyclist made his appearance. And then of course I joined the Local Defence Volunteers; and of course I didn't do it the obvious way – walking down to the village and enrolling at the village hall. My father did it for me, if not actually writing to the Commander in Chief Home Forces, most certainly writing a letter to somebody. . . .

I spent about eight months in the LDV (or Home Guard as it was later called) beginning with an arm band and finishing with a full denim uniform. It was not my first introduction to a soldier's life, for my OTC unit at Cambridge had already taught me how to slope a rifle; and the additional military knowledge I acquired defending Hartfield was only slight. However, there were two other things I learned – two new experiences – that were to be of the very greatest value to me.

The first concerned people. The England of those days was much more sharply divided into two classes than it is today. 'Good morning, Smith,' said the one. 'Good morning, Sir,' replied the other. Even when the two met as equals a certain inequality remained. Thus at Lords Cricket Ground they made their appearance through two separate gates, one labelled 'Gentlemen' the other 'Players'. Hitherto I had passed my life in a Gentleman's world, a world in which the Players existed only to serve our needs. Now, for the first time, I was to become a Player myself. In the Scout Hut at Hartfield the author's son would be lying down beside the cowman, he Jack, I Robin. It was a tremendous experience for me, an experience that seemed to be epitomized by my new name. Robin. No one had ever used it by itself before and I scarcely recognized it as mine. It was the name they had chosen for me and they couldn't have chosen better or done a kinder thing. With it they welcomed me across on to their side; and, oh, how gladly I went and how happy and proud I was to be among them, listening to them, learning from them. I learned much that I hadn't known before. I learned, for instance, that not all Players were contented with their lot. 'You see, Robin,' said Cherry, 'it's Them as makes the laws and We as have to obey them. Now we've got only two pleasures in life, you might say: our beer and our baccy. And when They want more money, you'll find it's always beer and baccy that they tax. And it's not fair on the Working Man.' I learned quite a bit from Cherry. He was something of the odd man out, the only one of us who seemed to bear life a grudge, who questioned and argued and said he didn't think it was right. A muscular man, he drove the coal lorry.

My other experience was of the night – dark, outdoor night. Hitherto when it got dark I had come indoors and turned on the light. It was the obvious thing to do. My parents and I would read, perhaps, for a while, sitting before the fire, then, one by one, go upstairs to bed. But now, while others slept, we in the Home Guard were watching, awake and alert, rifle in hand, scanning the skies for enemy invaders. And it was during these vigils that my love of night was born. When not on Home Guard duty I started going for night walks after dinner, up the road or along the lane, and occasionally even through Posingford Wood and so to the Forest. And I was delighted to find it neither frightening nor difficult, even without a torch. It was not that I could see in the dark especially well, but that I seemed able to sense my surroundings and so could move easily and confidently. I still feel this way about night, loving to be out in it, alone, the darker the better. Sight has gone. Sound now becomes all important, sound and a sort of sixth sense. The friendly hoot of an owl. The gentle munching of cows, or perhaps no more than their soft breathing coming from the other side of the hedge. Even the wind has its special night voice, a voice that seems to tell me that it is not just blowing, but up and *doing*, moving things around like a scene shifter on a darkened stage.

Walking at night I like to come upon the lighted windows of a wayside cottage, and to feel that behind the curtains is another world, a world bounded by four walls, a world of sight. I long to peer through the windows, and I know that even the dullest scene within would to me become high drama. I love, especially, returning home, to see the lights of my own house shining. So, I am sure, did the astronauts feel returning from the Moon, travelling through black space towards a waiting world. Soon they will once more be a part of that world. Soon I will be home, part once more of the indoor world of light and warmth. Such is a dark night.

But there is another sort of night, the night of the full Moon, a winter's night, of course, for only in the winter does the Moon ride high. And now you can see. Indeed, you can almost distinguish colours. Trees cast shadows and their leafless branches make intricate patterns on the roadway. There is a special oak near here that I like to visit when the Moon is full. I like to look up and see the pattern of twigs against the sky, and then down to see the pattern repeated at my feet. When the night is dark my world is small, no further than I can reach with my hand, and I prefer to keep to the valley bottom. On moonlit nights I like to climb out of my valley and stand on a hill top and reach up to the stars and feel myself part of a larger world, a world that embraces Moon and stars – and all Creation.

Guard duty over. Back to the Scout Hut. And now for the bread and dripping sandwiches that Mrs Wilson has prepared for me. No. Nothing to report. A quiet night. The Germans hadn't yet launched their assault on the Sussex beaches. ...

So, as that long summer turned to autumn and then towards winter, we waited. We waited for the German army; and we waited (we Milnes) for a certain buff envelope. The German army never came. The envelope did; and its contents informed me that I was to join a Royal Engineer Training Battalion in November.

The posting (it went on to say) was of course conditional on my passing a medical examination; and a further buff envelope instructed me to report for that purpose to a drill hall in Brighton.

I went. I arrived. I gave my name, age and other bits of information to a man at a desk, then perambulated the various medical booths within the hall, being measured at one, tapped on the knees at another, made to jump up and down at a third, and so on until I had done the round and could return to the man at the desk. I was all keyed up, all excited, fairly *trembling* with excitement in fact, for I was now very nearly a real soldier. The man at the desk passed me a slip of paper. I read it. It was my certificate, and it told me – and anyone else who might be interested – that, having been duly examined by such-and-such a board at such-and-such a place on such-and-such a date I had been placed in . . . the words dissolved as I stared at them: *Category C.*

Even now at the memory my fingers become moist, for it was without doubt the most terrible moment of my life. But . . . but . . . but . . . I could hardly speak. But what's supposed to be *wrong* with me? The man answered sadly that it was not for the board to say. I must ask my doctor at home. But what do I do now? Just go home, he said. The army wouldn't be needing my services for the moment. I blundered out blind with tears. . . .

What does a father do when he learns that his son is not fit for military service? Does he heave a sigh of relief? Maybe mine did, but it would have been a sigh quickly stifled by an understanding of how I felt about it, and by the thought that here was yet another opportunity for him to do something to help.

'We'll make a start by ringing up Dr Thornton tonight,' he said. It was almost as if he welcomed the challenge. If there really was something the matter with me, he would have it put right. On the other hand if the medical board had made a mistake, he would jolly well see that I went before another board. Now then: who would be the best person to fix this?

Lord Horder, physician to the King, adviser to the Government and chairman of innumerable medical committees, was at that time probably the most influential doctor in the country. My father wrote him a letter.

To our relief, if not to our very great surprise, the medical board *had* got it wrong. They had, quite understandably, mistaken my excited trembling for something rather more serious. It might have been only nervousness, but equally it might not. Better, as far as they were concerned, not to take a chance. Better to lose an able-bodied Sapper than to have to nurse a sick one. They were naturally reluctant to give me a second look over, and but for Horder's intervention, might well have refused. And the fact that all this wasted only a bare three months of my military career (but of course gave me an extra three months in which to perfect my carpentry) shows how fast things can happen if you pull the right strings.

So on a February afternoon behold a young man in a train speeding north. He is tall and thin, nervous and excited, and very, very happy. Behold also a middle-aged man in a Sussex garden. He too is happy, though in not quite the same sense. Content, rather. If the young man in the train is looking ahead to what might lie in the future, the other is probably looking back to what lay in the past. For the one a new world is just about to unfold. For the other a world is just ending.

He would write to me, of course, and I would write to him. He would be with me, or rather just behind me – as close behind me as the distance between us would allow. He would always be ready to advise if advice were sought, to help if help were needed. He would always understand.

He went indoors, found an atlas and opened it at a map of England. Newark in Nottinghamshire: here it is, on the River Trent. Here's where his next letter would be sent. To Sapper Milne, C. R., the Second Training Battalion of the Royal Engineers, Newark, Notts.

3. Training for War

'To people like myself,' wrote my father, 'the Great Sacrifice (the 1914-18 War) was not the sacrifice of our lives but of our liberties. Ever since I had left Cambridge I had been my own master. I fixed my own hours, I was under no discipline; no bell rang for me, no bugle sounded. Now I was thirty-two, married, with a happy home of my own and engaged happily in work which I loved. To be a schoolboy again, to say "Yes, sir" and "No, sir" and "Please, sir" and "May I, sir?" was no hardship to schoolboys, no hardship to a million men in monotonous employment, but it was hell itself to one who had been as spoilt by good-fortune as I.'

Luckily, when my turn came I was twelve years younger than he had been: I was still virtually a schoolboy. I was leaving nothing that I didn't want to leave. I was being diverted from nothing that I had set my heart on achieving. The road I had been following had died on me. Here was another road in another direction, inviting, exciting. I plunged happily along it.

Human beings are governed by two opposite instincts: the instinct to be an individual and the instinct to be gregarious. In each of us the one or the other is the stronger. My father was an individualist, and I took after him. At school, however, one is forced to be gregarious. I didn't resent this, but I didn't particularly enjoy it, and whenever I could I withdrew into my own private world. At my prep school it was largely an imaginary world visited at night before going to sleep; but at Stowe it was often real. On summer Sundays I would go immense solitary walks through the countryside hunting for birds' nests. If I had been a bird, I would have been a robin rather than a rook, defending my territory against all who would invade it, not living at the top of an elm tree with a lot of chattering neighbours.

But if school is a rookery, the army is different. In the army one becomes not a rook but a starling. One of the most glorious sights on a winter's day is to see a flock of starlings rise from a field, sweep through the sky, and then settle again a hundred yards away. A flock of rooks is a collection of individual birds; a flock of starlings in flight is a single entity, as if one single brain directs it, one single set of muscles controls its movement. Starlings can be individuals if they wish – as of course they are during the breeding season. And they can chatter together in groups on the lawn or on roof tops at any time of the year. But in the winter they set an example in precision of movement that a Company of Guardsmen on ceremonial parade can only stumble towards.

We arrived at Newark, straggling in off our various trains, variously attired, bearing assorted bags of belongings, and making our way in ones and twos up to the camp. We were all ages from twenty to early thirties, all heights and shapes, and we slouched, ambled, loped or strutted according to our build and the length of our legs. We had come from all parts of the country and had been in a variety of occupations. Some were builders, some navvies, some clerks, many were miners, one or two were Civil Engineers or surveyors. . . . I think I was the only one who had been nothing.

The following day we all bore at least a superficial likeness to one another, clothed now in khaki. And then began the process of turning fifty individuals into a single unit. It took a month. This was the basic infantry training that every recruit had to undergo before he could come on to his more technical training. And I enjoyed every minute of it. I was, of course, lucky in that I was one of the youngest and one of the more agile, and I was accustomed to living a day that began with a bell that got you out of bed and finished with a bell that meant lights out and no more talking. It was certainly harder for some of the others. Yet, as the weeks went by and we got fitter and tougher, and discovered that our bodies could do things we had never dreamt they were capable of (and do them moreover without protest), so we gradually developed a pride in ourselves as individuals, in our physiques, and a pride, too, in our corporate identity.

Then one day as we drilled on the Square, marching and counter-marching, sloping and presenting our arms, fixing and unfixing our bayonets, and finally standing-at-ease, standing-easy, our eyes were caught by another Section[1] of recruits also marching and counter-marching. Heavens, what a gangling, straggling, shambling lot they were! Their uniforms unfitting, their caps sitting awkwardly on their heads, their boots too big for their feet. Everything about them seemed awkward from the uncoordinated way they moved to the jackknives that dangled stupidly from the lanyards round their waists. Had we looked like that a few short weeks ago?

And it was then that we realized how far we had come, how much we were changed, and so took extra pride in the way we saluted when we passed an officer, in the way the toe caps of our boots gleamed in the sunshine, in the satisfying noises we could make when we smacked our rifles with the flats of our hands or brought our iron-shod heels down with a crack that set the tarmac ringing.

Of course there were moments when we complained, when we failed to see how the precise folding of a greatcoat could affect the outcome of the war. But when you realize that many of us had been dragged unwillingly from wives and families, conscripted into an army we didn't want to join in order to fight a war we didn't want to fight, and were now being shouted at by NCOs whom we

---

[1] The Royal Engineers prides itself on being different from the Infantry. Where the Infantry calls its troops to attention with the word ''Shun!'' Sappers use the word in full: 'At . . . ten . . . shun!' And where the Infantry divides its Companies into Platoons and its Platoons into Sections, we divided ours into Sections and Sub-sections. I say 'divided' because at some time during my military career – I forget exactly when – we had to surrender this particular difference. In this and the following chapters I use the word that was current at the time – in as far as I can recall which it was – I don't think it will cause confusion. As an officer I began by commanding a Section, later commanded a Platoon. It was not promotion – merely a change of name.

regarded as mere boys, it is surprising that we complained so little. There were many things that the army taught me – how to use a pick and shovel, how to tie knots, how to drive a car, how to handle a boat – that I have subsequently found useful, but of all the things I learned the most valuable was what I learned in the first month of my army life. The chain of command which starts with the General does not finish with the Private but with his limbs, and it is this last link that is the most important of them all. I learned the things my body could do and I learned to disregard its messages of protest. Just as a good officer is in command of his men, getting from them the maximum they can give and receiving in addition their loyalty and respect, so I learned to command my body and my body learned to obey.

Inevitably the training an army gives its troops is based to some extent on the last war it fought; and in 1941 our last war had been 1914-18. All we had learned as yet from 1939 had been how to retreat. So, not surprisingly, our only up-to-date training was in demolitions. For the rest we were taught how to dig trenches and how to prevent them from subsequently caving in; and then we made wonderful Boy-Scout things from long poles, bits of rope and pulleys. The tools with which we were eventually going to win the war – the mine detector, the bulldozer and the Bailey Bridge – had yet to make their appearance. But it didn't in fact matter that what we were learning was in itself so useless. The point was that we were being taught to work as a team. Once we had learned this anything new could be picked up in a matter of days.

But where, you may ask, does the Carpenter come in? What price *Modern Practical Joinery*? I must explain. In the army there is only one sort of infantryman. It makes little difference to what regiment he is posted, his work is much the same. But a Sapper can be posted to any one of a score of units each totally different from all the others. He can go to a Survey Unit or a Bomb Disposal Unit; he can go to a unit that looks after stores, or one that builds camps, or one that organizes docks or drives trains or makes roads. And all these are jobs calling for a particular skill, a skill which in many cases has been acquired in civilian life. Or on the other hand he can join a Field Company where he will be called upon to undertake a great variety of jobs according to the immediate needs of the formation to which his Company is attached. If the army is retreating at the time this will include mine laying and demolitions. If the army is advancing, mine clearing, road repairing, bridge building, operating ferries and so on. None of these jobs requires specialized knowledge, merely familiarity with the equipment – British or German – that one is handling. So a bricklayer might possibly find himself ultimately in a Company that spent its entire time laying bricks or he might never see a brick at all throughout his army career. A carpenter might be called upon to make roof trusses or lay floors or hang doors, or his special skill might be needed only when his Section wanted a new, portable, two-seater latrine.

And in order that, as far as possible, carpenters might be sent to units where they wanted carpenters, surveyors where they wanted surveyors, and so on, we were all, soon after arrival, trade-tested to see what special skills we had. And to this end No. 2 Sub-Section was fallen-in, right-dressed, open-order-marched, right-turned, and by-the-left-quick-marched down to a Nissen hut inside which there was waiting for us a small, elderly captain wearing the ribbons of the First World War. And one at a time we went before him.

'Sapper Milne.'

'Sir.'

'What trade?'

'Carpenter and Joiner, Sir.'

He looked at me, puzzled.

'What were you doing before you joined the army, Sapper?'

'I was at Cambridge, Sir.'

He looked at me, worried.

'You'd be better off as a clerk,' he said. 'Can you type?'

'A little, Sir.'

He had a large book on his desk before him and thumbed through it to the section on clerks.

'What is your typing speed?'

'Sir, I can't really type, and I'd much rather be a carpenter, please, Sir.'

He looked at me sadly, shook his head and sighed. For a dreadful moment my fate seemed to hang in the balance. I had so set my heart on being a Carpenter! It would be so awful to be made a Clerk and to have to sit at my typewriter while others were outside having all the fun! Then to my intense relief he relented. A pale, wintry smile came and went. 'All right,' he said, and thumbed through the book again to the section on carpenters.

'Now then, Sapper. . . . What joint would you use to join a trimmer to a trimming joist?'

I could hardly believe it! Immediately *Modern Practical Carpentry* (1906 edition) opened before my eyes. Chapter 2: 'Joints and Fastenings'. Chapter 5: 'Floors and Flooring'.

'Tusk tenon, Sir.' And I could have gone on to tell him how this joint was often constructed wrongly, through ignorance of the stresses it had to meet. I would not have constructed it wrongly. I would not have placed my mortice too low where the fibres of the trimming joist were in tension. . . . But he had gone on to the next question.

'What joint would you use between the lock rail and the swinging stile of a panelled door?'

Now it was the turn of *Modern Practical Joinery*.

'A pair of double tenons, Sir.'

In all I was asked six questions and to each of them George Ellis and I gave the answer pat. And if a seventh had been: 'What tool would you use for the preliminary dressing off of floor boards, &c?' and if I had answered that in Mr Ellis's younger days he had employed the adze, I am sure that the small, elderly captain would have been delighted. 'Quite right, Sapper, quite right. The army still employs the adze, and a very useful tool it is, too.'

But six were enough to qualify me. 'All right, Sapper. You have passed your trade test and your pay will be increased forthwith from two-and-nine a day to three-and-six.'

I saluted and marched from the room ablaze with pride and happiness.

Yet proud though I was, I was nevertheless conscious of not being quite the real article. 'You're a carpenter, too? What was your job in civvy street?' I dreaded this and got round it with much embarrassment and I hoped not too much mendacity. 'I was working for my father. He's got a farm.' It was accepted.

However, my real test came a few weeks later. We were on parade and had been inspected to see that we had shaved and had polished our cap badges properly. And then the Sergeant-Major struck terror into my heart.

'Fall out the carpenters and joiners!' he roared.

For a moment I hesitated. Would all now be discovered? Would it be safer to pretend that I hadn't heard (unlikely) or hadn't quite understood (no less improbable)? In the end I fell – and joined three or four others. 'You Sappers report to Corporal Morgan who will tell you what he wants doing.'

It was easy. No double tenoning, no adze work, just unscrewing beds and screwing them down again in different positions. I watched to see how the professional did it, then hammered my screws in with the best of them. That was the first and the last time that I put my trade to practical use during my five years with the Royal Engineers. I never held a hammer again.

Somewhere around late April or early May the whole Training Battalion left Newark and moved south to a large camp at Barton Stacey in Hampshire. The sun was shining, and, as we marched from the railway station along narrow country lanes, the hedges were ablaze with leaf. At one point my neighbour, looking around him at all that greenery, sang out: 'Hey, lads, what sort of a God-forsaken hole is this they're taking us to?' But God-forsaken though it was to most of us, to me it was like coming home: the warm, fragrant, friendly south, after my winter in the hard, urban, industrial north.

I have the very happiest memories of Barton Stacey, of visits to Winchester, of feeling the chalk downs beneath my army-booted feet. It was here that I became at last a fully trained Sapper; and here that, six weeks later, I emerged from another spell of training with the rank of Temporary Acting Unpaid Lance Corporal. Now

I was really someone of importance! I sewed on my stripe and swaggered about with immense pride. I was no longer one of a squad, falling in and being marched to wherever it was we had to go, no longer one of a flock of sheep. I was the sheep dog, moving up and down my column as the fancy took me, barking at them to keep them in order. 'Left, left, left, right, left.' I bawled. 'Come along. Move sharply there!'

And my sheep? They were a 'pre-OCTU' Class. That is to say they were an assortment of Sappers, Corporals and Sergeants, some very new to the army, others with quite long service, and now all lumped together as Officer Cadets. After six weeks at Barton Stacey they would be going on to Aldershot to one of the two RE OCTUs for a further six months' training, after which they would become Second Lieutenants. 'Left, left, left, right, left. You may have been a Sergeant last week but now you're only a Cadet. So chin in, chest out and swing your arms!' I might as well enjoy all this while I could, for I knew that it wasn't going to last, that my turn was coming, that the sheep dog would soon be returning to the flock. And so it was. When I had barked that Class out through the gates of Barton Stacey for the last time, I unsewed my stripe and became a Cadet myself. 'Left, left, left, right, left!' Now I was having to come-along-move-sharply-there. And six weeks later, on a cold January morning, the sky grey, the fields white with thin snow, I in my turn was marched through the gates, down the road, bound for Aldershot.

It was at Aldershot that I discovered the sort of soldier that I was never going to become. I could be Sapper Milne, one of thirty or so, indistinguishable from his fellows; and I could be Lance Corporal Milne, strutting about on his own. But I was no good at being Cadet Milne, an individual in a group. It was like being at school again, having to be gregarious, while at the same time trying to outshine the others. I had enjoyed being drilled as a Sapper. There was point to it then: we were being moulded into a homogeneous, cohesive body of men in which all individuality was suppressed. This was the way it was done, and one could take a pride in the result. But at Aldershot it was only for convenience that we were drilled as a squad, all doing the same thing to the single order of command. For the object of our training now was to turn us back into individuals. So I disliked our numerous sessions under the Senior Drill Instructor; and polishing my boots and my brasses became a bore. And as to the rest of my training, well, if I am honest and try to picture myself as I must have looked to my instructors, I wouldn't blame them if what they saw was a young man, a *very* young man, technically quite able, perhaps, but lacking in most of the more general qualities one looks for in an officer. ... So let me hurry on to the day when it all came to an end, a day at the beginning of July.

Here we were then, thirty or so infant Second Lieutenants, fitted out by the Aldershot tailors with Great Coat, Service Dress, Sam Browne and Peaked Cap. Where were we all going?

Well, there might have been a few of us whose specialized skills demanded that they were posted to units needing those particular skills. But for the rest we were just ordinary, moderately competent Engineers, with a rudimentary knowledge of building construction, mechanics, explosives, surveying and such like, and able to handle the equipment with which the army provided us. We could never have designed and built a wooden bridge across the Mohawk River, but give us the standard Folding Boat Equipment or Small Box Girder and a Section of Sappers under an experienced NCO and we wouldn't have disgraced ourselves. Some, of course, would have performed better than others. Some of us radiated self-confidence. Some of us were clearly born leaders. Others weren't.

It was generally accepted in the Engineers that the best jobs were those nearest to the enemy. So the best Cadets were posted to the Divisions; the less good went to Corps or Army Engineer Companies; the indifferent went to Line of Communication Units; the rather feeble, who needed a bit of extra experience before being given any very responsible command, went to the Training Battalions. And the most feeble of the lot didn't get a proper posting at all, but were sent here, there, anywhere – as Supernumeraries.

It was as a Supernumerary that Second Lieutenant Milne was posted to HQRE 56 (London) Division then at Sible Hedingham in Essex.

4. *Reflections on War*

It soon became clear why I had been posted to 56 Division: the Division was mobilizing for service overseas. This entailed – among other things – a sorting out of the troops and equipment that were to go from those that were to be left behind. For each unit would be leaving behind a rear party – consisting of the less young, the less fit – whose main task before being disbanded would be to tidy up. Here was a job just waiting for a Supernumerary Officer. Second Lieutenant Milne would take charge of one of the tidying-up parties.

So why didn't I? I was never told, and I shan't now attempt to guess. I shall just record the fact that one morning after breakfast the CRE, Lt-Col Keane, said to me, almost casually: 'By the way, Milne, would you like to come with us?' and I nearly passed put with pleasure.

At this point I must pause. You can if you like imagine the pause as taking place during my embarkation leave at Cotchford. During those seven days there would have been plenty of time for contemplation, for going through my thoughts and feelings and trying to understand them. And this is what I would like to do now.

So far the war had been for me no more than a succession of newspaper reports on the one hand and a sort of continuation of school on the other. Battles were being fought in Africa, in Malay, on the Atlantic, even in the blue sky over Cotchford, but the reality of war had not yet touched me. I had seen a bombed building or two on my rare visits to London – but it could have been the work of a demolition company. I had seen the remains, of a German bomber lying in a Sussex field – but it was no more alarming than a piece of rusting farm machinery. I had been taught how to use a bayonet, jabbing it into a straw-filled dummy – but the dummy didn't jab back or cry out in agony. I had yet to experience the real thing at first hand. I had yet to come face to face with fear.

This meeting was now not so far away. What would it be like? How would I react to it? Would I indeed survive? These were the three questions I was asking myself as I walked round and round the garden and then across the meadow, along the river, through Posingford and up to the forest. I was saying goodbye to it all. For ever? Yes, for ever. For of my three questions it was only the last that I could answer with absolute certainty. I would not survive. The thought didn't particularly bother me; for I had no very special reason for not wanting to die. The other two questions were much more important.

I can answer them both now; and to some extent I must try to do so.

If I were merely writing an account of my adventures, then the first question would be the one to engage my attention. Thus I did, and thus and thus and thus. But too many war stories of this kind have been written for me to want to add to their number. And in any case, compared with those epics that still tingle the blood, my story is tame and unexciting. So I turn rather to the second question: how did I react to it all? This is far more interesting.

Dare I suggest that it is not just more interesting, it is also more important? For if we are to prevent war we must first understand it. And in particular we must understand how it is that, while all reason is against it, yet instinct and emotion may draw us towards it, so that even someone who before 1941 and after 1946 could hardly have looked less like a soldier yet managed to find in those terrible years something of lasting value, something which, in its curious way, gave and still gives immense satisfaction.

War is like the application of heat to a chemical process: it speeds things up. It speeds up the progress of science, the march of civilization. This, I think, we all recognize. It also speeds up the development – especially the emotional development – of the individual. In a single year of war we can experience all the emotions of ten years of peace. They come fairly bubbling up within us. Indeed they may even come bubbling over, and in extreme cases the whole apparatus may explode. But if the bubbling is under control and is not excessive the outcome for the individual is not necessarily bad. I say this with great reluctance, hating to put forward anything that might seem a recommendation of war. Nevertheless it is, I think, generally true that good and bad can never be entirely separated from each other, that although at times the one may dominate the scene, the other will still manage to put in an occasional appearance. And this is true even of war. War is like strychnine. A poison, yes, and one wouldn't recommend that it should be put on sale in all grocers' shops. Yet this is not to deny that sometimes, in very small doses, there are certain ailments that it may help to cure.

Like so many of my contemporaries I experienced all the familiar, if today somewhat tarnished, emotions. The rallying cries of our leaders, the valiant deeds of our warriors stirred me profoundly. I had no doubts: the war in which we were engaged was a crusade against the forces of Evil, a conflict in which I must play my part. My king and Country needed me. So here I was eager to offer my services, proud that my offer had been – despite that first terrible visit to Brighton – accepted. *Dulce et decorum est.* . . . Oh, yes: all that sort of thing. Not expressed so crudely, of course, but felt, very deeply felt. The emotions that had stirred our fathers and our grandfathers before us, that had stirred young men from the beginning of time, were alive. Even as recently as 1940, even after all the disillusion of 1914-18, war still had that power over us.

The process of growing up is in part a process of getting to know oneself. Who am I? There is no one to tell us. We must find out for ourselves, and we can only find out by trial and error. This is often painful and the lessons discouraging. So the happy man is he who learns quickly and who then makes the best of it. I had already learned a number of things about myself. I knew that I was shy, emotional, young for my age, unadventurous, and that while others were covering themselves with mud and glory on the rugger field I preferred more peaceful surroundings. Frankly I was not the warrior type, not the stuff of heroes. Nor were these my only disqualifications. There was something far more serious, something that had dominated my life as a schoolboy and now seemed likely to dominate it in the army. My stammer. Even today it is painful to recall the pain – indeed the agony and the misery – that this used to cause me. There are some who can take what seems a grim pleasure in spluttering their way from word to word, leaving only their listeners to feel uncomfortable. But not I. And the memories of those battles with words, battles fought and lost, are with me still. At school I learned Greek. Today only a dozen words survive, one of which is *fronimos*. Its meaning is gone; its claim to immortality dates from the day when it took my tongue what seemed like half an hour to negotiate its 'comparative' and 'superlative' forms. And there were plenty of other, similar occasions, and would indeed have been more if I hadn't always done my utmost to dodge them when I saw them approaching. I knew my limitations. I knew when I was at my worst: reading aloud (which ruined Shakespeare for me), using the telephone, making polite conversation to grown-ups. And when I could I ran away.

So although, when contemplating my future military career, I might allow myself delightful Walter Mitty-like dreams in which single-handed I defied the enemy while bullets whistled past me and shells pattered around like hail, in more sober moments I well knew there were certain things that were quite beyond me. I might just possibly be capable of brave deeds, but brave words were out of the question. And so if, back in June 1940, I had attempted to assemble all my thoughts on paper, this is what I might then have written:

1. I want to do something as heroic as possible
2. I can't attempt anything that is going to involve much talking, particularly if it means talking into a microphone
3. If I can't fly a Spitfire myself, I wouldn't want to be the man who just oils the propeller for someone else to fly it. For this would make me miserably jealous

4. I don't really like being a member of a team. I'm happiest on my own
5. Does being nervous mean you won't be any good in battle, that you will go all to pieces?
6. I don't think it does
7. And I'm jolly well going to prove that it doesn't

To what extent did such thoughts point towards the Royal Engineers? Certainly to some extent they did, but equally certainly instinct and chance came into it. I did not know and I could never have guessed how unerring was that instinct, nor how, as a Sapper Officer with 56 (London) Division, I was to find exactly what I was looking for.

5. Flowers in the Sand

The Division sailed from England at the end of August. By the end of November we were established at Kirkuk in Iraq. We travelled by sea via Freetown, Cape Town and Bombay to Basra at the head of the Persian Gulf and thence by rail via Baghdad; and it was of course a thrilling and a memorable journey.

As with most of us it was the first time I had been abroad. Flying fish, coconut palms, date palms, Indians, Arabs, deserts and scorpions: I was meeting them all for the first time. This in itself was exciting enough. But, even more exciting, I was feeling myself part of something very much bigger than myself whose adventures I was about to share. There had been a party of Gunner Officers in our carriage on the train to Liverpool; two Lieutenants from the Royal Fusiliers had shared our cabin on the *Nieuw Holland;* at Cape Town the Divisional Commander himself had come aboard for a brief visit and I had caught a glimpse of him, a tall, stern, imposing figure. Royal Fusiliers, London Scottish Rifles, London Irish Rifles, Oxfordshire and Buckinghamshire Light Infantry, The Queen's Royal Regiment, Royal Artillery, Royal Corps of Signals: Company after Company after Company, each with its own special skills, its own history, its own traditions, thousands of men from all over Britain, all wearing the insignia of the Black Cat on their sleeves, all part of 56 Division, a Division that was setting out on a journey that would take it into who knew what countries through who knew what battles before it once again set foot in England: thus was the voyage out. And when, somewhere in the Indian Ocean, we heard on the wireless that 'powerful reinforcements' were about to reach Eighth Army in Egypt, we thrilled with pride. This was us!

But we were wrong. Iraq wasn't Egypt. Paiforce [1] wasn't Eighth Army.

The enemy we had come to fight was further away than ever. And on top of all this it was raining.

Four hundred miles can make a lot of difference. At Basra the desert sun had scorched down on our new solar topees, the desert sand had scorched up from beneath our feet – they said you could fry an egg on it – and desert flies, hovering in between, had accompanied every forkful of food on its way from mess tin to mouth. At Kirkuk it was English weather again, cold, grey and wet, and we were back in battledress. It was a bit of an anticlimax.

Why had we come to this desolate spot? For no very exciting reason that we could discover. Perhaps to guard the oil wells. Perhaps just to be handy in case we were needed. So what would we be doing while we waited? Train. Get acclimatized. Make ourselves comfortable.

Comfortable? We looked around. To the east, nothing. To the south, nothing. To the west, nothing. To the north – ah, yes: two things. An oil refinery and a line of mountains. With no other features on the landscape it was hard to judge distances. The refinery might have been anything from one to six miles away. As for the mountains, either they were distant and so surprisingly clear or they were near and so surprisingly small. In either case they were surprisingly regular, like the teeth of a saw. We looked at the ground. Flat as a board, baked hard by the summer sun, now beginning to liquify under the winter rain: mud. We sniffed the air. A strange, sickly, sulphurous smell: oil. Mud and oil: these were to dominate our lives for the next four months.

We were lucky. We were Engineers and therefore skilled at making things. We used the mud to make bricks. We used the oil to fuel our cookers, disinfect our latrines and mark out our football pitch.

We could call on bricklayers and carpenters, welders and tinsmiths.

[1] The first three letters, pronounced 'pie', stood for Persia and Iraq.

Our Company Commander had been a Civil Engineer and our Second in Command an architect. Indeed not only were we Engineers. We were the Field Park Company.

There are four Companies of Engineers in a Division: three Field Companies (one to each of the three Brigades) and the Field Park Company. The Field Companies do the work; the Field Park holds the stores and equipment. Field Companies live in their Brigade areas; the Field Park lives where it likes. In addition there is a Headquarters under the CRE, a Lieutenant-Colonel, which is usually to be found somewhere near Divisional Headquarters. In other words we were five quite separate groups living in five quite separate camps and going about our five quite separate businesses. I say all this so that those who are not expert in military matters will see how the Divisional Royal Engineers in one respect at least offered me the sort of environment I was looking for. I liked to feel myself part of the whole Division, yes, indeed: this satisfied an emotional need. But I did not like to be one of a large group of officers. And as a subaltern in the Field Park Company I was not. For there were only four of us.

We lived together (in the sort of comfort that only a professional architect could have designed and professional builders built) a little like the members of a Victorian family, close, happy, yet respecting our differences in age and rank. And we remained a united and happy family for over a year. Our Commander was Major Lake, a Territorial Officer, married, in his early thirties, reserved and meticulous. Second in Command was Captain Bertram, also married and with a young family, older, much more sociable. My fellow subaltern was Lieutenant Nelson, a Scot, efficient but aloof. I was closest to Bertram, who was to me something between elder brother and father – a relationship so firmly cemented during the war that it still survives. Lake steered the Company along efficient if unadventurous lines. Bertram added the occasional zest to relieve the boredom.

And of course there was boredom. I was the Bridging Officer in charge of the Bridging Section. In those days we carried Folding Boat Equipment, which is a sort of junior version of the better known Pontoon Bridge and was used for crossing rivers, and Small Box Girder, used for narrower gaps where a single span was possible. I was the Bridging Officer – yet I never built a bridge.

Bridges were built by the Field Companies. We merely supplied them with the equipment they needed. The best I could hope for was to be allowed to accompany it and watch them use it. But mostly I stayed at home waiting for it to come back to us, battered and in need of repair. Then I would set my Sappers to work to repair it, fitting patches over splintered wood, stitching torn canvas. It was work I could have done myself, and I longed to do it, to hold a chisel again. But it was their work, not mine, not an officer's. Mine was to walk up and down, up and down, seeing they did it properly.

I envied the Field Companies and I envied my own Sappers. A more enterprising officer would have gone to his OC and said: 'Please, sir, I am bored. My men are bored. Couldn't we sometimes do something a little more interesting?' But I was not yet very enterprising. Nor, I think, would I have found in Lake a sympathetic listener.

On one occasion the Engineers moved north into the mountains on the Persian border to practise bridging ravines and they took my Small Box Girder with them.

'Please, sir, can I go too?'

'No, Milne,' said Lake. 'An officer's place is with the largest part of his command. That is the rule.'

So I stayed behind, silently furious.

Dreary and monotonous, then, was the landscape all around us; and dreary and monotonous was my work. So all the more wonderful were those rare occasions when I *was* able to escape with my Section and be alone with them and enjoy a little independence and do something a little different in surroundings a little less drab.

Once it was to the Little Zab, the river where my Folding Boats were being used. More often it was to the range of mountains that lay behind the oil refinery. To my delight they were small and near. Their nearness made them accessible; they were perhaps no more than four or five miles away. Their smallness took nothing from their beauty, merely replaced awe and majesty with friendliness and intimacy. I preferred it this way. They were miniature mountains, toy mountains, and you could ramble and scramble happily among their tiny crags. Never mind what we did there; to be there on our own was all I asked for. When I first met them they were absolutely bare: bare rock on their summits, bare earth between. This very bareness was part of their charm: the charm of extreme simplicity and austerity. On a clear day it was a world of two colours only, pale brown and pale blue. Then, as the months went by, was added a third colour, the palest flush of green.

Of all my memories of Iraq this is the one that comes back to me unbidden year after year. During all the time I was abroad I was looking for reminders of England. Now that I am back in England my reminders come often from abroad. An early spring day, in late February, perhaps, the sky a palest blue, the bare hillside clothed still in its bleached winter grass: it is Iraq, not England, that I see.

We left Kirkuk in March, my feelings akin to those of the previous August when we had marched through Liverpool from the station to the docks. We left to begin a journey of epic proportions, a journey that can stand comparison with any in history. For it can proudly claim to be the longest approach march ever made by an army in all the annals of war. We left Kirkuk in March. Four weeks and 3200 miles later we were engaged in the final battle against the Germans in Tunisia. We paused only at night to sleep and for a few days near Cairo and again near Tripoli to rest, to repair our vehicles, to collect certain additional items of equipment, and to get ourselves into tropical kit. A few miles north of Enfidaville, with barely time to stretch our cramped legs or wash the dust off our bodies or shake it out of our clothes, the Division went into action.

Measure it by purely military, purely logistical standards and the journey was remarkable enough. Thousands of men, hundreds of lorries, trucks, guns, yes, even bridging equipment, travelling along desert roads, south to Baghdad, then following the oil pipe line across the sand to the hills at Mafraq in Transjordan; then down the steep descent to the Jordan valley; through Palestine, lush with orange groves, resonant with Biblical names, to Tulkarm where we learned our final destination. On again, green gradually giving way to brown until, after passing Beersheba, we were back once more in the desert, the Sinai Desert, soft sand, wind-blown and a sandstorm waiting for us to show us how it was done. Over the Suez Canal and into Egypt, where we paused and took the opportunity to pay a quick visit to Cairo and glance at the Pyramids. Then on, following the coast road so familiar to the soldiers of Wavell and of Rommel, past undistinguished settlements that had lived their private lives in a thousand years of obscurity and whose names had then been suddenly trumpeted round the world: el Alamein, Solum, Tobruq, Benghazi. . . . Then, after a few days at Azizia near Tripoli, to the final lap: Ben Gardane, Gabes, Sfax, Sousse and ultimately, for 563 Field Park Company, a salt marsh just south of Enfidaville.

But of course it was more than just a succession of staging posts, more than just a Grand Tour, more than just being part of one of the largest caravans ever to cross the desert: it was the feeling that we were not just on the move but moving in the right direction – oh, so important, this – moving simultaneously towards the war and towards home. Home. When I had left England it was with the certainty that I would never return. Now, although there was still an undefeated army between me and Cotchford, I was facing in the right direction, moving in the right direction, and my thoughts could fly ahead of me. And so in my letters I could write about my home-coming, as certain now that I would one day see Cotchford again as I had before been certain that I would not.

Yet even this was not all that the great journey had to offer. It was for me something at once intensely beautiful and intensely dramatic, and I saw it through two pairs of eyes, the eyes of a soldier and the eyes of a traveller. War and peace side by side, each with the power to move and inspire.

I could feel wonderfully military – the Great Commander – as I led my Section of Bridging lorries out on to the road to take their place in the mighty convoy. But at the same time I could notice here and there the minute, fragile swords of grass that had suddenly begun to prick through the bare earth. At one of our wayside halts in Transjordan I found a tiny anemone, the brightest crimson, like a drop of blood. I picked it and pressed it and sent it home in a letter. At the top of Solum Pass my soldier's eye was awed by the sight of a great column of German vehicles, battered and burnt, strung out along the roadside, while my traveller's eye was held by the sea. There it lay, a thousand feet beneath us, looking exactly as Tennyson had once seen it.

The wrinkled sea beneath him crawls. . . .

It did exactly that.

Then on to Benghazi where, next to the corpse of a German tank, I found a lark's nest bubbling over with young life. War and peace, side by side, the one however devastating never able to obliterate the other. So it was then. So it was always to be.

Thus day after day we snaked our way across the desert. The desert! O evocative word! What a flood of memories it brings back! Monotonous? Barren? Mere sand? No! Varied and beautiful and inspiring almost beyond belief!

At times it was absolutely flat and hard, so that, standing on it, I seemed to flow out across its surface and to possess it right to the very horizon. As I marched over it, the hard sand beneath the heel of my boot sent pulses up my leg, and my boot became, not something I wore, but a part of my body. Boot and leg were one and the pulses coming up from them gave them strength. I could have marched to the rim of the world, so strong did I feel.

Elsewhere the sand was soft and rounded like the human form, like someone asleep. Watching it you could sense its breathing, and at the wind's caress it gently stirred.

Elsewhere again it was a desert not of sand but of stones, a desert of giant marbles of all sizes but uniformly round and brown. Some were the size of tennis balls, some as big as footballs, some even bigger. I rolled one over to see what lay beneath it.

And elsewhere again the desert was a vast and dazzling garden.

How fortunate we were! For eleven months of the year the desert lives up to its name. Then comes spring and for a single month it is ablaze with flowers. This was the very month of our great trek.

And so it was seldom that we did a day's journey without at some point coming upon clusters of flowers, waiting beside the road, waiting, so it seemed, to watch the procession go by and to wave and cheer its passing. Drifts of flowers and the trailing debris of war: now the one and now the other, and each in its way deeply moving to one who was seeing both for the first time. Then, as we approached our journey's end, came the distant but ever-growing sounds of war. And thus we reached our salt marsh, where, to the banging of guns could be added the singing of the little black crickets that dodged in and out of the heather-like scrub that flourished in the sand.

North of Enfidaville our infantry battalions were hurling themselves at the enemy. South of Enfidaville the Field Park Company sat down to wait. Well, at any rate we had all arrived, and that was a considerable achievement. My bridging lorries had been old when they left England. They had been landed at Suez and had crossed the desert to Kirkuk in November. And now, hammered once again by the rough desert roads, choked by the all-enveloping desert dust, they had just endured an even longer journey. Some of them were very, very lame, but at least they could all move.

Did anybody want any of them? Happily, they did.

On the main road beyond Enfidaville a bridge had been blown up by the Germans. It was a bridge over a wadi, and to cross the gap a Box Girder would be needed. It was to be built as soon as it was safe to do so, and meanwhile my lorries were to go forward and wait in readiness.

'Please, sir, may I go with them?'

'No, Milne,' said Lake.

'*Please*, sir!'

'No, Milne. You remember the rule. An officer's place is with the larger part of his. . . .'

How easily I might once again have submitted! How nearly I did! And what I would have missed if I had! But I was growing up at last. I had been on the leading rein quite long enough. I was beginning to want my freedom. An officer may be in command of a considerable number of men but his independence may be very limited. He commands but he is also commanded. A Sapper Officer is fortunate in that although he is given orders he is seldom supervised. How he carries them out is his own affair. Up to this point I had needed supervision. Please, sir, what shall I do? And Lake had told me. Now I no longer wanted to be told. In any case I was feeling my way towards my own rule, one that was to become my guide from then on. An officer's place is where the work is most exciting.

So I stood firm and in the end I was allowed to go. And thus it was I had a seat in the front row of the dress circle when the curtain went up on the last Act.

A roll of drums. . . . a crescendo of sound. How else can you attract an audience's attention, still their murmurings, bring them, tense, to the edge of their seats, breath held, eyes staring? Not drums here in North Africa, of course. Aircraft. Bombers. High up in the sky. Coming from behind us. Flying, calm, unhurried, majestic, towards the enemy's lines, to the hills where they were entrenched. Then a sudden spurting of brown smoke from the hills, a line of smoke where the bombs had fallen, and a few seconds later a long, low roar. The smoke hung like a cloud, then drifted and thinned and vanished. . . . All eyes were on the hills.

And then quite suddenly, as the desert had flowered a few weeks before, patches of mauve and yellow and spots of red appearing in the brown sand, so did the enemy hills flower now. Not mauve and yellow but white. White flowers like snowdrops, in ones and twos and then in tens and twenties, covering the bare brown slopes. For a brief moment we were mystified. Then we understood. It was the end. The German and Italian armies in Tunisia had surrendered.

We made our way to the roadside, staring up the straight, shell-holed road that ran from Enfidaville north to Tunis, from the British lines to the German lines. And in a little while a column of men came into sight, marching towards us. And behind them we could see another column ... and another ... and another. Now the first column was nearer and we could see on either side of it a single soldier with a rifle slung over his shoulder. Now it was abreast of us. Germans. Another column of Germans and another. Then Italians. Was it really true, as I remember writing in a letter home, that the column was led by an Italian General so perfumed that I could smell him as he passed?

I turned to look the other way, back down the road towards Enfidaville. How deserted this road had been when we had driven up it! Beyond the town there had been a notice warning us: 'Keep moving. This road is under shell fire.' It had been a little frightening, a little eerie, but intensely exciting leading my small convoy to our first adventure. The road deserted, the desert deserted, no sign of life anywhere.

How different it was now! For now had come a third and final flowering of the desert; and as I looked back – and later as I drove back – I could see that it was alive with soldiers, British soldiers, clusters of them, all along the roadside, lounging and laughing, with forage caps at jaunty angles and cigarettes between their lips.

6. *The Lull*

Shortly after the surrender I was ordered to explore a certain track and see if it passed through any minefields. I took a small party of Sappers and together we set out.

Right back to the distant days of 1940 I had always seen mine-clearing as the sort of work I might enjoy, and in my Walter Mitty daydreams it was always for this that I had been awarded the Victoria Cross. In the early days of the war it was in fact the only Sapper-work that regularly made the headlines: mine-clearing in the Western Desert and bomb disposal in London. And of the two there was no doubt which place had the greater attraction: Africa had lured me since I was a child. I had no idea how bombs or mines worked but I imagined that they were set off by some sort of ingenious device involving either wires and batteries or levers and springs, just the kind of thing I had enjoyed inventing and making as a boy.

So here was my ambition: to find a lot of mines and defuse them, preferably in moderately heroic circumstances. And since the opportunity for this sort of work does not often come the way of a Bridging Officer in a Field Park Company, I knew that sooner or later I was going to want to get myself posted to a Field Company. I was not in any particular hurry about this; I was very fond of both of my fellow-officers and of the men in my Section, and so, provided I was not madly jealous that the subalterns in the other Companies were having a much more exciting time, I was content to wait. My goal was only one step away. When a vacancy occurred I would be an obvious candidate. Section Commander in a Divisional Field Company: this was the height of my military ambition. The next step above that, to become a Captain and be made Second in Command of a Company, was both totally beyond my abilities and totally lacking in attraction. Seconds in Command were concerned solely with administration, talking, not doing, being clerks not carpenters.

Meanwhile, any opportunity that presented itself for playing around with mines and learning a bit more about them, found me all eagerness. And, as it conveniently happened – and I don't think it was the result of any special agitation on my part, for I was too shy to agitate much – opportunities did present themselves. One of my first tasks on arriving at HQRE in Essex had been to set up an exhibition showing various British explosive devices. Then, soon after joining the Field Park Company, I had attended a short course on bomb disposal. On the *Nieuw Holland* I had been invited to give a talk on mines to a group of Gunner Officers. (Help! I've never done this sort of thing before. Will I stammer? Luckily a small explosion during the course of my talk – and I cannot now recall if it was accidental or intentional – diverted attention from my nervousness and helped to put me at my ease.) Then, on our journey across the desert, I and some other officers had spent a day being introduced to all the many varieties of German and Italian mines that we were likely to come across. And it was here that I had discovered yet another pleasure that mine clearing had to offer.

In England I had seen only British devices. Oh what crude inartistic things these now seemed compared with what we were being shown. Beautifully designed, beautifully made, the German devices were works of art. One's fingers yearned to touch them and hold them and caress them and generally fiddle around with them, as one's fingers sometimes yearned to play with a beautifully made child's toy. This beauty of theirs not only made them a delight to handle, it also made them very much safer. The steel balls that were trapped in grooves until you depressed a spring-loaded plunger, and which then escaped into holes: you knew exactly that it would all work as it was meant to work: you could trust it not to catch you unawares.

Lastly, when we had arrived at Enfidaville, Lake had told me to assemble my own collection of enemy mines and arrange them for demonstration to other units. So in theory at least I was by now quite an expert. All I needed was the practice.

And now here it was and you can imagine with what eagerness I set off with my small party along the unknown track, mine detectors and other paraphernalia at the ready: you can imagine my excitement when, sure enough, at a certain point, there before us lay the hoped-for minefield.

I walked onto it, my heart no doubt racing in a way that would have set doctors in drill halls in Brighton shaking their heads. I walked onto it as I had been taught to do, wielding a light, metal walking stick to ensure that I didn't put a foot wrong. And there all around me, so easily visible, quite disappointingly easy to see in fact, were the mines. Like a botanist looking down at the flowers round his feet or an astronomer looking up at the stars above his head, I knew them all. All were friends. All were familiar. . . . *All*? No not all. And in an instant I was Keats' astronomer, seeing his new planet; for there at my feet was a stranger.

I lay down beside it, comfortable and relaxed, and very slowly, very delicately began to clear the sand away from round its edge, feeling round it with my fingers, feeling down, feeling how the lid fitted over the top, very gently lifting the lid to see how it moved, to guess what might be underneath. . . .

Most mines are laid with the sole intention of deterring the trespasser, or of catching him out if he refuses to be deterred. An incautious foot or an incautious wheel will set them off, but anyone wanting to make them safe and remove them can do so quite easily. One in a hundred, however, is different, and is specially designed to catch the man who tries to disarm it. So I had to assume that my stranger was the one in a hundred. I had to test the lid very carefully. I had to slide my fingers gently not just round the edges but underneath in case there were any surprises. And I did it all slowly, lingeringly, to spin out the pleasure.

It was, of course, one of the other ninety-nine. The strange lid lifted easily off the strange body to reveal four very familiar igniters that were all too easily made safe and then all too easily unscrewed. And that really brought my small adventure to its prosaic end – except that the mine was indeed a new one, and became known as the Africa mine. I don't pretend to have been the first to have discovered it – just one of the first. It was certainly extremely easy to deal with and the story is really only worth relating as an example of what I have so often met in life: beginner's luck. For there can't have been many sappers who, going onto their first minefield, were rewarded with the added bonus of a brand new mine.

Those were happy, relaxed, high-spirited days, the days that followed the German surrender in North Africa, and we felt on top of the world. Then suddenly we were plunged into black despair: the Division was ordered back to Tripoli. How vividly I recall our feelings and how utterly illogical they were. The enemy had been cleared from North Africa. Our next battles were likely to be taking place in Europe. The crossing to Europe could just as easily be made from Tripoli as from Algiers. Yet Algiers was our magnet. To travel north and west was to advance. To go south and east to retreat. It was almost like being sent back to Kirkuk for another spell with the oil wells, almost as if we were in disgrace. I wonder if the Divisions of First Army, marching eastwards, felt the same in reverse. I wonder if for them Tripoli was always the magnet.

Well, if I had set my heart on seeing Algeria, by an extraordinary piece of good luck and bad management that was just what I was going to do. No sooner had we completed the long trail back down the desert road and established ourselves in our new patch of sand than the order came that all our bridging equipment was to be handed over to 51 Division at Sfax. I can't now remember – if indeed I ever knew – how Lake took this news: whether or not he felt that the whole Company if not indeed the whole Division was now about to disintegrate. One always tended to view orders that came from on high rather critically. And no doubt we would have commented on the fact we had driven through Sfax less than a week ago and had we known then could have saved ourselves a six hundred mile journey. But as far as I was concerned, having never had any great affection for my lorries, I felt no great sorrow at their loss (for it was only the lorries I was losing, not their drivers). Here in the soft sand they seemed particularly unlovable as they wallowed and floundered like great whales stranded by the tide. Almost the only direction they seemed capable of travelling in was vertically downwards, as they gently subsided into graves dug by their futilely spinning wheels. If somebody else wanted them, they were very welcome. So I didn't resent that I had to go back up the road I had so recently come down. Far from it. For I would now be on my own. For the first time in my life I would be leading my own convoy. Allow four days up, taking it slowly, and then two days – my drivers riding as passengers in a single lorry – for the return. Say a week in all – a nice little excursion. Back by next Tuesday, then.

It wasn't like that at all. It was much – oh, very much – nicer. Oh, kind and thoughtful army to have ensured that when I reached Sfax 51 Division should have moved to Djidjelli in Algeria, 400 miles further on.

I've already described one long journey. This one was very similar, but there were two important differences.

First, my bridging lorries, if they had been slowly dying before, were now on the very point of death. It was no longer possible to carry out quick repairs at the end of the day's run. Often it meant lying up for several days while local scrap heaps were combed for bits of spring or a slightly younger carburettor; so that I suppose our journey from Tripoli to Djidjelli took in all about a fortnight.

Secondly – for me the vital difference – for the first time in my army life I was in complete command of my Section. No longer was I being watched over by Major Lake, carrying out his orders. Instead I was making my own decisions in a situation that no one had foreseen. I didn't ask Lake what I should do; I sent him a signal from Tunis telling him what I proposed to do. I wasn't following a given route; I acquired maps and chose my own. Thus day by day we limped westwards, travelling as far as we safely dared, then choosing somewhere to camp for the night, replenishing food and petrol, carrying out repairs. Only one thing did our expedition lack: confidence that what we were doing needed to be done, that the goal was worth the effort. Indeed in our hearts I think we all knew that it wasn't.

And how right we were.

We dragged ourselves into Djidjelli and I went off in search of the Field Park Company.

Of course they knew nothing about us and of course they didn't want our bridging. So I found a quiet corner where it was in nobody's way and left it. Perhaps it's there still.

We left Tripoli on September 1st. We left by sea. I had enjoyed my stay in Africa. I had seen a lot of exciting country. I had made friends with desert rats and chameleons. I had discovered a new mine. I had caught malaria. I had been stung by a scorpion. And all this qualified me for the Africa Star and made me feel quite the desert veteran. The only thing I hadn't done was to fight any battle, but that was surely to come quite soon.

As for our bridging, all was well in the end; for on the open deck of our Tank Landing Craft, next to a Platoon of anti-tank guns, were eight new lorries. And the bridge they carried was the Bailey.

7. War – The Events

At about 8 o'clock on the morning of September 9th we drove ashore. This was two hours later than had been planned and so gave the sun time to get up and bring light and warmth to the lush, green countryside. There was a short strip of grey sand and then we were on to a road that ran parallel with the coast – a narrow road, really no more than a track, with a stone surface. After a little the road turned inland past a field of tomatoes – those plum tomatoes we today meet in tins. Here they hung red-ripe on their bushes, and every now and then were baskets half filled – yesterday's harvest that we had so rudely interrupted.

So this was Italy. A flat plain dotted with occasional white-walled, red-roofed houses. In the distance blue-grey mountains. On either hand small fields, richly cultivated, so lush, so green, the air so heavy with the sweet breath of all their vegetation, that this was my first and most overpowering sensation. We drove inland a little way, then found a patch of grass that was to be our home for the next few days, and settled in to make ourselves comfortable and await events. . . .

How tempted I am to go on like this: revisiting the apple orchard where the small boy came to give me my first lessons in Italian; or walking again beneath the tall vines, reaching up to help myself from the bunches of grapes, small, black, sweet and juicy, that hung overhead; or seeing at night, all silent and mysterious, the rounded hump of Monte Mango, while from the silent village at its foot rose the heady smell of newly pressed wine. This was the Italy of my letters home: all peace: no guns. It is the Italy that I remember most vividly and to which I have returned year after year. Even at the time, even during the war, I was able to look back on the country we had come through a bare month earlier and see only its beauty, all else having faded. It is so much of the truth – but of course it is only a part.

I have a collection of poems. They were sent to me by their author when he discovered that he and I had both served in 56 Division. He had been an infantry officer with the Queens and his poems were bitter and brutal, recording only the ugliness of war. For, yes, in spite of the vineyards and olive groves, the war in Italy was indeed ugly; and so his poems contained much that was true. Much but not all.

A year ago I was sent a typescript to read. It was a more or less factual account of his experiences in the Italian campaign written by a fellow Sapper; and he recorded neither the beauty nor the ugliness. Instead, he saw it all as a game, with himself the hero dashing from adventure to adventure, blazing away at the Jerries, being stonked, diving for cover, but always coming up with a grin and a quip. I tried to read it, but couldn't. I wanted to cry out, 'It was *not* like this. War is *not* a game.'

And this set me wondering: what was the truth, the *whole* truth? I needed to find out, because I needed to make sense of that extraordinary period in my life: twenty-one crowded months, probably the most formative twenty-one months I shall ever know. So I began to think about war in general – real war, I mean, not just the training and manoeuvring that I have described so far – and about my own personal experiences in particular. And the more I thought, the more I came to see that my Sapper friend's account was every bit as truthful as my own apple orchards and vineyards or the ugliness recorded by an infantry officer. Reluctantly I had to admit that war is indeed an exciting game; that children with their plastic guns ('Pow, pow! You're dead.') and schoolboys with their Thrilling Tales of Great Battles are visiting real, not fantastic worlds; and that it was just such a world that we all, to a greater or lesser extent, found waiting for us in Italy.

So the truth about war as the soldier sees it is, it seems to me, three-sided, like a triangle. You can label these three sides 'The Adventure of War', 'The Horror of War' and 'The Fruits of War'. Each of us had our own, unique triangle, its shape depending upon our nature and upon our experiences. What shape was mine?

To answer this question I must sort out my various memories into three piles and then examine each pile separately. And since this will mean upsetting their chronological sequence, it might be best if I begin with a very brief description – a sort of campaign map – of the route I took on my journey from Salerno to Triest.

On September 9th, 56 Division landed on a strip of sand near Salerno on the west coast of Italy just south of Naples. Three other Divisions landed alongside us – one British and two American – and together we made up the newly formed Fifth Army under the American General Mark Clark. A few days earlier Eighth Army under General Montgomery had crossed from Sicily to land on Italy's toe; and in between these two events the Italians had surrendered. I was still in the Field Park Company but our bridge now was the Bailey.

The landing was not seriously opposed and it was not until several days later that the Germans attacked very heavily and all but drove us back into the sea. However, we recovered, and then advanced quickly to Capua on the River Volturno, building a number of Bailey bridges on the way. Shortly after the crossing of the Volturno and to my great delight came my posting to 220 Field Company, where, a couple of weeks later, I was put in command of No. 1 Platoon.

We were now in mountainous country repairing narrow mountain tracks and occasionally clearing minefields; and soon we met a new enemy: rain. Rain that sent torrents swirling down the mountain side to sweep away our patched up bridges. Rain that turned firm roads into a swamp of mud.

Then came the attack on the Gustav Line, a line that stretched from the famous Monte Cassino down the Liri and the Garigliano to the sea. Our sector was on the Garigliano about a mile from its mouth and here on the eve of my father's birthday I built and operated a ferry. At the end of January came the landing behind the German lines at Anzio, and with it the wildly optimistic hope that Rome was about to fall. Alas, the beachhead got stuck. The Germans counter-attacked even more strongly than they had at Salerno and 56 Division had to be withdrawn from the Garigliano and shipped from Naples to reinforce the besieged garrison. We were at Anzio for six weeks and during the middle two of them acted as infantry. During our stay we neither advanced nor retreated, merely weathered the storm; and we were indeed glad to get away alive. We returned by ship to Naples, drove to Taranto, where another ship took us to Egypt for a badly needed rest.

Then followed leave in Cairo, training on the banks of the Suez Canal, more training near Gaza, a visit to Jerusalem, an exercise that took us from the Sea of Galilee down the Jordan to the Dead Sea (where we had a swim), and finally more training up in Syria. My furthest north was Beirut, where I got my hair cut. Then the long drive back through Palestine, across the Sinai Desert to Port Said, and thence by sea to Italy. We were now in Eighth Army. At Rome we were inspected by King George. At Assisi we paused to make our final preparations. At Pergola I celebrated my 24th birthday with a Bailey bridge. And then, a little to the south of Urbino, near Fossombrone, overflowing with optimism, we hurled ourselves at the German's Gothic Line. Our optimism lasted ten days, and as the grapes ripened again, came the bloodiest of all our battles.

Near Sant' Arcangelo on the edge of the Plain of Lombardy I was wounded. I was evacuated to Fano where a piece of shrapnel was taken out of my head, then flown to a hospital at Barletta. I convalesced among the *trulli* of Alberobello and sometime in December rejoined the Division at Forli. I spent a short time with HQRE and eventually moved to 221 Field Company as Information Officer. It was now January and the fighting had died down: rain and extensive flooding made movement very difficult. In April came the spring offensive that was to bring the campaign in Italy to an end. 56 Division was on the coast north of Ravenna and advanced up both sides of Lake Comacchio and through the 'Argenta gap'. By the end of the month all was virtually over. We crossed the Po without opposition and were at Rovigo on the Adige when the Germans surrendered. Thence we hurried to Trieste to keep the peace between the Italians and the Jugoslavs.

I was at Trieste for just over a year, returning to England and civilian life in time to celebrate my 25th birthday with my parents at Cotchford.

8. War – The Adventure

I had just recovered from malaria and was enjoying a week's sick leave in Tripoli when I learned that 56 Division was to take part in the invasion of Europe.

Oh, how my heart leapt at the news – as it had leapt back at Sible Hedingham when I was asked if I would like to accompany the Division overseas, and as it had leapt at Kirkuk when we received orders that we were moving to the Middle East for an important operation. But our voyage from England had taken us only to Iraq, and our journey to Africa had given us only the last few days of the Desert War. As yet we had done very little, and nothing to be especially proud of. We had yet to prove ourselves. Now at last was our chance, for this was surely the 'Second Front' that everyone had been talking about, clamouring for, for so long; and we were to be the spearhead of the attack, the vanguard of a mighty army that was to sweep across Europe. All that we had suffered hitherto – the boredom and the depression – served now only to intensify our feelings of excitement and elation. All was well. We were not a third rate Division fit only for garrison duties. The High Command had faith in us, and we would not fail them.

Such were my emotions, and the emotions, I suspect, of most of us; and so, as we set about preparing ourselves for 'D' Day,[1] our lives were filled with a sense of purpose. We were on the move again. We were riding the crest of a great wave that was fast heading for the shore. As yet the precise location of that shore was

---

[1] Not to be confused with that other 'D' Day, which took place nearly a year later – the landing in Northern France.

unknown. But the wave had a name. Its name was 'Avalanche', and the very word set my blood a-tingle.

Thus an important part of me was seeing myself not as an individual but as a member of a vast body of men and was feeling a thrill of pride that I wore the Black Cat on my sleeve. Never mind what I personally did or failed to do. History was about to be made. The Black Cat Division would be making it. And I would be there. 56 Division poised at Tripoli; the Light Brigade lining up at Balaclava; the British and French armies before Agincourt: the mood is the same. Bugles call, drums roll, voices shout, metal rings against metal, and slowly, rank by rank, section by section, company by company, we move into place A pause, a moment of silence and then . . . we're off! And as we surge forward and fling ourselves upon the enemy, we know no fear. We are not ordinary men with ordinary emotions. We are in the grip of a new and strange and wonderful emotion and it intoxicates us. Flashing swords, rattling machine guns: only the weapons are different. The thrill is as old as Man.

Yes, whatever happens afterwards, it starts as an adventure; and certainly I joined most enthusiastically in the general excitement. But there were moments when I had to admit that my own particular share in the adventure was going to be extremely modest. While the subalterns in the Field Companies were spending their last few weeks in Africa arming themselves with grenades and Bangalore torpedoes, practising leaping into the sea and dashing ashore through the waves, I had little to do but sit in my tent and feel envious. There was nothing special that I needed to practise. No one was likely to need a Bailey bridge on the beaches. So I had to draw what consolation I could from the fact that I was at least to be in the Company's Advance Party – under Captain Bertram – that I and my bridging lorries would be travelling in a Tank Landing Craft (which had a glamorous sound to it), and that we would be going ashore soon after dawn. Here was something to cheer me up. To have been in the Rear Party, to have travelled in a troopship, to have landed tamely long after all the fun was over: that would have been misery!

So, as the great fleet crossed the Mediterranean, I was feeling happily heroic.

Once we were safely, away from land, sealed orders were ceremoniously opened and we learned that our destination was a place called Salerno not far from Naples. Apart from a storm, our voyage was uneventful.

My lorries were lined up on the open deck and with them was a troop of anti-tank guns. I had a bunk in the wheelhouse and, some kindly organization having provided a small library, spent idle moments reading Hugh Walpole's *Jeremy at Thrale*, and then – with a few more idle moments still left – went on to *Mr Perrin and Mr Traill*: but alas there was not time to finish it, for, at 3 o'clock in the morning on September 9th, the great Avalanche swept ashore. Five hours later Lieutenant Milne, stepping daintily from ramp to sand, didn't even get his boots wet.

Here then is one aspect of the adventure of war, one mood that infects us. It is a mood that carries us, high-spirited, through the preparations for battle and into the battle itself, and it is a mood that entirely obliterates fear. How long it lasts and whether it ever recurs will depend on our individual fortunes. The fighting at Salerno was very fierce and many must have quickly moved to the second side of my triangle, from adventure to horror. But I was lucky. Bridges were not wanted and so I had little to do, and having little to do, I did not therefore make a very important target for the German guns.

The mood that carried me to Salerno, though it evaporated temporarily during the dull days that followed, quickly reasserted itself when we finally burst through the ring of mountains and spilled down into the Plain of Naples. Now came the Great Advance, the road choc-a-bloc with vehicles, looking like Oxford Street during the rush hour: a gigantic, solid, steel caterpillar grinding and crunching its way forward, and I a part of it, caught up in it, I, too, with my bridging lorries, leaving the rest of the Field Park far behind, all on my own now, grinding my way forward with the tanks and the carriers and the guns. Oh, it was indeed marvellous to be there.

Thus we advanced, almost unopposed, to the Volturno; and, once through the mountain pass, I was racing ahead to provide the bridges that enabled the advance to continue. Yes, I was lucky. This part of the Italian campaign might have been designed especially to suit the Bridging Officer of a Field Park Company. Never again in Italy were so many bridges needed. Night after night I was providing them. And when at last we moved into a different sort of country, out of the plains and into the hills, away from broad tarmac roads among narrow, stony mountain tracks, when at last no more Baileys were needed, then (so it almost seemed) the High Command said: 'Milne's job is over. He can now be posted to a Field Company.' And I was, and the adventure continued.

But what about the enemy, you may ask; what about the fighting? It's easy to enjoy it all when you're not being shot at.

True, but an exploding shell doesn't necessarily bring the adventure to an end. Indeed sometimes quite the reverse.

There was a game we used to play at school in which, greatly daring, we danced over the borders of our own home-ground on to the free-for-all ground in front of us. 'Can't catch me! Can't catch me!' we cried as we danced forward, inviting pursuit. 'Oh, can't I!' cried the other fellow. And then the chase, scampering, dodging, until, if we were lucky, flushed with excitement, panting with exhaustion, we were safely home again. This was the game we played with the Germans. Of course, the stakes were higher. But the stakes were high anyway; so there was nothing to lose making it into a game. There were two forms: in the one you hoped you would not be seen; in the other you hoped you would not be hit. The first was best played at night; the second in daylight. And since I played both on the Garigliano – and something else besides – it might be worth while to see what happened there.

It will be remembered that the Garigliano formed the seaward end of the Gustav Line. We reached it in December and by that time I was commanding No. 1 Platoon of 220 Field Company.

I can't remember now the name of the village we had moved to. It might have been Laura but I rather think it was one a little further to the south. At any rate it was down in the plain and the climate was noticeably milder. The move from Roccamonfina was a move sideways, not an advance. The advance had got stuck at Monte Camino. We were now regrouping, ready for the big attack. In front of us the ground was flat and open. Somewhere ahead was the river, and here, if anywhere, was the line that separated the two armies. Beyond the river the plain continued a short way and then came the mountains. We could see the mountains, which meant of course that they could see us. So there wasn't much we could do in daylight – except enjoy the gentle, mellow peacefulness of our surroundings. Only at night did we become soldiers, sallying out to work on the various tracks that criss-crossed the plain and led to the river.

Then came my first patrol.

It was, of course, to the river. For the river was the first obstacle to be crossed. Deep and slow, it flowed between high banks some two hundred feet apart – and somewhere along its course we had to construct a ferry. Where? That was the question. Our maps gave us a clue. Aerial photographs gave us another. But only by going to have a close look could we be quite sure. So, on a succession of nights, one or another of us went. I was still fairly new to the Company, not very experienced, and so it was only natural that Major Smith kept the most likely place for his own visit, did the thing in style, swam the river and won the Military Cross. The place I was sent to look at was never, I guess, more than a faint possibility. It was where the railway bridge had been demolished: there and another place about fifty yards upstream.

I dressed for the part: jersey in place of tunic and something woolly on my head. Some of us wore special shoes with rubber soles so as to make less noise, but I never did, for I had a sort of superstition about my boots: I felt safe in them. Then I set out, calling first on the infantry Company that was looking after that section of the front, to pick up my guides. Not only would they know the way but, more important, they would ensure that whatever happened on the river I was at least not mistaken for a German on my return. All was quiet, they said. No German patrols had been reported on our side of the river. Good. We'll be gone about an hour.

I was now crossing that strip of land that separates the two front lines. In the First World War it was called 'No Man's Land' for it was a land inhabited only by corpses, and anyone who ventured there risked becoming a corpse himself. I can't remember what we called it in Italy if indeed we called it anything. I'll have something to say about it later. Here let me say only that at night it was utterly silent, utterly deserted and, so it seemed, utterly untouched by the noisy, messy battling armies that flanked it on either side. I was on a narrow track that ran between raised banks, heading for the river, feeling (of course) very excited, looking (had anybody been watching) probably mildly ridiculous. For I was – or felt I ought to be – ready to take instant action should a patrol of Germans be lying in ambush behind the next tree. Thus I advanced with knees slightly bent, pistol in hand, and my two guides following behind.

About fifty yards short of the river we stopped. Here I went on alone, moving very cautiously on hands and knees. Yes, we had come to the right place, for there was the tangled mass of the bridge, half in the water, half out – and totally obstructing any possible ferry. However, let me at least be able to say I had done the job properly: very gently I pulled myself forward to the water's edge and dipped in a finger. . . .

Such was my first patrol. I had not been spotted, and I returned home safely, feeling very pleased with myself.

Then came the big attack. More guns, Major Smith told us, would fire tonight than had fired at the opening of the Battle of El Alamein: and immediately I felt a return of the thrill I had felt before Salerno.

My Platoon was to build and operate the ferry. It was late evening, already dark, and in the darkness we were making final preparations with the lorry that was to carry our equipment, when the Hour came, the Conductor brought down his baton, and with a crash the whole percussion orchestra sounded forth. The noise was terrific, thumps behind us as the guns fired, flashes and crashes ahead of us as the shells exploded, and the sky above scratched all over with lines of tracer. I had heard it before like this one night at Salerno. It was like a symphony: lasting as long, the instruments almost as varied – for each type of gun has its own individual voice – and the effect every bit as dramatic and moving. Then I had been in the audience, no more than a listener. Now I was a participant; and so, as we made our way down to the river, my Platoon on foot, the lorry creeping along beside us, it was as if we were marching to the sound of drums and cymbals, and my feeling of intoxication reached its climax.

We built the ferry. Things went wrong, of course, because things usually do go wrong. It doesn't greatly matter. Indeed, it is often quite a good thing, for the more there is to think about and worry about, the less time there is to feel afraid. On this occasion our lorry – for reasons, best known to its driver – went into a ditch and couldn't get out. So all our equipment had to be carried the last two or three hundred yards. However, all was ready on time. In fact it was the infantry who kept us waiting. For it was not until 8 o'clock in the morning that the far bank was reported clear of Germans and we were able to cross over and complete work on the other side.

Thus the ferry, and all told it provided me with a good range of experiences until, very suddenly, very unexpectedly and, as it happened, quite pleasingly dramatically, I left it.

It was about a week later. I had been doing something on the far side and was returning in my jeep. There were three or four vehicles ahead of me waiting to cross; and as soon as I had joined them we had our first shell. It was quite a small one, as shells go, and it travelled in a leisurely way so that you could hear the thump as it was fired and then the singing as it approached, before the crash that announced its arrival. The vehicles backed down the track out of the way, but I stayed by the river – I forget now why, possibly because I was in a hurry to get across. One shell isn't much to worry about and there might not be any more. But there were; and then happened an incident that in retrospect – and I have reflected on it many times since – still leaves me wondering, groping for an explanation.

There was a ditch beside the track that would provide the cover I needed while the shelling lasted. I got into it and stood there waiting for the thump that would announce the approach of the next one. Two other soldiers were in the ditch with me; I was facing the river and they were behind me. Then something told me that it would be better to face the other way. Perhaps I wanted to see who my companions were or perhaps I wanted to face the gun so as to hear it better. I began to turn round: a simple enough thing to do, something I must have done a million times before, and no particular difficulty doing it while standing in a ditch, but this time I found myself moving rather more slowly, rather more thoughtfully than usual. Weight on to right foot, left foot off the ground, left leg turned, then gently lowered – as if I were on the parade ground learning it by numbers. ... And as I lowered my left leg I heard a sound. No, not the boom of the gun that I had been listening for; something much nearer, much more unexpected, much more menacing: the sound of metal against metal coming from beneath the sole of my foot. Metal studs clinking against something metal on the ground. I knew what it was at once, drew back my foot and looked down; and there sticking out of the ground, quite meaningless unless you were familiar with them, scarcely visible even then, were three little black wires about an inch long, the three prongs of the igniter that the Germans used on their 'S' mines. A tiny push, the merest fraction of my full weight, and the igniter would have exploded.

As I said earlier, I never fancied getting a pair of rubber soled patrol boots. This was why.

And now the dodging game began. I shouted to the two soldiers to get out of the ditch and together we ran back up the track to a farmhouse. There I found a slit trench and jumped inside, whereupon the gun shortened its range and began firing at the farm. One of its shells scored a hit and I saw somebody being carried away bleeding. As I will explain later, I always found this sort of thing horribly upsetting. A game is a game, no matter how dangerous, but once somebody gets hurt, it stops being a game and I hate it. So I left the farmhouse and ran back to the river. The next shell joined me there, which was flattering in a way, but which set me a problem, for the ditch was mined and I knew that the fields on either side were mined too. So where did I take shelter?

There was just one possibility: in the middle of the track was a small crater where a few nights previously a tellermine had exploded. It was about three feet across and a foot deep. With another shell announcing its approach I climbed in and curled up. Yes, I was still very much the target and the crater wasn't deep enough. A few yards away was what was left of the jeep that had set off the mine and strapped to its back, still surviving, was a shovel. I unfastened it and set to work to dig. The next shell was nearer but my hole was deeper. The shell after that was all but a direct hit. I could have stretched out my hand and touched it, but luckily my hole was by now deeper still. Nevertheless, I reckoned I'd had enough and that the time had come to make a dash for Home.

The ferry was on the far side and was no use to me. But, in addition, we had rigged up a device for getting foot passengers across, consisting of two small boats, a length of rope and two pulleys. You got into one of the boats, pulled on the rope and away you went; and as you moved out from the shore so the boat on the other side was pulled towards you until, in mid-stream, the two passed each other. Thus when you had arrived at the far bank, the boat that had started there was now on the near bank ready for the next lot of passengers.

This was my way to safety, and the only question was whether I could get across in time. I hoped I might just be able to, and raced to the water's edge. And I most clearly remember my thoughts as I did so. I was remembering something I had read about many years before: that if you were very frightened because, for example, you were being pursued by a bull, something called adrenalin was automatically pumped into your blood, giving you extra energy, extra speed to escape from danger. Now here was a moment when I ought to be very frightened and most certainly needed extra speed, so it would be an interesting experiment to see if adrenalin came to my rescue.

Thus it was in something of an experimental mood that I jumped into the waiting boat and heaved on the rope. And I was greatly disappointed to find that, so far from having extra energy, my arms and legs were heavy as lead, my muscles made of jelly. My only consolation was that I seemed able to think extra clearly; for as I heaved I was calculating that it might be possible to save a few seconds if, in mid-stream (and despite the proverb that advises against it) I changed boats. This would save the time taken to pull them past each other and avoid risk of entanglement. I moved up into the bows ready for a quick scramble. . . .

I was Home and the game was over. I had won and the Germans had lost! Was I too quick for them . . . or had they just run out of shells? I don't know, and it doesn't matter. It was an adventure with a happy ending – but the happiest part was yet to come; for at the top of the home bank I found Major Smith, sitting on the edge of a slit trench waiting for me.

'Hullo,' he said in his dry voice and with the very slight smile that, as a Regular Soldier, he just occasionally allowed himself. 'You've been having an exciting time. I was afraid I was going to have to win the Military Cross coming to your rescue. . . .'

But it was not to watch my antics that he had come down to the river. It was to bring me news that I was being sent to Capua on a Bridging Course. The course was to last a week and I was to leave first thing in the morning.

I have already, I hope, made it clear that danger and fear are not related. And so far I have described situations which, though possibly dangerous, were never fearful, situations in which, as it were, danger was so well disguised that we never recognized it. But there were, of course, many situations, many periods when the disguise wore thin, when Death – our own or the deaths of others – began to show through and chill our blood. What then?

The first thing was to arrive at a proper understanding of danger, to realize that what seemed dangerous quite often was not, or was not if you took sensible precautions. On arriving at Salerno we should have immediately dug ourselves slit trenches. We didn't, paid for it, and learned our lesson. Inexperienced troops, though often wonderfully fearless, could at the same time be foolishly careless of their lives; and then when things went wrong they would panic. With greater experience we learned that lives were important. We did not take unnecessary risks, became steadier under fire and were not scared by mere noise. And just as, during our recruit training we had learned to take a pride in our physical abilities, so now we took a pride in our courage; and this helped to keep us even steadier. Thus we enlisted pride and commonsense; and, since the more allies we had the better, we looked for things to distract us and we learned to laugh as much as possible. When all this began to fail us we set about inventing disguises. War was not war; it was a game of rugger, fast, tough, exciting, with a good chance of a bloody nose or a bruised shin, but nothing worse. Or alternatively (and this I think was the disguise most favoured by the British) war was a party, a children's party with crackers and sparklers, but all really rather tame and boring to the adult. 'What was it like?' we would ask the returning warrior. 'Oh, quite a party,' he would reply with a drawl. 'Bit noisy at times.' No more than a noisy party. No one could possibly be frightened of that!

But in the end – if one survived that long – all distractions and disguises wore thin. In the end we had to stare the monster in the face, and this was the real test of our courage. I was lucky. Mine was only a little monster: big enough and fierce enough to satisfy me that it was real, all right, but not so big that I couldn't – most of the time – outstare it.

And now I must tell what I saw.

9. War – The Horror

In war you may be killed or wounded. But people are killed and wounded every day on our roads and we don't talk about the horror of driving. The horror of war is not what it does to the human body (which anyway it probably does only once if at all) but what it does to the human spirit. It is the sight (and sound and smell) of the dead and the injured, the fear that what has happened to them will happen to you, together with all the feelings of revulsion and despair aroused by the human carnage and general destruction that go to make war's horror.

In this respect we were luckier than our fathers. Our war was infinitely less horrible than theirs. At no point in the Italian campaign did we lose faith in our cause or in ultimate victory. At no point did we feel that our lives were being uselessly sacrificed by an uncaring High Command. Though at times our spirits may have been low, at no point did they reach total despair. And this I say loudly and clearly because I cannot begin to write about the horrors of the war in Italy, still less about the horrors of my particular part in it, without first making it absolutely plain that, though the same word may be applied (for lack of another) to the Battle of the Somme, its meaning is totally different.

A small incident comes to mind. It was during my bridging course at Capua. One evening after supper the officer in charge was talking to a group of us, recounting his experiences during a training exercise at Aldershot. With sparkling eyes and obvious relish he was telling us how live rounds had been fired over his head. Oh, yes, he, too, knew of the excitement of coming under fire. He too had his story. And I remember so vividly my reactions both at the time and later, discussing it with a colleague: amazement, almost indignation, that he should have offered this to us who had just come from the Gustav Line! That is why, ever since, I have always been so reluctant to talk about my own blood-curdling adventures. And if I attempt to do so now – because I must – it is with the full realization that they are very small stuff compared with what others suffered. I say this mainly to excuse what follows. But it is also an opportunity to record what are, I suspect, fairly general reactions to our own personal war experiences: pride and a sense of superiority if the hardships and dangers we had to undergo were greater than the other man's; humility sometimes amounting almost to feelings of shame if they were less.

The horror of war has two components: revulsion and fear. The two are quite different and could be encountered quite separately, and when separate they were not too hard to bear. It was when they were together that they became so formidable. For then Death was tapping us on the shoulder saying, 'Look! What I have done to them I can do to you. What I have done here I can do again.' Sickened at what we saw and at the same time sick with fear we did indeed feel more than doubly sick.

I remember my first corpse with that clarity that is reserved for all 'firsts'. He was Sapper Pockett, and I even remember his name though I have no cause to, for he was not one of our Sappers, not even in the Division but from a Construction Company. I had never known him alive and saw him dead for only half a minute. There he lay, along the roadside. Someone passing by had chanced on him and, seeing him to be an Engineer, had come to us; and Major Lake had sent me to cope. But what did one do? I really had no idea. Have a look, for a start, anyway: so I had a look. A shell had landed just in front of him and blown him over so that his head was broken and spilled like an egg that has been dropped on the floor. I wondered what would happen if I tried to get him into my truck, what sort of mess it would make of us all; and I recoiled at the prospect. In the end I left him and went to find a Burial Unit. Here I met an officer whose stammer was even worse than mine – which helped to restore my morale. He asked only one question. 'Is he in one p-p-p-p-p-p-piece?' Good for Sapper Pockett. Apart from a missing arm, he was at least that.

Sapper Pockett was fresh. The Corporal – whose name I forget, if indeed I ever knew it – was stale. He had been wedged in the iron ladder at the top of a water tower for several days before I was told to try and get him down. The ladder, originally vertical, had been bent and now overhung at its upper end, making it anyway unpleasant enough to climb. But far worse than this was the smell and the dripping that came from the object at the top. Let me forestall the anticlimax: I didn't succeed. It was the Caserta fire brigade that got him down in the end – and the weight of his crashing body broke their ladder. On my own, with only a rope, I could never have done it. But at least I tried. I got right up beneath him, tied myself to the ladder, and then, with both hands free, tied a rope to his ankle. Drops of clear pink liquid were coming off him all the time, but I had fastened a handkerchief over my nose and mouth, wore a gas cape over my head and shoulders and my glasses protected my eyes. Then I untied myself and returned, weak and trembling, to the ground. We pulled the rope. But he had been dead too long and his decaying flesh was moist and slippery. Boot and sock came off and fell uselessly at our feet.

Thus my initiation; and how fortunate for me that both incidents occurred when there was no danger and no fear. It was only revulsion I had to face, and to my great relief I had faced it well enough. They were only small ordeals but most valuable in the self-confidence they gave me.

To some extent, I suppose, the mind protects itself automatically from what it fears to contemplate. A doctor can look upon a battered body and see it only as a medical problem. My corporal was a problem in engineering. When a mine exploded beneath a jeep one night on the Garigliano (and we have already met both the mine's crater and the remains of the jeep) my attention was so riveted by the banshee wailing that came – I eventually realized – from its horn that it was not until I had stopped the horn by ripping out its flex and then put out the fire that followed, that it occurred to me to wonder what had happened to its driver. And then I remembered the torch-like object that had been tossed up into the air by the explosion. Presumably that was he, in which case what was left of him was now lying in a minefield. There was only one thing I needed to do: make quite sure he was dead. I blessed the darkness and I blessed the minefield, for I would not now be inspecting the tattered remains of a human being, I would be spending the next few minutes trying not to trip over unseen tripwires or put my foot on unseen igniters, which was quite sufficient to occupy all my attention. And when that had been done I could return to my ferry and forget the whole incident.

If there wasn't a particular problem to distract attention, my mind would fasten onto minor details. A line of dead Fusiliers on a hillside and it was their boots that I found myself thinking about. Socks and boots were such homely, ordinary, personal things, so much a part of everyday life. You put them on in the morning and took them off at night, and the socks had holes in the toes and the boots were worn down at their heels. Somehow it seemed incongruous that you should continue to wear them when you were dead. . . . And on another occasion, when my Corporal, Bob Whalley, was hit in the throat and collapsed on top of me and bled to death all over me, what struck me as interesting was that even in his dying gasp, 'Oh, oh, oh.' I could still detect his North Country accent.

But on the whole I didn't meet death too often. Today one pictures the crowds that gather round a road accident eager for a sight of the victims. It was not like that during the war. Nobody concerned himself with what was not his concern and, as Engineers, our concern was with things not people. So the dead we ignored. In any case it needed only one person to put on a bandage, two to carry a body. More than that just got in the way.

Thus was a thoroughly untough soldier gradually toughened up until in the end he was able to cope with fear and horror simultaneously. I remember on one occasion in north Italy seeing a wounded man being helped out of a tank. It must have been at least a hundred and fifty yards away and I have no particular recollection of the shell or whatever it was that hit him. I just have this very clear picture of two figures on top leaning down and then lifting up a third figure and that third figure was – or seemed to be – red. The incident concerned me not at all; the sight was far too distant to be in the least horrible: had the man in the middle sprained his ankle and been wearing a red jersey, he would have looked no different. The reason for my sudden wave of nausea was because of what had happened five minutes earlier. I had been near a farmhouse that had suddenly come under very heavy mortar fire. I ran inside, took refuge in what turned out to be a stable, lay on the floor and hoped for the best, while the shells came crashing down outside. It was fairly frightening while it lasted and it seemed to last ages. A small distraction was that I found I was sharing the stable with a cow and so was able to wonder what would happen if the cow suddenly started charging about. Since this would have made my position even less comfortable, it was a distraction of doubtful value. However, the cow seemed remarkably placid. ... Eventually the storm came to an end, and I was able to go outside and look around. Apparently not much harm had been done: none of the machine gunners who were occupying the farm had been hit. The only casualty so they told me was the Italian farmer himself who had tried to make a run for it: silly man; he should have stayed put. So I left the farm, slightly shaken but with light-heartedness once more surging back. 'Can't catch me!' I had got away with it again. ... And then I saw the man in the tank. And the message was plain. 'War is not a Game. War is real. Shells can kill. Next time it might be you.' And immediately I felt awful.

But however unpleasant it was to see death or injury, fear was our worst enemy: fear of our own death. It was fear that made us go to pieces. If we ran away it was because we were afraid.

'I would it were bed-time, Hal, and all well.' Thus Falstaff to Prince Henry before the battle of Shrewsbury. And if I were asked to give my reasons for believing that Shakespeare himself had on some occasion taken part in a battle, these ten words would be my proof. How deceptively simple they sounded, yet what a chord they set reverberating! How well I remember this yearning for bed-time as, cold and frightened ('But it's not really cold, so why am I shivering?') I set out on an enterprise I knew was going to be unpleasant. Bed-time! All the bedtimes of happier days, right back to my childhood, came in a great procession before my eyes, and I reached out towards them – almost literally, for I could feel the muscular spasm – as if I were trying to grasp them and heave myself through the next few hours to the security that lay on the other side.

It was like this at Teano. It was like this on a number of other occasions, too. But in one respect Teano was (thank goodness) unique and that is why I would like to say what happened there.

It was just before I left the Field Park Company all eager for the more adventurous life I would surely find in a Field Company. My Bridging Platoon was in among some olive trees just north of the Volturno. The rest of the Company was still in the Caserta area south of the river. The Division was pushing ahead against increasing resistance towards Cassino. That night a bridge was to be built at Teano.

I should have been excited. I might well have felt jealous that once again I would just be a spectator while another officer did the work, had all the fun and got all the glory; but at least I should have been excited that here was something happening and that I was taking part in it. Better surely than sitting under an olive tree feeling frustrated. I had felt excited enough on all previous occasions. There had been the Division's first ever Bailey bridge at Battipaglia. I had been there. We had built it in daylight and the Germans had shelled my lorries – not seriously, I must admit, but enough to boast about afterwards. And there had been several more bridges after that as we crossed the Plain of Naples, all of them built at night, all of them uneventful, uninterrupted. There may have been moments of jealousy. There may have been moments of acute boredom as, with nothing to do, I stood idly watching while others worked, or wandered off on my own into the dark and paced up and down and thought about this and that and looked at my watch and wished time would go a little faster and that I didn't feel so sleepy. But at least I was up near the front doing important work; and so, all in all, life was good and I was happy, and the more bridges they wanted the better.

So why didn't I rejoice tonight? Why did I suddenly feel afraid? I had never felt afraid before. Why now?

Was it because the officer who was to be in charge was himself afraid and his fear was catching? Or was it instinct, the instinct one has that thunder is in the air, that a storm is about to burst. One did seem to develop a sort of subconscious barometer that warned of danger. Mine had been high for so long. Now it was suddenly falling. . . .

It had always seemed the natural thing to accompany my lorries to the bridge site, even though there was so little for me to do when I got there. I suppose that if something had gone wrong it might have been useful to have had an extra officer around. But normally there wasn't anything that one of my corporals couldn't do equally well. So if I went, I went because I wanted to not because I had to. I wanted to see what was happening and I wanted to be with my men. After all that was my rule: an officer's place is where the work is most exciting. So what good reason was there for not going tonight? None.

But equally there was no good reason why I *should* go; and I began to produce arguments for staying behind. I had always been in charge in the past: well, why shouldn't someone else be in charge for a change. Why shouldn't Corporal Quick take the lorries up? He could do it equally well. And the experience and responsibility would be good for him. There was nothing special about this particular bridge, no reason really for supposing that it would be any different from all the others. So why should I have to spend a boring, wearying night doing nothing when I might just as well be in bed.

I went to Quick and gave him his orders. And then, to show how little I had been persuaded by my own reasoning, I told him not to wait until all the lorries had been unloaded so that they could return in convoy – as we had always done in the past – but to send them back one at a time as soon as they were ready to leave. 'Don't hang around up there,' I said. 'They can easily find their own way back.'

Thus I hoped I had covered myself whatever happened. My conscience could now rest easy.

Away they went, and I retired to my tent and lay on my bed and tried to convince myself that I had not been a total coward, that the night would be peaceful and all would be well. I lay awake listening. Yes, as I thought, not a sound to be heard. They had already been gone some time and the first empty lorry would be due back any minute. The minutes dragged by but no lorry came. The hours crept slowly towards midnight, then even more slowly onwards, onwards towards another day. Did I sleep? I doubt it. What time did they get back? I can't remember. What happened? What I knew would happen, only worse. They had been shelled continuously; a number of Sappers had been killed; Quick had been wounded; there were two dead bodies in one of the lorries; the bridge had been abandoned.

Pathetically, I tried to sound surprised. . . .

Fear of what might happen: that was one sort. Fear when it was actually happening: that was another.

There were many varieties of bang, some more unpleasant than others. An approaching shell is a little like an approaching dog. One dog in a thousand may bite, one in a hundred may growl, the rest wag their tails. If you've met the dog before, then however uncertain its temper and even if it growls a little, you'll have learned how to treat it and you'll probably not get bitten. If it's a stranger, you are rather more apprehensive. 'Good doggie, good doggie,' you say hoping to convince it that it is one of the well behaved nine hundred; and if it then growls, you fear the worst. So it was with shells. Very few actually did any harm. Most would approach with a not unpleasant singing sound wagging their tails in a friendly way, and once we were used to them they were not particularly frightening. A few came tearing at us like an express train and were much more alarming. And a few were fitted with ingenious devices. After all, if a shell isn't going to hurt you, it is at least something if it scares you. Better a dog that barks than one that wags its tail where burglars are concerned. So there were the 'moaning minnies', fired from mortars in batches of ten, and which, as they approached us, sobbed crocodile tears at the havoc they were about to create. And there were the air bursts – shells that exploded in mid air, and, whether or not they were more lethal, certainly both sounded and looked much more menacing. But even those that sang could on occasion bite, and so we searched for additional reassurance. 'Good shell, good shell,' we said. 'It's not us you're after, is it? It's those poor devils over there.' And we could thus feel ourselves to be, not intended victims, but spectators, which was much less frightening. And if an accidental one came close and made us duck, we could tell ourselves it was a mistake, not meant for us at all, and we could almost forgive it.

When one was up and about it was never too bad. For it was not expected that we should work when a storm was raging. The infantry could make a dash for it and risk getting wet. Tanks had their armour to keep them dry. But Sappers worked in the open, slowly, carefully, often in quite large groups, and with nothing to protect them. So when a storm broke we took cover and waited until it was over. After all, the German guns only had a limited number of shells. Even if they could see us they could never afford to fire at us all the time. There were other more important targets.

But in bed at night it was very different. 'I would it were bedtime, Hal. . . .' Yes, indeed, but only if all were well. It usually was. Nights were usually quiet – but not quite always; and then bed could be the most miserable of places, with nothing to distract one, nothing to do but lie awake and a-tremble waiting wretchedly for the next explosion. And oh, how close and menacing they always seemed on these occasions. No chance now of persuading myself that they were being aimed at someone else: they were being aimed at me and I knew it! If I could have got up and gone out and looked around, I might have convinced myself that this was not so; but it needed more determination than I possessed. And so I lay there waiting and waiting for the nightmare to come to an end. . . .

Thus our encounters with fear passed through three stages. In the first, we barely noticed it: war was an adventure and excitement dominated our emotions. In the second stage the excitement had worn off, fear was present but we were able to control it. In the third stage the strain began to tell. War was now no longer a game, nor could we fool ourselves that it was a party. It was just thoroughly stupid and thoroughly bloody. At the start, filled with confidence, we had walked upright, chin up, chest out, like soldiers on parade. Later we had developed a permanent stoop. We walked with knees bent, eyes to the ground, measuring the distance to the nearest hollow, ready for an instant spring. In the end we didn't bother. It wasn't worth it. If you're going to hit me, do it now, for Heavens sake, and get it over. . . .

It was October, 1944. We were down in the Lombardy Plain. We had fought our way from bloody ridge to bloody ridge, up and down, up and down, with always another one ahead of us. And then at last we had fought our way through to the Promised Land, only to find it no Promised Land at all but another, even nastier battlefield.

We were down in the Plain of Lombardy and my Platoon was in a farmhouse and just outside was a field of aubergines. We were preparing our midday meal, cooking it in a German Field Kitchen. This Field Kitchen didn't really belong to us. We had taken it over from a Platoon of a Field Company in 78 Division, back at Taranto four months previously. They were leaving Italy for the Middle East. We had just arrived back; and so we were inheriting all their vehicles and equipment. But the Field Kitchen was a little different: they had captured it and so it was their very own and only lent to us on the understanding that they could reclaim it on their return. They were now back, and a message had just come that their Platoon Commander was at Company HQ all eager to bear it away.

I went round, feeling thoroughly cross and uncooperative.

'I'm sorry,' I said, 'it's in use at the moment. It's got my men's dinner inside it and I'm not handing it over until they've finished with it.'

'But I've got to get it back at once,' said the subaltern. 'I must have it right away.'

'I'm sorry. You can't. You'll just have to wait – or come another day.'

Three officers, standing in a group, arguing irritably, all a little on their dignity: a nice target. A ranging shell landed nearby.

When dogs are on their dignity nothing less than a direct hit with a bucket of water will break up the argument. So it was with us. In my case, it was partly the argument, partly that the honour of the Division demanded that I didn't make the first move, and partly that I was past caring anyway; and I expect it was much the same with the others. 'Wounded' and 'Killed in Action': familiar words in those days, and to those who saw them day after day in the newspapers recalling perhaps those pictures of battles in which men are firing guns at each other at point blank range, horses are rearing, swords are flashing and it seems unlikely that there will be a single survivor. How different is modern war! At times how unglamorous! One might be wounded charging the enemy with a tommy gun, but one was just as likely to be struck down while sitting on the latrine. Indeed, in our case, more likely. For it was the odd and the unexpected shell catching us when we were least expecting it that so often did the damage. Nearly all my Platoon's casualties occurred in circumstances that were far from glorious, and I was no exception.

The other shells had landed with a crash. The one that finally settled our argument made, so it seemed to me, no sound but a puff, a sort of buffet somewhere behind my head. I scarcely heard it. I never saw it. And, luckily, I never even felt it.

His lips curling in a cynical smile, the god Mars distributes his rewards. For some they are appropriate – for after all he must retain the respect in which men hold him, retain his authority over their lives. And so for some it is the well-earned medal or the hero's death in action. But for others. ... One by one we come before him and hopefully we hold out our hand.

When my turn came he saw before him someone who, for all

his attempts to look like a soldier, yet remained a faintly ludicrous figure. And so, being in one of his kindlier moods, he gave me what I wanted just when I wanted it. He took me gently and he pressed his thumb into the back of my head, not too hard to hurt, not too deep to leave more than a small but permanent dent.

A few days later my parents learned that I had been wounded and placed on the 'seriously ill list'. But by that time I was feeling nothing but a deep sense of happiness and pride.

10. *War – The Fruits*

In the old days you plundered the towns and raped the women. Loot and sex were the fruits of war. And to some extent – sanctified by history though fortunately greatly modified – these were two of the fruits of our war in Italy. There were brothels in Naples and elsewhere (though I was too young and innocent to know anything about them), and if we didn't exactly loot, we certainly 'liberated', which was much the same thing.

But there were other fruits as well. I have already mentioned some of the differences between the Italian Campaign and the First World War. Another difference is that, while our fathers were fighting in a country whose utter destruction had reduced it to a lunatic's nightmare, we were advancing through changing landscapes some of which were among the world's finest and were quite untouched by the fighting. Even at its most battered and depressing Italy would still have seemed a paradise compared with Flanders mud. The apples we picked from the trees, the bunches of grapes we picked from the vine: yes, these were among the fruits of our war. But so too was the apple orchard. So too the view from the vineyard.

Most of us – even, had he been there, that recruit who had described Barton Stacey as a god-forsaken hole – must have felt that Italy was a pleasant country to fight in. To someone who loved the countryside as much as I did, it was more than just that. And to me personally, it was more than just more: it was something else besides.

What happened at Montefiore will illustrate what I mean.

We captured Montefiore on September 3rd, 1944, and with its capture our hopes for a quick breakthrough to the Po, to Venice, indeed to Vienna, reached their height. The following evening a small and select column of vehicles formed up along the narrow road that led to the town, and among them was a detachment of Engineers under my command consisting of a bulldozer, a scout car with a sergeant and three or four men, and my jeep with its driver.

Our object – wildly optimistic as it turned out – was to force our way quickly through and past the German defences where they appeared weakest and make a dash towards San Marino. Looked at in cold blood it was an alarming prospect. Had we known just how strong these defences were, the prospect would have seemed even more alarming. But we didn't know and our blood was still hot; and I was both delighted and excited to be taking part.

I have already mentioned the importance of a little confusion, and the confusion with which this enterprise started most certainly helped to make it much less frightening. On the other side of Montefiore was the river Conca. The river was crossed by a bridge and the bridge – naturally enough – had been demolished. Here then was the first obstacle that my bulldozer and Sappers would have to negotiate before the column could proceed. We ought, therefore, to have been at the head of the column. Alas, we were near the tail, and the road we were moving along was extremely narrow. How, in the rapidly waning light of day, does one get a bulldozer past a troop of field guns jammed nose to tail? That was my first problem. Slowly, with many apologies and much backing and bumping, jeep and bulldozer made their way up the line, and, as darkness descended, entered Montefiore.

Montefiore was like the setting for the second act of a Verdi opera, dark, mysterious and intensely dramatic; its paved streets barely wide enough to accommodate my bulldozer; its buildings rising sheer on either side; no light, no sound, no sign of life. Was the town deserted? Were its inhabitants all a-bed? Or were they up and alert, watching anxiously from behind barred windows? Slowly we creaked our way through, ours the only noise in the surrounding silence. ... And then, round a corner ahead of us, entirely blocking the way, as solid, as lifeless and seeming almost as large as the buildings it was wedged between, was a vast Churchill tank. It was just what I needed and I laughed aloud, then clambered up it and knocked politely on its roof. . . .

Night had fully come when at last we reached the river. The Brigadier was waiting for us and he was in a hurry. I was given no time to reconnoitre: I was told where I was to make my crossing and so I set my bulldozer to work cutting a ramp down to the water's edge, while impatient staff officers paced up and down. I was not happy about it: there was too much soft earth and not enough hard rock. Vehicles were going to get stuck. I'd seen this happen so often before. However, I had no choice and we did the best we could and it certainly *looked* all right; and then the Brigadier was back again. Montefiore on its hill lay behind us; ahead was a plain, and through this plain ran our road. But over on the left was a great ridge and on its highest point perched the village of Gemmano. The village and the ridge looked down on us, silent, brooding, powerful, watching us – so it seemed – as we scratched away at its feet. 'That ridge,' he said, 'is Boche-held. I must be past it by first light.' So my bulldozer and I had to leave the river and hurry along the road to look for the next obstacle.

We were now ahead of the column. I was riding on the bulldozer beside the driver and the open road lay before us, faintly silvered as the beginnings of light began to creep back into our world, and utterly deserted. In the dust of its surface I could just detect a single set of track marks: someone had been here ahead of us, perhaps one of our carriers. But of him there was no sign. There was no sign of life anywhere, just the two of us racketing down the road, while above us loomed Gemmano ridge. The night air was cool and fresh and invigorating; it was the first time I had ever ridden on a bulldozer; and I wanted to shout and sing, I was so happy.

Of course you can say that it must have been exciting to be out in front of an advancing army, leading the way, and that so long as there was no shooting there was no reason to feel afraid. On the other hand you must concede that my bulldozer was a large, vulnerable, and – if not visible in the darkness – at least a very audible target; that there were certainly German guns in the hills, quite possibly a German tank waiting at the far end of the road, to say nothing of German mines. Was it just excitement that made me so completely unafraid and happy? Or was it something else?

Let me just finish the story first. Some way down the road we came to another blown bridge, a small one, crossing what was little more than a ditch, and we set to work to cut a diversion round it. But before we had finished, a despatch rider came up with an order that we were to return: vehicles were getting stuck and we were needed to tow them clear. So back we went, and it was just as I had feared: the ground was far too soft; and while the bulldozer got working with its winch, I walked up and down the river to see if I could find a better place. But by now bright patches were coming in the sky. It was too late. The guns were turning round and going back. We were all going back, dispersing, getting under cover. For if daylight came to find us still lined up on the road to the river there would indeed be a massacre.

So, through the failure of my ford, the operation had to be abandoned. And as it turned out, this was just as well. Gemmano was indeed 'Boche-held' and just how strongly we were now – at a staggering price – to find out. From an olive grove I watched the first attack, in battalion strength, go in . . . and fail. For the second attack – in brigade strength – they needed my olive grove for their machine gunners. So we were ordered to withdraw behind Montefiore, and – giving us the merest sip from the tankard that others were now about to drain – our progress was speeded by a shell that killed one of my corporals and two of my Sappers.

That was the end of it as far as I was concerned, indeed almost the end of it as far as the Division was concerned; for that attack too failed and the Division was moved to another sector. When the little village of Gemmano ultimately fell – not to the Ox and Bucks who had made the first attempt, not to the Queen's Brigade who had made the second attempt, not to 46 Division who relieved us to make the third attempt – but, ten days after my night ride, to 4 Indian Division, it had claimed the lives of well over a thousand men. I say this to put my own small adventure into perspective.

Nevertheless, tame though that adventure was compared with

what our infantry did and suffered, Gemmano became for me a name to remember, a place where (or near where) many things happened.

For it was here that I experienced not only the Adventure of War, not only (when that adventure had come to an end and the German shelling had started) the Horror of War, but also the Fruits of War.

For yes, it was indeed this third side of my triangle that had made me so light-hearted on my night-ride down the deserted road. Afraid? What was there to be afraid of? There may have been men crouching behind guns, but dwarfing them was the town of Montefiore behind us, was the great ridge that flanked the plain we were driving through, were the olive trees and the vineyards that lay around us. In the dark I could scarcely see them, but in the dark one's awareness comes through another sense, a sense I had discovered four years earlier at Cotchford: one *feels*. And I felt all around me the Land of Italy, and I knew that it was both powerful and benevolent. Some in my position might have felt this great, all-pervading presence as a Person, might have given it the name of God. I didn't because this was a word that held for me a different meaning, one that was associated with Church Parades, sermons and childhood beliefs that now seemed false. For me it was never a Person. Indeed I scarcely questioned what it was for I never really thought about it at the time; and it is only now that I am trying to sort out my various experiences that I have come to see that, of the many fruits that Italy had to offer me, this was the greatest of them all.

I found it that night below Gemmano. I found it not just where one would expect to find it – in the picturesque countryside and in the fine views of distant mountains; not just when the guns were silent – as we crossed the Plain of Naples or made our way north to the Gothic Line through Umbria and the Marches. I found it even at Anzio.

The British have always felt an affection for their disasters. If two names survive from the Italian campaign, the first is certainly Cassino, the second is probably Anzio; and both were equally awful. We were taken to Anzio by Landing Ship from Naples and we brought with us no illusions. We had been told the worst: that things had gone badly wrong there, that the Germans were attacking very powerfully and for the first time in the campaign were using aircraft on a considerable scale, so that we were likely to be bombed as well as shelled.

If a disaster is of one's own making, one feels perhaps some responsibility for putting it right; but this was somebody else's fault, nothing to do with us at all. We were just being called in to pull their chestnuts out of the fire; and we felt no enthusiasm for the task. So we arrived in low spirits, and the sight of the bombed and battered town did nothing to reassure us. As we drove in convoy through the cratered streets my mouth was dry and my stomach tight. But out in the country on the far side reassurance came with a flood; for the countryside was not Italian – it was *English*!

I don't suppose that anyone today, visiting the fields and woods that were once the Pontine Marshes, would be particularly struck either by their beauty or by their Englishness, but this was what most forcibly struck me, and the difference it made was immense.

I remember in particular the day the order came that we were to stop being Engineers and take over a section of the line from an infantry company. Then indeed we knew that the situation was desperate. The one great blessing that Engineers enjoy is that, whatever the hazards of our work, when it is done we can return to billets that are always both comfortable and safe, and there we can relax. This is a blessing totally denied to the infantry who must sleep where they work and live where they die. So here we were, our tents left behind, our vehicles left behind, our cookhouse left behind, marching up to the front and to who knew what dangers and discomforts.

It was beginning to grow dark when we halted, the first stage of our journey completed. I have no particular recollection of the place, just of a slit trench three feet wide and six feet long with a thick bed of straw at the bottom. I climbed into it and found it more comfortable than any bed I had ever known. I lay there luxuriating in the comfort, then slipped peacefully and happily to sleep. In the middle of the night there came a hand on my shoulder and a voice in my ear: it was time to get up. We – the Platoon commanders – were now to be shown the next stage of our journey, memorizing it so that we could then guide our platoons forward to the green hillside beneath whose grassy surface we were to spend – like moles – the next two weeks. And as I moved along the footpaths, beside the hedges, across the fields and through the copses I might have been walking through Sussex countryside, so friendly did it all feel, so much like home.

This inspiration that I drew from my surroundings was always strongest at night and particularly when I was alone. I suppose this is only natural, for then there were no distractions: no voices to listen to and none of the sights of war – the incredible mess that is made not just by the fighting but by the mere presence of an army in occupation – to spoil the view. And so I felt it most when perhaps I most needed it: out on patrol in the silent country that lies between the two sleeping armies. Alone in the dark, yet not alone, for all around me were the hills. And the rocks and the trees and the bushes and the grasses were there as they had been for hundreds upon hundreds of years. The war was only a tiny thing fought between two tiny armies. Italy herself was at peace. We could kill each other; we could batter the landscape and destroy its buildings; we could litter it with our bodies and with all the debris of our fighting; we could shout ourselves hoarse. But we could not touch the peace that lay around us, in the distant mountains, in the little rounded hills, in the lush valleys, in the vineyards, under the great chestnut trees Peace, beauty, sanity and a great and all-pervading Benevolence: almost always, almost everywhere these were with us, and they dwarfed the lunacy and ugliness of what we were doing.

All my life I have found reassurance in the countryside; have found sorrows and anxieties benefitting from a walk through a meadow. In the past if I had been asked to explain why this was so, I think I would have ascribed to the meadow a fairly passive role. I went to it; it did not come to me. I knew what it had to offer; it knew nothing and cared nothing for my needs. Nor would I have credited it with offering anything more than I was conscious of: pleasant sights, pleasant sounds, pleasant smells, something to take my mind off its particular worry, as refreshing and restoring as a cool drink on a hot day. So it had seemed at Cotchford when I was a boy. So it seemed in Italy. In Italy I certainly needed all the reassurance I could get; and I found it there. But if I had thought about it at all (and I didn't think about it much) I would have said that the mountains were no more than kindly spectators at the drama that was being played out up and down their slopes – not participants.

Today I am not so sure. Or rather if I believe it with my head I might dispute it with my heart. Today I am less of a mathematician less of a scientist than I once was and I don't listen only to reason, sometimes I prefer Shakespeare.

> The night has been unruly: where we lay,
> Our chimneys were blown down; and, as they say,
> Lamentings heard in the air; strange screams of death,
> And prophesying with accents terrible
> Of dire combustion and confus'd events
> New hatch'd to the woeful time. The obscure bird
> Clamour'd the livelong night: some say the earth
> Was feverous and did shake.

Let the geologist with his seismograph and his Richter scale say what he likes, this is what happened on the night Macbeth murdered Duncan.

Scientists can tell us a lot but they cannot tell us all. Sometimes the poet can tell us more. And just as I prefer a poetic to a scientific account of an event that occurred in 1040 so I prefer a poetic to a scientific interpretation of what happened on the night of March 24th 1944.

We had just come back from Anzio. Our landing ship had taken us to Naples and from there we had driven to Nocera, a town about twelve miles away on the edge of the Plain, to begin our four months' holiday. I remembered Nocera. My bridging lorries had spent a night in a jam factory there back in October. It had been a happy and memorable occasion. Two days earlier we had crossed the mountains at San Severino, had looked down on to the Plain of Naples and had seen in the distance the famous Mount Vesuvius. 'See Naples and die,' they say; and whatever exactly is meant by that, I think we all felt that here was a historic moment in our lives. And the view lived up to the expectation: so green, so peaceful after the noise and destruction of Salerno. An island of peace, it looked. And over to the left, the Lord of the Island – the volcano – unmistakably regal with its crown of white cloud floating just above its head, the only cloud in all the blue expanse of sky. So it was only proper that our guns should have fallen silent and that the two battling armies should be crossing this holy place on tip-toe, their squabbling not to be resumed until the Plain of Naples lay behind us and Vesuvius was out of sight.

Thus it was on my first visit to Nocera; and now here we were again, conquering heroes, proud of our exploits, swaggering back.

Oh, bliss! We had got out of Anzio alive! For six weeks we had scarcely taken off our boots, let alone our trousers. We were filthy. Our clothes were filthy. And now, waiting for us at the Italian army barracks where we were to be billeted, were hot baths and new clothes. I threw away a shirt that had become more black than khaki. I threw away, more sadly, a jersey whose many holes I had darned with such loving care. And more sadly still I threw away my officer's peaked cap. I had bought it so proudly at Aldershot; I had worn it so proudly ever since; I liked it battered, but now it was battered beyond wearing. And I emerged, like a butterfly from its chrysalis, not quite sure if I was still the same person.

Nevertheless, this was undoubtedly an occasion that called for a little celebration; and so that evening Major Smith invited his fellow officers to join him for dinner at the Albergo Capuccini in Amalfi.

I have no memory of the meal, only of the drink that followed it. A stirrup cup, one for the road, what shall it be? Cognac seemed appropriate: seven cognacs for seven brave soldiers. We stood in a group in front of the glowing embers of a fire feeling very happy and pleased with ourselves. We're just back from Anzio, we had told a couple of Canadians. 'Gee, Anzio! That must have been tough! We were on the Sangro,' they said. 'That was tough, too, but, boy, Anzio must have been a whole lot tougher.' It was nice to see how impressed they were. . . . And now here were our drinks. We raised our glasses. Cheers! I took a cautious sip. I was not much of a drinker in those days. It was only four months since I had ventured my first glass of wine; and my monthly entitlement to gin and sherry had always been passed to others. So it is not surprising that the cognac seemed about as drinkable as undiluted liquid fire. Luckily my companions were also finding it stronger than they had expected. We struggled on, sip by sip. Brave soldiers don't surrender; veteran fighters can take their liquor. But in the end I had to give up.

'Throw it on the fire, then.'

'All right,' I said, 'I will. Fire to fire: that's where it belongs.' And with a theatrical gesture I did.

Immediately a great sheet of flame leapt out into the room, grabbed the drink and swallowed it at a gulp; and seven brave soldiers recoiled. . . .

Thus the Prologue. Now the Play. It is night. The scene is a mountain top; and here another fire that had been glowing quietly has suddenly flared. . . . Look, here it comes again, blood-red and molten, retched up out of the ground, spilling over, pouring down the mountain side, setting the vines alight, crackling and writhing, pressing on over their twisted, blackened bodies, pressing relentlessly forward, an irresistible tide that burnt and flattened all that ay in its path. . . . We could see it from Nocera. We watched it from a landing window on our way up to bed. We missed the detail, of course, for it was twelve miles away. But the blood-red fire was plainly visible, rising up, spilling over, pouring down. And we knew that it came from Vesuvius and that Vesuvius was erupting.

I lay in bed. . . . I cannot swear to pyjamas and sheets, only to bare toes, iron bed, white-washed ceiling and a solid roof above that. A pleasure to be lingered over, like the first night of the school holidays. . . . I lay in bed luxuriating, and in no hurry to go to sleep. . . .

I lay in bed. . . . I had been asleep and now I was awake and could continue luxuriating. There are few greater pleasures than lying in bed in the early morning knowing that it is an hour before one need get up. After six weeks at Anzio to lie in a bed that was clean, that was dry and that was safe, and then to become conscious of the sound of rain beating down on the roof overhead, to hear it fairly rattling down and to know that it couldn't reach me: never in my life had I known more blessed luxury. Even today the memory of it is unrivalled, undimmed. . . .

The door opened and someone came in.

'Half past six, sir.'

It can't be! It's still pitch dark.

'Have a look out of the window, sir.'

I went to the window and looked.

There was a layer of cinders on the sill and the street outside was black.

I dressed and went outside. Cinders crunched underfoot as I crossed the yard. Cinders flying like hailstones stung my face and hands and caught in the folds of my tunic and in my hair. Shielding my face I looked up at the sky. A great black cloud, blacker than any I had ever seen, stood over us. At first I thought all the sky was black. Then I saw that the cloud was wedge-shaped, streaming out to us from Vesuvius, over us and away to the south east where it became tinged with brown. On either side was blue sky. I stooped to pick up a handful of cinders. They were hard, like clinkers, mostly the size of small peas but some as large as hazel nuts.

The rain of cinders continued all day. The black blanket grew thicker: two inches, three inches, four inches. We stayed indoors. If we ventured out it was with hands in pockets and tin hat on head. Cinders were still flying when news reached us that roofs were collapsing and at once a party of men armed with shovels went up on to our own roof; and as they shovelled so more cinders fell.

At 7 o'clock in the evening the sky cleared. The storm had lasted fourteen hours and our shroud was seven inches thick. Next morning we set to work to dig ourselves out. Bulldozers were busy on the main road two hundred yards away and it took us a whole day to reach them. The following day we left, driving carefully down the narrow track through the black streets.

On the main road I had my last view of Vesuvius. All round us the countryside was in mourning: black vineyards, black fields, black mountains. Above us was the blue sky. And in between the two was the volcano. A veil of smoke draped its summit, and, rising above, piled majestically fold upon fold, towering up into the sky and looking as solid as the mountain beneath, was a gigantic pillar of cloud.

There it stood in its glory and its triumph. A geological phenomenon, and no more than the merest coincidence? No! The Lord of the Plain had spoken. The Land of Italy had delivered her judgement. Like naughty children we hurried away.

11. War – The Lesson

I have often looked back on my five years in the army, on my four years with 56 Division, on my two and a half years in Italy; and sometimes I have felt that they were five wasted years, years that could have been better spent qualifying for some profession, years that put me at a disadvantage compared with those who, younger than I, had missed the war and got ahead: sometimes I felt that I was one of war's casualties. But that mood passed. At other times I looked back with private pride and satisfaction on what I had done. It had not been much really. But I was proud that I had started in the ranks, proud that I had spent so long overseas, proud to have been in 56 Division, serving in Italy throughout the campaign, proud to have achieved my ambition of commanding a Platoon in a Divisional Field Company, and very, very proud that I had been wounded. At other times I was grateful that during those four years abroad I had seen so much of the world: Cape Town, Bombay, half a dozen different deserts, and Italy. Italy in particular. At other times I just felt how lucky I had been to have found so much that was good, so little that was bad: that those five years had provided me with a foundation stone, strong and lasting, on which to build my adult life. And at times – and especially at this very moment – I looked back with an agonizing realization of the price that had been paid. It is this realization that has made these such difficult chapters to write: for how could I describe my many blessings when others had known only the curse of war. If I had received, they had paid. That I might come home, they had stayed behind.

So I must end with two small memories, both from Anzio, both from the time when we were pretending to be infantry. Yes, pretending. For let me make it quite clear that we were never the real thing. We never did what they did. We never suffered what they suffered. We couldn't: we weren't good enough. We just occupied reserve positions behind their front line. And when that line was dented, it was not we but the real infantry who had to counter attack to restore the situation. And one evening, as the sun was setting, we watched the counter attack go in.

We had been warned to expect it, and now here it came: men carrying rifles, men dragging Bren guns, half walking, half running, hurrying up the hillside. We could hear them panting, see their grim faces as they came hurrying and stumbling by. Then they dropped to the ground, while another group came up and passed them. Thus they moved up the hillside, taking it in turns, one group hurrying forward while the other group lay on the ground ready to give covering fire. At the top of the hill was a gate on to a road. They had to go through this gateway, and they did it as they had been taught, fanning out, slipping through one at a time, careful not to bunch. And so they passed out of sight ... but not out of memory. Shortly after they had disappeared the German 'defensive fire' came down all around us, and it was very heavy indeed. Later I helped some of the wounded back. Had they achieved their objective? I don't know. But I do know that every objective that the infantry was ever set had always to be paid for: that of those who set out in the evening not all would have breakfast the following morning. The question was not: 'Should a price have been paid?' but: 'Was the price too high?' With the Engineers it was never like this. If we paid it was with sweat, not blood. Blood was never part of our bargain, for our objectives could not be achieved – our bridges not be built, our roads not be cleared – if we got ourselves killed. It was our duty to stay alive; theirs, not ours, to die. Loose coins in a pocket, they were, loose change. How much? One Lieutenant, two Corporals and ten men? Fair enough. Quite cheap, considering.

Let no one ever recall his exciting, his heroic or his funny adventures in the war, without remembering the Infantry. There is nothing exciting, nothing heroic, nothing funny about struggling up a hillside lugging a Bren and then getting yourself killed as you reach the top.

My other memory is of four Spitfires. They came in a line, flew over our heads, wheeled to the left and then, one at a time, dived and dropped their bomb. Up they came, one at a time, surfacing; and now they were in a circle, flying round, and each, as it came again to the target, dived. They had dropped their only bomb; so now they fired their machine guns. Four identical planes flying round and round, but with one great difference. The leader when he dived, dived steeply, almost vertically, dived so low that he almost vanished behind the trees; the other three made shallow dives. One deep, three shallow. One deep, three shallow. One deep ... and as I watched the leader go down for the third time, I noticed that he was wearing a red carnation in his cockpit, a carnation that grew and grew. . . . That was all – except for a splash of dark grey smoke coming up from behind the trees to mark the spot where he had landed. . . .

And I remembered J. F. Roxburgh preaching a sermon at Stowe. It was the first time I had heard him preach and it was on Armistice Sunday, 1934.

'In war,' he had said, 'it is always the best who die. . . .'

Interlude. *Hedda*

I stood at the top of the steps and watched her go – a great white moth fluttering away into the darkness – down, down, down, between walls afoam with wistaria. I stood there until the darkness and the town had swallowed her up, then turned to climb the hill, the first stage of a long journey that would take me across Europe, across the Channel, back to England, back to Cotchford, back to civilian life again.

But I would return. We had agreed to that. I would return in the spring. And meanwhile there would be her letters and the feeling that I was getting things ready – qualifying for a job, finding a job, finding a home – getting things ready for the day when I could invite herb to come and join me. If our ways were to part, if seven hundred miles were to come between us, it was only for a little while.

Yes, it was not only war that I had found in Italy. It was love – and that too for the first time. Love and war and all the complicated, conflicting, tumultuous emotions that each engenders, both were there waiting for me. The one had claimed a piece of my head; the other, less literally, now claimed a piece of my heart.

Hedda was one of a group of Italians whom Harry – in ways known only to people like Harry – had managed to organize. There were about eight of them in all, two married couples and four unattached females. Hedda was the youngest, a year younger than I. The others were quite a bit older, somewhere between late twenties and mid forties, I would guess. And to welcome them to our villa on the hill above Trieste were the seven of us, the officers of 221 Field Company. And thither they came on Saturday evenings, to eat, to talk, to dance, perhaps to listen to some music, or swim in our swimming pool.

I was not present on their first visit. I forget now what particular excuse was given – headache, pressure of work, calls of duty. If Harry wanted to import a gang of popsies, that was O.K. and just the sort of thing Harry would want to do, but count me out. I don't dance, thank you very much, and I don't particularly enjoy female company, thank you very much, and I don't fancy spending my evenings necking with signorinas who don't speak my language. This was my reaction. And so my heart sank when I was told that the party had been a success and that they would be coming up again next week.

'Oh, and Chris, there was one who would have been just right for you. We told her all about you and she wants to meet you. She's at Venice University studying English.'

Then I hope you told her that I don't dance.

'That's all right, Chris, she wants someone to help her with her English. You ought to be good at that. She's quite a smasher, by the way.'

Oh, shut up, Harry.

One of the blessings of being an Engineer officer was that dancing didn't need to be one of our accomplishments. This was because of our domestic arrangements. As I have already explained, each Company lived on its own, and so, if we ever had an Officers' Mess, it never held more than seven of us, not enough, mercifully, to justify the appointment of an Entertainments Officer eager to keep us all entertained. Only once did one of our Colonels attempt to bring his officers under a single roof, and that was when we were in Palestine. The attempt was resented and was a failure, but before we broke up and went our individual Company ways again, he did manage to organize one dance for us. Attendance was more or less obligatory. 220 Field Company was allotted seven young ladies from Tel Aviv. One of them was to be mine.

'But I don't dance. I can't dance. I just don't know how to.'

So Jack took me in hand and taught me the two-step, and together we had two-stepped round the Company lines after dark the night before, until I thought I had mastered the quarter and half turns. Thus my armoury when I was presented to my partner consisted of the two step as taught by Jack and the waltz as vaguely remembered from my prep school days. But when the band struck up I lost my nerve and had to confess that the waltz was all I could manage; so we sat side by side, until a recognizable waltz turned up, then took the floor. This was it. We stood opposite one another. I clasped her. I knew what to do with my hands. Now for my feet. I looked down at them, hopefully, encouragingly, and they began to tremble and make little spasmodic movements. Oh I knew how to do it perfectly well really. One two three one two three, it was easy once you had got going and I could whirl her round the floor until we were both giddy. It was just knowing how to begin, which foot and when, and getting her to do it too so that we didn't collide. The dance was now in full swing, carefree couples were spinning by, but we were still motionless, locked together, paralysed. . . . In the end I said 'Sorry. We don't seem to be getting on very well' and she said 'No we don't, do we?' and we returned to our seats. . . . I was naturally reluctant to repeat that sort of fiasco again.

Luckily dancing (said Harry) formed only a small part of the evening's activities; and so on the second occasion I agreed to be present.

Looking back on it afterwards I had to admit that I had quite enjoyed it. The Italians had been a jolly, friendly lot and some of them had been able to speak a little English. Hedda had been there and she was indeed most attractive, and being in her company had given me a pleasing and quite new sensation. It was all rather exciting, and to my surprise I found myself looking forward to the following Saturday when they were due to come again.

So it all began. My fellow officers were either married or engaged or at the very least had girls waiting for them in England. Only I had never had a girl in my life. Only Hedda was the right age for me. And so it was natural that we should be paired together and not surprising that the others should take a delight in watching and encouraging our progress. So it all began, at our villa on the hill; and Saturday was the day that I lived for.

Then, with approaching exams making a convenient excuse, another day was added. The place this time was her home in Piazza Garibaldi. And after work (and with a message that I would be out to supper but might like something to eat when I got back) I slipped off and made my way down into the town. Oh well worn track! How much happiness in anticipation did I carry down you, how much happiness in retrospect carry up, and how many hopes and fears did I turn over and over in my head as my feet, left to themselves, followed the familiar route! Today, looking back on those springtime years I can't help feeling a little sad that most people now do it all so differently. Were we innocent? Were we immature? Were we old-fashioned? Probably all three. But how-fortunate for us that this was so and that we were thus able to share together those incredibly happy months and leave behind no regrets. Our lives came together, ran side by side, then separated; and mine most certainly and hers too I am prepared to swear were vastly the richer for the experience.

I rang her bell, then climbed her stairs, and usually it was she – though sometimes her grandmother – who opened the door to me. And then we were alone together in a little room furnished with a settee where we could sit together side by side. How did we spend our time? As innocently as anyone could wish, more boringly than anyone would have thought possible, yet as pleasurably as any courting couple ever had since the world began.

In between visits we wrote each other letters, each in our own language; and thus we learned about each other and about those things that are in any case often easier to express in writing, and especially so if conversation is difficult. And in between visits and letter-writing, and with the help of a *Teach Yourself* book, I set out to learn Italian.

Already, as I have said, I had fallen in love with the land of Italy. Now, in Hedda, through Hedda and because of Hedda, I began to love and understand the people of Italy. To the troops who had landed at Salerno they had been Wops: Wops who had run away when the fighting had become too hot, Wops who had surrendered, Wops who had changed sides when it had suited them, Wops who preferred a life of idleness and ease, reclining in the sun while others worked, Wops who in many ways were little better than the cows or pigs or chickens that so often seemed to occupy the ground floors of their houses. Wops and Wogs, Italians and Arabs, there really wasn't much to choose between them. Who can blame us if this was how we saw them. It was, after all, the picture painted for us by our politicians, and one all too easily acceptable to a victorious army striding across a defeated country.

Understandably, too, we thought of all Italians as a single people, and, first impressions being strongest, judged them by what we saw down in the south. Now I learned for the first time that Italy, so obviously one country on the map, had been a nation for less than a hundred years; that there were very great differences between the Italians of the north and those of the south; and that in Trieste in particular, though all spoke the same language, there was a mixture of races. Hedda herself was partly Austrian. Others were partly Slav. Others again were Italians from elsewhere who had moved in when the town had been annexed after the First World War. Gradually I began to understand how it was, how it had all happened, how they felt about it, and gradually I began to share their feelings and their aspirations.

I never learned to talk Italian very fluently because I was still not very fluent even in my own language and found foreign languages a great deal harder to get my tongue around. But I could read. I read about the Risorgimento. Garibaldi became my hero and Abba's *Da Quarto al Volturno* one of my best loved books. I learned about the Medici, and years later was able to declaim – with an Italian student on a rowing boat on Lake Orta in front of Lesley – Lorenzo's famous poem. I followed the adventures of Don Camillo and *I Promessi Sposi* before either had become known to English readers. And of course I went to opera after opera after opera, enjoying what went on, not only on the stage, but also in the auditorium. There is drama in Verdi but there is drama too in the queue that forms up outside the opera house – as indeed there is drama everywhere in Italy whenever two or more Italians are present, be it in a railway carriage or the wilds of the Abruzzi.

Thus did my two loves – for Italians in general and for Hedda in particular – grow side by side steadily stronger, until at last the time arrived when the second felt enough self-confidence to make its first public appearance. Hitherto our meetings had been confined to the villa and to her apartment. Now came the next step. Some military purpose – I entirely forget what – took the Company for a week to San Dona di Piave. At the same time a need to call on her University took Hedda to Venice. And there we met. There in Venice, where we were both unknown and so unlikely to bump into friends, we first perambulated the streets arm in arm. There in Venice we shyly but proudly proclaimed to the world around us that she was my girl and I her man.

What young man does not feel that his love is unique? What middle-aged man does not look back on his first romance with exquisite pleasure but at the same time with the realization that every other middle-aged man can do exactly the same. The only thing that was unique about my love for Hedda was that up to then I had never even remotely experienced such sensations before. The emotions themselves were ordinary enough: I loved being with her, being close to her, feeling that she was a part of me and I a part of her, proud to feel that someone so lovely was mine. And as the bond between us strengthened so the future became more certain. Yes, we would marry – one day, when I had established myself in a job and had a home to which I could invite her. Understandably she needed that, and only when I had provided it would I feel that I had proved myself and earned my reward. Yes, I would labour for her, but not for seven years as Jacob had for Rachel or as I would need to if I were to become an architect. I couldn't exist that long without her. Two years at most was all I could wait.

Cambridge wanted me back. It seemed silly – and here I agreed with my father – having got so far not to go on and get my Degree. But a Degree in what? Apparently all I needed, after war service had been taken into account, was a year's residence followed by a single Part in any Tripos. What Tripos? Mathematics was out, and none of the related subjects interested me in the least. So it had to be something I could tackle from scratch and scrape through after a bare eight months of study (for term started in October and exams were in May). There seemed to be only one possibility: English Literature. I had not specially enjoyed English at school. But then what had it amounted to? Swatting up Cobbett's *Rural Rides* and *Macbeth* for the School Certificate, reading Shakespeare aloud in class (and praying that I would not be given a part) parsing, précis writing, a weekly essay. Surely this was not English Literature. Surely more important was my love of Dickens and Hardy. I hoped so. And since the only purpose of my taking a Degree was to be able to call myself a graduate, I also hoped it wouldn't matter too much if all I got was a Third. Then, armed with my Degree, I would find myself some sort of job, perhaps one involving a bit of writing, and then – yes, *then* – she would join me.

And meanwhile? Should we become officially engaged? I, impulsive, was willing, She, wiser, was not.

It was in Venice. We had agreed on the time. We had agreed on the place. I forget now what the time was, only that I was there a quarter of an hour earlier in case she should be early too. But I could show you the place, at the far end of the Piazza opposite St Mark's. There I stood; there I paced up and down with ever-growing anxiety while clock bells chimed out the passage of time. I knew where she was staying, for I had delivered her safely back there the evening before. And Laura was with her, so that if anything disastrous had happened between then and now surely Laura would have come to tell me. Yet all the same I was anxious. Perhaps she had been taken suddenly ill. Perhaps she had not told Laura where our meeting was to be. . . . Another chime. She was now an hour late, a whole hour. Fear and anger in fierce competition with each other were boiling up inside me. And then I saw her. . . .

Oh familiar emotions! The flood of relief so quickly drowned by the flood of anger, and then the lingering resentment that she should have done this deliberately. I was good at being resentful;

I was well able to remain silently furious for the rest of that wretched day. Of course in the end I relented. Of course in the end our affections were restored and indeed seemed even greater as a result, as if the bond between us had been tested and the very testing had given it added strength. And yet in the turmoil of my emotions a tiny seed of doubt had been sown.

Never before in my life had I needed to understand the feelings and emotions that governed the life of another person. If someone behaved in a certain way, they just did, and that was that. If I would have behaved in a different way, it was because I was a different person. That was that and it didn't greatly matter. But with Hedda it did matter. It did matter that she should have deliberately chosen to cause me pain and ruin our afternoon together. I did need to know why. And so I needed to build a kind of working model of our relationship that I could study and make sense of; and in the end the model I made pictured her as a wild pony and me as its trainer. Gradually I was taming the pony, but with its taming came the loss of its freedom, and every now and then it would rebel, and just as I thought it was mine it would kick up its heels and gallop away. But it would come back and I would try again and one day it would submit and I would have succeeded, and then it would be mine for ever. That was how we were: she the pony, I the trainer; and it raised a question. Was I a pony-trainer by nature?

The answer was no. She groped for a word to describe what I lacked and came up with two: *noncuranza* and *disinvoltura*. And I have to grope a little to find the English equivalents of what she meant. Self confidence, nonchalance, an easy manner but with a slight hint of superiority and superciliousness, the manner that in a restaurant needs only a raised forefinger to bring waiters hurrying across to you, that in a queue automatically finds you at the front without anyone quite knowing how you got there. I knew what she meant. I had met it in Germans.

Perhaps in my smart officer's uniform I had looked more the masterful husband she needed, the husband she and others could admire and respect. Perhaps therefore when I made my promised reappearance in March, 1947, but now wearing grey flannel trousers and a tweed jacket, she began to have doubts. We met in Venice. We had made no particular plans. Perhaps we might stay in Venice, perhaps go to Bolzano: we could decide when we met, and the decision was really hers. We met, and her decision was to return to Trieste where she could introduce me to her various friends and relatives: this she felt was the proper thing to do. And because there wasn't a spare bedroom in her apartment, she had found me a nice hotel. 'You don't mind, do you? After all, we will be spending the rest of the day together.' I only minded a little bit and tried not to show it.

So we travelled to Trieste by train; and since I was now a civilian and the town was still occupied by Allied troops, I had to acquire an entry permit. She knew where I had to go to get it and together we went; and it was just as such places always were in those days, a milling crowd of Italians and somewhere out of sight in the distance an official behind a desk taking no notice of them. The perfect situation for testing one's *disinvoltura*. 'Say you are English and go up to the front ... of *course* you can ... of *course* you must ... of *course* it's all right ... you'll never get your pass if you don't. *Please* ... to make me proud of you.' So I had to. '*Permesso ... Scusi ... Inglese ...*' I muttered my passwords and edged my way forward. It worked. As the waters of the Red Sea had fallen back on either side to allow the Children of Israel to pass through, so did the flood of gesticulating, chattering, *documenti*-clutching Italians give way before the Englishman, and I passed dry-shod to the man at the desk. The Englishman secured his permit, honour was satisfied, praise was awarded, smiles returned; but I suspect that we both knew that the Englishman who had pushed his way to the front of the queue was not I. And so, although my visit was a happy one and although when I said goodbye to her we were outwardly as confident about the future as we had ever been, I think inwardly we both wondered if we would ever meet again.

We didn't. For another six months we continued to write to each other and I continued to think of her as my fiancée. Then, without too much heartbreak and with no ill-feeling, it came to an end.

I last heard from her on May 7th the following year. It was one of a number of letters I received around that time from various of my friends. For sentimental reasons I kept them all and so I kept hers; and the other day, thinking I might find it there still, I looked, and there it was, the last to reach me and so at the bottom of the pile

A te e a Lesley i sensi della mia più viva simpatia e auguri vivissimi per il vostro fidanzamento avvenuto al 17 aprile.[1]

To discover what you are you must also discover what you are not. To learn what sort of husband you might make you must learn what sort of husband you can never make. Hedda taught me this. She taught me a lot of things: about Italy, about Italians, about women, about love, about myself. She even succeeded in teaching me the two-step. She helped to loosen the bonds that tied me to my father, and she prepared me for new bonds, bonds that have tied me now for nearly thirty years in a happiness that I could never have found with her.

On July 24th, 1948 I married Lesley.

[1] To you and to Lesley my warmest affection and best wishes on your engagement announced on 17 April.

PART TWO

The Road to Work

1. *A Walk Through the Hills*

On a spring day not long ago Lesley and I set out to climb a mountain. We drove our hired car along a narrow road to the point at which it entered a beech forest; and here, where the smooth tarmac gave way to rough stones, we parked, got out and set off on foot. The road continued uphill for a while, and though it was not particularly pleasant to walk along, it was at least going in the right direction, upwards, and we were happy and hopeful. But after a little it went through a cutting and then began to descend. It was a twisting road and the trees were close at hand on either side, and so we could not see what was around the next corner. So, for a while, we were able to hope that the descent was only temporary, the climb shortly to be resumed, for the road must surely lead to the mountain top. But at each turn the descent became steeper; and the lower we went, the stonier and dustier and drearier the road became and the lower fell our spirits, until at last we stopped. Where was it taking us? What should we do? At the point where we were standing it did a sharp turn to the right, but down through the trees on the left we could see a small patch of sunlight, a small grassy glade in the middle of the forest. It was some way beneath us, for the ground here fell away steeply, and if we scrambled down to it we would have lost even more height and be even further from our mountain top. But it invited us and so we went. And there for a while we sat, in sunshine once again, and drank a little wine and ate a little bread. Then, after we had rested and were refreshed, came the question: Where next? Up or down, back to the road – or what? At the far end of the glade was a very faint track, really more of a gully washed out by winter rains than a path worn by man. It continued downhill; but by this time we had abandoned the hopes we had set out with. Instead we would follow our instincts, going where the going seemed most pleasant, taking whichever path seemed the most inviting no matter where it might lead us. And so we followed the gully, and it led us to another glade, rather larger than the first, and at the far end of it, there was our stony road again. Bother!

Then I noticed something. On the far side of the road the ground, rose to a line of beeches. But it was only a line: there were no trees beyond them, for between their trunks was the sky. We crossed the road and clambered quickly to the crest of the ridge. And there below us lay an immense plain. It was about half a mile wide and it stretched away into the distance. It was clothed in short green grass, like a lawn, and it undulated gently like a giant sea, each wave crest a foam with an outcrop of white rock. We stood for an instant, then, as we slithered down the little slope on to the grass and out into the full sunshine, so our spirits soared with the lark that rose from the ground ahead of us. We need search no further: we had found what we wanted.

We set off, keeping at first to the troughs between the waves, and at first they were grassy. Then suddenly we came upon one that was all purple and mauve: pansies in such profusion as I had never seen before, never imagined possible. We walked through them, treading on them, then sat down among them, drinking in their colour so thirstily it seemed we were absorbing it not just through our eyes but throughout our entire body. And not until this great thirst was quenched did we go on. And now we were like two dogs following a scent, or rather each following its own scent, for we no longer moved forward side by side. And indeed we were on a scent, the scent of wild flowers, hunting for new ones to add to our collection; and every time one of us found one we would stop and I would bring out my notebook and write down a description and make a guess at its family and perhaps do a quick sketch. Then on again, this way and that, up and down, wherever there was the promise of something new to find; and it was Lesley who made the discovery we had been hoping for: spring gentians, the most brilliant of all the gentian family, as if the entire sky had been distilled to provide the crop of colour with which their starry faces were painted. Here were half a dozen, growing among the rocks.

Then on to the next hillock and here were so many gentians there was just not room for them all, and some had slipped off the edge and were growing in the grass at the bottom, where, against the green, their colour was if possible even more vivid.

Then came the stop for lunch, choosing a place that looked inviting and where we might be sheltered from the wind, but not knowing until we had opened our bags and spread out our picnic that we had chosen a place where fritillaries grew. There were three flowers we had been specially wanting to add to our list, flowers we had met on other occasions, past holidays, and hoped to meet again: these were two of them. The third was the narcissus.

After lunch came the storm, and though it never reached us, it stood between us and the sun and hung its gauze curtain over the mountains and rumbled and muttered threats that could not be ignored. If it swept across the plateau as we feared it might where could we shelter? We looked around and there seemed to be only one place: on a distant hill stood the remains of a small stone hut. Thither we went. The hut itself was of little use, but standing there we saw something else. We had come to the edge of the plain. Beyond the hut the ground dropped away steeply and suddenly to a narrow valley. On the other side of the valley the beech forest began again. Here among the beech trees was the shelter we were looking for, and all we needed now was to find a way down, somewhere where the slope was not too precipitous. Lesley found the place and we set off.

And so, just as the forest had led us to the plain, the plain in its turn now led us to the valley. Having shown us its delights, it now showed us the way forward to whatever was to come next. But before it took its leave of us it had one final delight in store, kept back to the last possible moment. As we made our way down between the rocks to the waiting valley, Lesley saw them ahead of her, waving white heads at her, so perfectly placed, so perfectly timed, we were almost expecting them: our narcissi.

In the valley stood a man, the first human being we had set eyes on since parking our car, a small, solitary figure who looked from a distance as if he had come from the opening paragraph of a Hardy novel: someone, clearly, not to be ignored. We approached him and learned that he was a cowherd out looking for his cows. All day – so he told us – they were free to wander as they pleased. Then in the evening he would come for them to lead them back to the place where they spent the night, a place back down the valley where there was a spring. We had seen a cow from the plain and pointed out where it was. There were another five, he said, smiling, and went on his way to find them; and we moved on towards the sheltering trees.

The storm never came. It moved away down the mountains and in a little while the sun reappeared. We lay in the green grass on the edge of the forest, drank a little more wine and added a few more flowers to our list, then looked at the time and decided we ought to be making our way back. But which way? We could retrace our footsteps, meeting again our narcissi, our fritillaries, our gentians and our pansies, but this would be a little dull. We had seen them once and didn't specially need to see them again. The alternative was to keep to the valley, skirting the edge of the forest, and thus work our way round to the point where we had first left it. And this was what we chose to do. And so, without intending to or expecting to, we came to the spring. There was no doubt about it: there were the cows and there was the water, looking at first like a little stream threading the grass, until we noticed it was not moving, held in the valley bottom. We passed the cows, crossed over the water, climbed a short way up the slope on the far side and sat down. What else could we do? For here was a natural open-air theatre, with a back drop of beeches, a sloping grassy stage, and glinting water to give the impression of footlights. The cows were already on the stage. We took our seats, not knowing that this was only the start, that the show was just about to begin.

A fanfare of trumpets? You could call it that. It was the whinny of a horse; and then round the back of a hillock they came, a troop of horses, mares and their foals, a dozen or more, moving towards us, then stopping to take up their position on the left of the stage. A pause; and then the next arrival, coming this time from the right. More cows, lots of them, the mothers walking in stately procession, their calves frisking and galloping, showing off their paces. Horses in a group on the left. Cows on the right, spreading across, moving down towards the footlights as if to take up their positions for the opening chorus.

'All we want now,' said Lesley, 'are the Indians.' And as if in answer to her words a column of smoke rose from the trees on the far left. . . .

A day to remember – and also to ponder on. There was nothing special about what we had seen. The flowers were there for anyone to find. They had been growing there maybe for centuries, and every year had made their annual appearance. Nor was there anything very special about the cows or the horses. Here was the spring to which they returned every evening as the sun began to go down. Their entry had been dramatic, but then they were Italian cows and Italian horses and drama is in the Italian blood. The only unusual thing about that day was our presence on the scene. And so, as I pondered, I found myself stringing together the apparently chance happenings that had brought two people who had set off from their hotel after breakfast with every intention of climbing to the top of Monte Camiciola to find themselves instead seated in a tiny valley hidden in the middle of a beech forest at just the very moment when the daily drama was about to begin.

Such were my first thoughts, and I recorded them on our return to England. It was a story with a moral perhaps, the moral being that it is not always a good thing to have a preconceived idea of where you are going, that sometimes it may be better to take life as it comes, set your sails according to the winds that blow, go with the tide, follow your instinct, choose the grassier, less trodden road, if that is the one that appeals to you and choose it for its own sake and not in the hope that it might lead anywhere very special.

It was not until some months later that I saw the episode as something else. I saw it as a microcosm of my career.

What young man leaving University with a Degree (even if not a very good one) has not aimed for the mountain top? My aspirations were vague. I had no very precise idea where I wanted to go or by what route, just that I wanted to climb, and I was willing to take any path that appeared to lead upwards. The road I chose was broad and stony and well worn, for many had travelled that way before me. It took me to London, into the forest, away from the sunshine. But where else could one go to seek one's fortune? I turned my back on the valleys where lesser mortals laboured, and strode confidently forward.

Then came disillusion. The road that had started off with such promise, levelled out, then began to descend; and there was no escaping from it, no path however narrow that would take me upwards again. Down I went getting more and more depressed, until I saw a glade, a gleam of sunshine, offering a moment of pleasure and a ray of hope. Now I had left the road. I had resigned from one job and been sacked from another. Now, unable to find anyone willing to employ me, I was on my own and having to make the best of it.

Thus I came to the plain. It was not what I had set out to find. It was well below the mountain tops. It was a modest plain but it offered me what I wanted. Here, out in the sunshine away from the forest, I was free, my own master, going where I pleased, following my instinct. With new and unexpected delights waiting to be discovered round every corner, what more did I need? Selling books in Dartmouth, what happier occupation could I find.

Then after many pleasant years of bookselling, came the curtain of cloud that obscured the sun. ... But it would have been time to leave in any case, for my plain had been explored: I had found all that I had hoped to find, all it seemed possible to find. So I left not unwillingly. I could no longer be a full-time bookseller. I didn't want to be a part-time bookseller, nor, luckily, did I need to be. I knew what I wanted to do instead. The valley lay beneath me green and inviting. I climbed down to it. Here were new delights waiting to be discovered, new treasure. I walked along it a little way, then sat down. I was fifty-four. It was late in the day. The sun was already losing its heat. But I had timed it nicely. . . .

2. Downwards

On a May morning in 1947 I made my way to the offices of the Cambridge University Appointments Board to begin my search for a career.

What sort of a job had I in mind? I really had no idea and hoped they would make suggestions. I could list my various qualifications – a good scholarship in mathematics followed by a bad Degree in English Literature; it was up to them – I hoped – to tell me in what direction they pointed. There was only one direction I would utterly refuse to consider. I would not – could not – become a teacher. Teaching meant talking and my voice was still not to be trusted.

Just as every seed has somewhere written inside it the most exact details of the plant it will eventually become, so it must be with the human being. We may carry our hopes with us to the grave but often it will be like hoping that the apple tree will one day produce a crop of plums. No doubt a perspicacious interviewer could have read it all in the young man who sat before him, and no doubt my interviewer did in fact read a lot of it. But would it have helped if he had told me what he saw?

When one is twenty-six and in love, a year is a lifetime, and it was just as well I did not know what lay ahead of me: that it would be four years before I found a career I was going to be happy in, that this career would be in bookselling, and that I would have to wait nearly thirty years before my own first book got into print.

So my interviewer was tactful and I came away confident that before long something would turn up, something that, in some modest fashion, would blend Newton with Shakespeare. Though there might not be many such jobs, there were surely not many graduates who could rival my particular qualifications. The road to the mountain top had entered the forest. It was a little hard to be sure exactly where it was leading, but never mind: it was going uphill; and I strode happily along.

A couple of months later I was in London in a bedsitter. The hunt was now on in earnest. The first application forms had been filled in and shortly afterwards the first letters of regret had been received. And so it was thought (meaning that my father thought and I agreed) that I ought to move to where the prospects were brightest, where interviews would be a bus ride rather than a train journey away. So I said goodbye to Cotchford and left home. And among the few possessions I took with me was my typewriter. I would need it for writing letters, of course, but I would also need it if, in the intervals between interviews, I tried to write other things as well.

'I want to be a writer.' I suppose I had said that first at the age of eight or thereabouts, and I had certainly said it again at the age of twenty-five while I was in Trieste. What is a writer? If I were asked now I would say that he is half of a partnership, the other half being enough readers to keep the first half in business. In those days I might have answered more naively that a writer was someone who wanted to be a writer. So I sat at my table in my bedsitter and wonder what to write about.

Another definition of a writer might be that he is someone who transforms experience into words. He can either do this very rapidly, as a reporter does at a football match, or he can digest his experience more slowly and more thoroughly as does a novelist. At the age of twenty-seven I possessed neither a stock of experiences on which to draw, nor the ability to go out into the world and seek new ones. I wished to write in the privacy of my room – and I had nothing to write about. So I wrote about nothing. After all this was what, forty years earlier, my father had done, and done both well and successfully.

I tapped away at airy nothings, sent them off an got them back.

First study your market: this, of course, is the golden rule, and if I had done so I would have seen that I was living in the past. In 1947 as far as light articles were concerned there was no market to study: current tastes and the paper shortage had seen to that.

Then came my first job. It was with the Central Office of Information, the civilian heir to the war-time Ministry of Information. The first Labour Government was in power grappling with the first of the succession of economic crises that have plagued government after government ever since. 'The balance of payments', 'higher productivity', 'fair shares for all', 'the Nation's housekeeping'; the phrases were fresh in those days, and the problem seemed simple enough, the remedy obvious. All that was necessary (so we thought) was to ensure that everybody knew and understood. So speakers were sent out, and wherever they could find an audience – in factory, canteen or parish hall – and whenever they could make their voices heard above the clatter of machinery, knives or knitting needles, they would explain it all in simple, homely terms. The words were theirs; the facts and figures were ours. This was the work of my section and I enjoyed it. And since I was occasionally allowed to attend Government Press Conferences, I had the added bonus of being able to boast of encounters with Cabinet Ministers, and this made me feel pleasantly important.

So I was happy: happy, that is to say, while I was busy. But gradually the work began to run out. Whether this was because our speakers were themselves the victims of the austerity they urged on others or because one crisis was so like the next that the same speech served them all, I cannot now remember. All I do remember is increased periods of idleness; and it was then that I learned – if I had not already learned it at Kirkuk – how hateful it is to have too little to do.

At first it was pleasant to alternate between work and idleness. Both were welcome, the one providing a relief from the other. But gradually I began to resent the work. The less there was, the more I resented the fact that there was so little and so resented even the little that came my way. At first the crosswords I did, the papers I read and the letters I wrote were all done a little guiltily, a little surreptitiously. Later they were done ostentatiously, provocatively, defiantly. And included among those later letters – and giving me particular pleasure in that they were written during office hours – were answers to advertisements, applications for other jobs.

I joined the John Lewis Partnership early in 1949. John Spedan Lewis, the Chairman, had great faith in the product of our Universities; so my Degree in English Literature undoubtedly helped, but my chief qualification – as it had been when I joined the army – was my carpentry. For it was as a trainee furniture buyer (or possibly furniture designer) that I was engaged. Indeed there were several similarities between 1949 and 1941. Another was that my training did not aim to fit me for a specific appointment but merely to give me all-round experience and competence; and yet another was that I started in the ranks.

So on the appointed day I reported to Mr Jackson, manager of the Lampshade Department at Peter Jones, and thus found myself doing – for the first time perhaps, but not, as will be seen, for the last – the one thing I had vowed that I would *never* do. A year or two previously I had gone into the electrical department of a big store to buy a light bulb, and while waiting to be served by a young man elegantly dressed in black jacket and striped trousers, I had myself been mistaken for a shop assistant by an old lady wanting a vacuum cleaner. That was when I made my vow.

Was it just his clothes? Certainly the clothes we wear have a powerful effect on our personalities, and so on our relationship with one another. The army realizes this when it dresses its troops in uniform and then allows its officers a rather smarter uniform. Dictators realize it when they give jackboots to their supporters and remove the braces of their enemies. The king is more kingly under his crown, the fool more foolish in his ill-fitting trousers. How great a transformation can one achieve in this way? Can any fool, suitably dressed, become a king? Could I, in black and grey, have walked the soft carpeted floors of Harrods with confidence and poise? Probably not. Clothes can accentuate: I doubt if they can change. The seed, the potential must be there in the first place.

So, as the elegantly dressed young man handed me my light bulb,

I was conscious of a vast gulf between us, a gulf that could, of course, have been summed up by that single, haunting, Italian word, *disinvoltura*. I felt it then acutely. What is odd is that I didn't feel it at all during my first day at Peter Jones. Instead I felt only my feet.

I enjoyed selling lampshades. I enjoyed the companionship of my fellow assistants: they were a cheerful, friendly lot. And I enjoyed serving customers. Altogether it was a good and happy start to my new career.

There is no need to retrudge every step I took from Department to Department during my year and a half with John Lewis. I can list about fifteen of them which would seem to indicate that I spent about a month with each. I can't think it was anywhere near as long, so perhaps there are some I have forgotten. I learned a lot, most of it at one time or another to come in useful. I learned many practical things – though not, alas, by practising them, for I was never allowed to do, only to watch. Watching the expert throw a handful of tintacks into his mouth and then bring them forward one at a time between his lips, I learned how to upholster a sofa. I learned how to make loose covers – and later put theory into practice on our own armchair at home. I learned how to French polish, how to make curtains, how to paint straight lines – and the lines that still decorate the chest of drawers in our bedroom today are testimony to that particular lesson and to my enthusiasm at the time.

I learned how curtains were hung and pelmets fixed, and accompanied the hangers and fixers as they went from house to house, and occasionally ('Here's something for the boy') picked up a tip when the job was done. And I learned – though I've yet to find a use for these particular skills – how to apply gold leaf and how with a feather dipped in paint one can imitate the effect of marble. In a different field I learned how secondhand furniture was bought and I accompanied buyers on their visits both to private houses and to auction rooms. I helped myself to books from the Partnership library and learned about Chippendale, Hepplewhite and Regency. I visited two factories near High Wycombe and watched machine tools in action, to excellent effect at one, to appalling effect at the other. I read *Partnership for All* and was as favourably impressed by what Spedan Lewis was trying to do as I was unfavourably impressed by the way he wrote. But of all the things I did and saw, the most important of them all came when I was told to design a dining-room suite.

I wonder if the Departmental Manager who gave me this particular task realized at the time how totally unequipped I was to tackle it. At home I had made small pieces of furniture – stools, shelves and so on – and I had altered and repaired larger pieces. But I had never *designed* anything in my life, that is to say I had never taken pencil and paper first and made a drawing. My furniture making started with a plank of wood and a saw. Consequently not only did I not know how to make a scale drawing; I had no idea of the sort of shapes, proportions and dimensions that were appropriate to chairs and tables. Though I might have been able to measure and copy, without a pattern to follow I was helpless.

This must have been all too obvious to him as soon as he saw my efforts. He made little comment. What was there to say? Instead he lent me a book to read, a large and beautiful picture book of modern furniture; and from the moment I opened it I began to have a feeling for furniture that I had never possessed before, a feeling that could perhaps be summed up by the word 'love'.

Up to then I had 'liked' the furniture my parents had in London. It was mostly old, Italianate, and painted with gay floral themes (for my mother hated what she called 'brown wood'); and I had liked the rather more rustic furniture we had at Cotchford. I didn't specially like but I was beginning to know something about the various second-hand pieces we sold at John Lewis, and I knew that I disliked most of what we sold in our new furniture departments. Then I opened my book and for the first time met Gimson, Waal and Barnsley. For the first time I saw beauty – not just prettiness – in proportion, in shape and in the very nature of the wood itself, and I saw this flowing from something that had its source in a rural past where beauty lay not in ornament but in simplicity. I saw twentieth-century inspiration coming not from the nineteenth but from the sixteenth century. But in 1949 this new found love was virtually confined to illustrations in books. Outside books, in shops generally and in John Lewis in particular, 'second-hand' meant eighteenth and very early nineteenth century, and 'new' meant either 'repro' with its stained wood and cabriole legs or 'contemporary', splay-legged and pale. Furniture design was at its lowest ebb. Only in the Craft Centre near Piccadilly could I see on exhibition individual pieces of furniture, handmade, beautifully designed and following in the tradition of those early twentieth century masters. It was at the age of eight that I first learned the pleasure of handling tools, finding in wood something satisfying to cut and shape. It was at John Lewis that I discovered the added pleasure that could come from good design. There was pleasure in the making: this I knew. There was beauty in the shape and in the material: this I now discovered. I won't pretend that I went home and set to work on my own dining-room suite: I've yet to do that. It was just that where before there was a single seedling growing, now there were two.

These were the things I learned about the world around me. But I also learned something about myself. I learned that, much as I might enjoy myself with a chisel and a plane, even with a hammer and a mouthful of tintacks, I would never be at home in John Lewis. It was as it had been at OCTU: I impressed my various Departmental Managers as little as I had impressed my Officer Instructors, and for almost exactly the same reasons. Like Hedda they too had a word for it. It caught my eye as I glanced at one of their reports: a French word this time. *Gauche*. Just as I felt ill at ease in Service Dress, so would I have felt ill at ease in a Business Suit. Service Dress was obligatory, the Business Suit optional. They urged me to buy one but I never did: and this in itself probably told them all they needed to know – that I was unable to become one of them, that I would always remain an outsider. The shop assistant, poised, polished and self-assured, from whom, years before, I had bought my light bulb did in fact typify what I would never be. I imagine that this was blindingly obvious and I don't suppose that Spedan Lewis when he sat down to dictate his letter to me had a moment's hesitation. It was not a letter that I welcomed at the time: nobody likes to be given the sack. Gratitude came later, when I had found what I was looking for and realized what a stony path I had escaped from.

His letter was waiting on the mat when Lesley and I arrived home after a holiday spent at the village of Laveissière in the Auvergne. In spite of the fact that this holiday had been punctuated (or rather I had been punctuated) by a succession of boils under my left arm, it was, and remained, one of our happiest and most memorable. And this was fortunate not only because the memory lingered on to warm the bleak days that were to follow. There was another reason. I had got the sack. I was out of work. I was beginning to feel that nobody wanted me. I was beginning to lose confidence in myself. There was now no doubt about it: the road was going downhill fast.

It was at this point that we saw our glade.

From time to time Lesley's parents used to come to London and stay with us in our flat in Chancery Lane. It wasn't just for the pleasure of seeing their daughter that they made the long journey from the Isle of Wight. It was to perform on the BBC. They wrote stories and talks, and from time to time came to London to broadcast them. And so, when the moment arrived, Lesley and I would put one or other of them into a taxi and then, an hour later, switch on the wireless. And as I listened to the familiar voice, so I knew that of all the things I could never summon the courage to do, giving a talk on the BBC headed the list. Reading aloud – whether from Shakespeare in class, from the Bible in Chapel, or from a list of names at roll call – was the one thing I had always, determinedly, unashamedly and usually with very great success, done my utmost to avoid. Reading aloud into a microphone, with the thought that there were thousands listening to me at the other end, would have been the ultimate refinement to the torture.

But this was not to stop me from *writing* a talk. Probably it wouldn't be accepted; and even if it were, no doubt they could arrange for one of their professionals to read it.

During our holiday we had had a small adventure. Setting off one morning to climb the Puy Mary we had been caught in a violent storm, and seeing a small solitary stone hut ahead of us on the hillside, had hurried towards it. Inside we had found two men and all the apparatus for making and storing cheese. So I wrote a little piece called 'The Story of a Cheese' and sent it off to a BBC friend. To my delight it was accepted; to my horror I was invited to read it. 'But I can't possibly. I can't read. Couldn't you get someone else to?' His answer was a very firm No. I looked at Lesley in despair ... and surely one of the bravest things she has ever done was to offer to read it for me. This she did: she not only read it beautifully, but during the rehearsal they discovered that the script was a couple of minutes too short. So, with the clocks ticking away towards the fatal hour, she wrote an extra paragraph, spliced it in and polished round the edges so that the join didn't show. The BBC gave us £15, and I reckon that her share was about £13.10.0. But we didn't divide it up. Instead we went round to the Craft Centre and had a coffee table designed and made for us by Robin Nance.

If that was Lesley's bravest moment, mine came shortly afterwards. Buoyed up by hope, humbled by shame, I wrote another talk – this time about painting a meat safe. It too was accepted – and I read it myself on Woman's Hour. I stammered during the rehearsal, but not during the performance. I then wrote and gave two more talks.

Such was the sunlit glade in the middle of a very black forest. For when not writing, I was answering advertisements and being interviewed – with total lack of success. Indeed my search at one point took me – unwittingly – to the very brink of that path that so many once-proud ex-army officers had followed on its sad journey from hope to despair: at one point I found myself in the office of the Sales Manager of a firm of encyclopaedia publishers. Kind man: he knew, and he knew that I didn't know, and he sent me away.

Finally, in desperation I grew a moustache, and after nursing it in private for a day or two, took it out and showed it to the world. It was scarcely visible, being gingery in colour, so I darkened it up with some of Lesley's mascara. The moustache marked the nadir in my fortunes; and I find myself now wondering how many moustaches owe their origins to some period of depression in the lives of their owners and were grown initially more as a gesture of defiance than anything else. Mine lasted a fortnight. It was totally out of character, totally idiotic, but it served its purpose. For with its removal I was able to make a fresh start. I cannot recall exactly the succession of events that led to the decision. 'Two roads diverged. ...' Does the wise man standing at the junction attempt to draw up a balance sheet? I never have. Indeed I dislike making conscious decisions at all. I prefer to wait until either the matter decides itself or instinct prompts me. Just as the right key slips easily into the lock and turns the wards smoothly and sweetly, so, without effort and without forcing, should one know what to do. On this occasion the two roads were very unequal. I was in my glade. It was either back to the stony track I had left or on through the trees with scarcely the ghost of a footpath to reassure me that here was a way forward that led anywhere at all. Would I have ventured that way if I had been on my own? I think not. Happily, both in London in 1951 and in Italy in 1976 Lesley was with me. On both occasions it was a shared conviction that this was the right course that made the decision so easy, so inevitable.

On August 1st, 1951, I shook the dust of London off my feet and, clutching our bowl of goldfish, caught the train from Paddington to Kingswear where Lesley, who had gone on ahead, was waiting for me.

3. *Lesley*

To be socially graceful one must not only say the right thing but say it at the right time, and this is what I am bad at. The right time comes, but the conversation flows on without the hoped for lull, and the right thing remains unsaid. It is so often like this with me and it was like this in the last chapter. Lesley slipped quietly into its pages and I never properly introduced her. So I must do so now.

In the early days of our marriage people would ask us: 'How did you two first meet?' And I would say: 'I invited her to supper. We had dried egg omelette and chips. I made the omelette. She made the chips.' In those days this was an adequate explanation – adequate as far as it went, I mean. Dried egg powder was to be found on every larder shelf – and little else. Today I would perhaps need to explain that in 1948 eggs were so scarce that they were known as 'shell eggs' and the ration was one a week. No guest would have expected her host to feast her on a fortnight's supply.

Of course I would then go on to add that she was my cousin. This was how I knew of her existence. I knew her address too; and having nothing better to do at that particular time I thought it might be interesting to discover what she looked like. So I wrote her a letter.

She was a cousin on my mother's side, a de Selincourt: and de Selincourts were not always on speaking terms with each other. In particular my mother hadn't spoken to her brother Aubrey for about thirty years. That was why we had never met before. It was my Grandfather's second wife, Nancy who, in an attempt to bring us together, had given me my cousin Lesley's address.

I was in London, living alone in a flat in Chancery Lane, working at the COI. She was in London, living with a friend in Claverton Street, working in the showroom at the Cambridge University Press. At 7 o'clock on Thursday February 5th, 1948, she knocked on my door.

Well, she could certainly fry potatoes: a useful accomplishment. And no doubt, lying in bed that night, she pondered over the fact that I could certainly make dried egg omelettes. But as she didn't like omelettes, even shell-egg ones, I doubt if this made me immediately more desirable than any of her other young men. Come to that, I wasn't particularly keen on chips. But I had recently taken my farewell of Hedda and my heart was vacant.

You can use a diary in one of two different ways. You can use it as a journal to record events that have happened: or you can use it as an engagement book to remind you of events that are still to come. I use my diary in the second way. In fact I can think of only one single entry in the past thirty years in which I recorded an event that had already occurred. Nevertheless, dull though they are to re-read, limited almost wholly to dentist's appointments, with day after day left blank, I do not like to throw them away at the end of the year but add them to the growing pile that I keep in my chest of drawers. And it was here that I have just found my diary for 1948, the oldest of them all and unique in that, being a present from Hedda, it is an Italian one.

So I can report that on Thursday, February 12th, I had supper with Lesley at Claverton Street; on Sunday, February 15th we went to Kew Gardens; on Monday the 16th we went to a play and on Thursday the 19th we met for lunch. Nevertheless it was not really, as this might seem to suggest, love at first sight, but rather the discovery that we liked doing things together. Particularly we liked doing nothing much together.

Although Lesley had an older sister, a four year gap and a great difference in temperament lay between them. So, like me, she had led the life of a solitary child and like me she had enjoyed it. We had both of us been brought up in the country, both of us had spent long, happy hours wandering alone through fields and woods, sitting alone under trees, lying alone in the grass. Like me she preferred animals to humans. Our discovery was that though we were both solitaries we liked being solitary in each other's company. We enjoyed walking together along a country footpath, we enjoyed sitting together on a sofa, we enjoyed lying together beneath a hedge. Together we were yet separate; touching, yet silent; she and I each engaged with our own thoughts – yet lost and lonely now without the presence of the other.

'Lesley lunch' says my diary. I was working in Baker Street, she in the Euston Road, two stops away on the Tube. If it was sunny we could take sandwiches into Gordon Square or Regents Park. If it was not so sunny we could go to a pub near Warren Street Station where we could get a good meal at a modest price. 'Lesley 6.30'. This would be at Chancery Lane, of course, so that we could be on our own; and then I would escort her back to Claverton Street on the bus.

On Sunday March 14th there is a complicated timetable indicating a trip on the Green Line to West Wycombe. On Friday March 19th there is the entry 'W'loo Platform 7, 6.15', indicating my first visit to the Isle of Wight to meet her parents, my first meeting with my Uncle Aubrey. On Saturday April 10th are the words 'Sir Charles Napier Hotel, Spriggs Holly'.

Of all the things I enjoyed doing in the country, a longish walk was what I enjoyed most, for not only could I then be a naturalist looking out for interesting birds, I was at the same time an explorer, finding my way. I shared my father's passion for maps and map reading, for planning a route and then following it. The best route was a circular one, out one way, back another, and as far as possible following footpaths rather than roads. Lesley and I had already discovered the Chilterns on our visit to West Wycombe in March but the walk had been a short and simple one. It was time to try something more ambitious. If it turned out a success, I might even look upon it as a sort of omen for the future.

The Green Line Bus took us to High Wycombe and a local bus took us on through West Wycombe to Stokenchurch. From there a footpath led across country to the tiny hamlet of Spriggs Holly[1] and here, no more than a modest country inn despite its grand name, was the Sir Charles Napier Hotel. A friend of Lesley's at the CUP had recommended it. He had recommended well.

The following day, in perfect spring weather, we set out on our walk. I had planned it the evening before, planned it on my own, as I liked to do. I understood maps. Lesley didn't. We set out towards Chinnor Hill in Bledlow Great Wood and made our way to where the ground falls steeply to the valley of the Thames. From there we took a track diagonally down the slope to the village of Bledlow and then by footpaths came to Saunderton. This was the limit of our walk. Of our return journey I am less sure. I know that at one point we came to a wood where the path was indistinct and I was in fear that we might lose our way. And I know that, almost at the end, the path ran up beside another wood towards a gate in a hedge. Beyond the hedge was the road. Once on the road it was half a mile back to our pub. So we had done it. We were practically home. I looked again at my map to be quite sure and found that the wood we had been walking beside was called Venus Wood. Beyond the gate on the other side of the road was a little corrugated iron chapel. Here undoubtedly was the right place and the right time for saying the right thing; and for once I was not going to miss it. I had navigated her through the Chilterns. We had done the entire homeward journey with arms round each other's waists and her head on my shoulder. If I could navigate her so successfully and we could walk like this so happily through the spring countryside, surely we could go on together a little further.

I stopped just short of the gate and we turned to face each other. 'Will you marry me?' I said.

'Of course I will, darling,' she answered.

In my diary on April 11th occurs that retrospective entry, the only one I have ever made. In ink are the words 'Got engaged!'

---

[1] The Ordnance Survey today spells it 'Sprigs Holly'. I rather think that in 1948 it was spelt 'Sprigs Alley'. However, I prefer the spelling I recorded in my diary.

4. *Westwards*

On March 3rd, 1951, the following advertisement had appeared in *The Bookseller.*

> Partner wanted: Young man, well educated, with initiative, offered one-third share in West Country bookshop. Ability to drive essential for developing travelling bookshop to remote parts. Home given with some social life. Capital required, minimum £350.

At the end of my long, stony, downward road, here was the signpost, its message the famous and familiar one that had first appeared in the columns of an Indiana newspaper exactly a hundred years earlier: 'Go west, young man.'

A fortnight later we were in a train heading for the Cotswold Bookroom in Wotton-under-Edge near Gloucester. Dr Paxton had apologized for the fact that he would not be there to greet us as he had a christening that afternoon, but his wife would be in the shop and would look after us until his return. *Dr* Paxton? DD, presumably. The local vicar? We pictured an elderly clergyman and wondered what sort of books he would want me to drive to remote parts with. . . . So it was a delightful surprise and a great relief to find that the Paxtons were about our age and that he was a prep school master. Not DD but PhD. Not christening anybody: being christened himself ('. . . and a great mistake,' as he confessed many years later).

Though we never went into partnership with them, John and Joan Paxton were exactly the people we needed to find. The jump that we were eventually to make, from London to Dartmouth, from the security of being employed to the insecurity of being self employed, was greater than we could have managed on our own. We needed an intermediate stepping stone and a helping hand. For this the Cotswold Bookroom was ideally placed, almost exactly midway, geographically and metaphorically between the world we were leaving and the world we were going to. And as for the Paxtons, two kinder and more helpful people, both then and still, we have yet to meet. Though we briefly contemplated the idea of opening a companion shop in the nearby town of Chipping Sodbury, John, who was an economist, knew that there wasn't really enough money in it to support the two of us with no other source of income.

But if the idea came to nothing it pointed the way ahead. Inspired and encouraged by the Paxtons' enthusiasm, by their evident enjoyment of what they were doing, by what they had already achieved, by their faith in what it was possible for a small-town bookseller to achieve and indeed by their whole attitude towards life generally, and bearing with us their promises of help and advice whenever we should need it, we returned to London convinced that this was the life for us, that we would snap our fingers at London and at all those employers who had refused to employ me, and open our own bookshop in a town of our own choosing.

Today the road westward is lined with young people, their belongings on their back, their worldly wealth in their pocket, boldly thumbing their way towards new hope and a fresh start. Where are they bound for? What will they do when they get there? Anywhere! Anything! Were we more timid twenty-five years ago? Had my generation less self confidence, less optimism? Possibly this is true generally. Certainly it was true of Lesley and myself, and the reason lies partly in our nature and partly in social attitudes. Yes, we were timid and we did lack self confidence. But at the same time, in those days and even at our level, *noblesse oblige*: which meant that I had to earn a living and earn it in a way that was considered appropriate for someone with a University education. Failure to do this mattered very much. Failure in London was bad enough. To leave London and then to fail would have meant an ignominious return – and that would have been very much worse. An employee can always blame his employer: the self employed has only himself to blame.

'Really,' said my mother some two months later when I announced our plans, 'it does seem a very odd decision.' And of course in many ways she was quite right.

In 1945, when my father had suggested to me a career in publishing, I had said what I thought of the business world. Five years later, the business world – in the form of J. Spedan Lewis – had said what it thought of me. The antipathy appeared to be mutual and it was indeed odd that I should be trying again to do something I both despised and was bad at. But that was not all. There was something even odder in my choice. There were two things that were then overshadowing my life and that I needed to escape from: my father's fame and 'Christopher Robin'. Yet, here I was apparently deliberately seeking out his shadow so as to work beneath it, choosing a trade that would put me on public exhibition as Christopher Robin, wrapping up the books he had written. Was it that I was deliberately turning to face the dragon that had been pursuing me? I must be honest and confess no such courageous intention. I was running away, all right. I was running away from London.

London was the scene of my father's successes. London was the scene of my failures. Neither Lesley nor I had any love for the place, and every weekend we used to escape into the country. What was there to keep us here? Why should we not make our escape permanent?

'But what made you choose *Dartmouth*?' So often we have been asked this question. Our London friends wondered why we had chosen a place they had never even heard of. Our Dartmouth friends wondered – in our early days at any rate – why we had chosen a place where the prospects of making a fortune seemed so remote.

Looking back, I still think we chose as intelligently and as carefully as we could. Certainly as it turned out we chose extremely well, but equally certainly a large amount of luck came into it. I doubt if any modern 'feasability study' could have offered us a town in which both bookselling and living have been such a pleasure for so many years.

This was how we went about it.

First an atlas. The whole of England lay before us, but instinctively our eyes turned to the southern half. We were southerners. Cambridge was my northern limit; Oxford, where she had been born, was Lesley's. North of that, despite our Scottish blood, lay foreign country. Anywhere south of London we could feel at home. South of London yet at the same time well away from London. This sent our eyes westward. Lesley had been brought up in Dorset and the Isle of Wight. Her father had a boat, and from sailing holidays she knew the Dorset and Devon coast. I too had holidayed in Dorset and Devon. Lesley had a special fondness for the sea and I was very happy to share it with her. A coastal town, therefore, somewhere between Weymouth and Plymouth. Large or small? Small for choice, to be as different from London as possible and because there was inevitably going to be a sort of amateurishness, a sort of tweediness, about our shop that would be out of place in a big town where smart suits were worn. A small seaside town then, a holiday town that would give us a bit of extra business during the summer. A town that didn't already have a good private bookshop. . . .

So first the atlas to list the towns. Then a gazetteer to tell us their populations. Then a guidebook to describe their appearance. And lastly a classified telephone directory to locate existing bookshops. This gave us about half a dozen possibles. Back to the telephone directory for local estate agents; and finally a dozen letters.

This, when I am asked, is my story. But there is another story I would now like to tell. It is a detective story and I wrote it during those bleak days when I was still searching for a London job. The *Evening Standard* was at that time running a series and was welcoming contributions from their readers. They didn't welcome mine, and I resurrect it now, not for its intrinsic merit, which I am prepared to accept is slight, but for a reason which will emerge.

The story was built round an idea, and the idea was this. A murder is to be committed. It is planned to look like an accident. Fate, watching from the wings, decides to lend a hand. Unknown to the villain his victim meets with exactly the accident that was being prepared for him. The victim dies. The villain of course is innocent. But alas, the ingenious scheme that was designed to make murder look like an accident now makes an accident look like murder. And so the villain is arrested. Ironic – or so I hoped. . . .

I need not fill in the details, except to say three things. First, the victim was to be pushed over a cliff. Secondly I wanted a wild flower. And thirdly I wanted a name.

The flower had to be a rare one such as one might hope to find growing on cliff tops by the sea. It also had to be an attractive one such as a keen gardener might wish to dig up to plant in his own garden. So I went to a public library to search through books on wild flowers: and in the end I found just what I wanted: the white rockrose.

The name was the villain's name. I wanted a collection of letters that sounded possible but in fact was not a name at all. And for this I went to the London telephone directory to check that it wasn't there. And the name I failed to find was 'Prout'.

Soon after our arrival in Dartmouth I made two discoveries. The rare white rockrose grows on the cliffs at Berry Head. And there were Prouts all round us.

It was almost as if Dartmouth had known all along that we were coming.

5. Setting up Shop

It was of course a big event in our lives, opening a bookshop in the West Country, and one that we might in later years like to look back on, reminding ourselves exactly how we set about it. So I bought myself an exercise book and began keeping a journal.

The exercise book still survives and in this chapter I record some of my entries.

1951. May 9th. Among all the unlikely premises that we have been offered – the cafés, the fishmonger's shops, the butchers (complete with marble slab) and the guest houses – are three possibles. Two of them are in Brixham and one in Dartmouth. And since Brixham and Dartmouth are neighbouring towns, we felt they might be worth a visit. So, leaving Lesley behind – for she is still working – I catch a train from Paddington, arrive at Brixham and meet Mr Webster, estate agent. He is short, fat, bow-tied and exuberant. He takes me to a boarding house that is off the road and miles from shops. But never mind. 'Brixham is expanding' and there would soon be shops all round me. Sorry! Can't wait – and anyway it's too expensive. Next he offers to show me another boarding house 'belonging to a lady in the theatrical profession who has been told by her husband to sell out at any price so that they can go touring'. However, she is out. So he takes me on a guided tour of the town, nudging me in the ribs to draw my attention to Brixham's fleet of 27 taxis, to the best grocer's shop in England, to the new car park, etc., 'Brixham,' he assures me, 'is fast coming to the fore!' I mention that I am going on to Dartmouth tomorrow. 'Dartmouth!' he cries in horror. 'Dartmouth is *dead*!' He takes me to my hotel and we part. After supper I call on the actress. Nice house – but it is a shop I'm wanting.

May 10th. I meet Thomas John, estate agent. He shows me a place but advises against it. 'Position is everything for your business,' he says; and I'm sure he's right. Then he tells me that a baby-linen shop in a better position might be closing down. He goes to find out, while I walk along the cliffs in the sun. On my return he tells me it is indeed closing 'but the owner won't be hustled.' I leave Brixham, catching a bus an hour later than I had intended.

The bus takes me to Kingswear and I stand on the ferry slip looking across the river to my first view of Dartmouth sparkling in the sunshine on the other side. A dead town? From here it could hardly look more inviting. I cross on the car ferry, walk along a narrow street – and there on the corner facing me is the very place I have come to see. What a position! I call on Victor Newton, estate agent, and he tells me that the owner waited until 11 o'clock but has now gone out and won't be back until 7.30. We go to inspect. It is called Fairfax Sports and is as crammed with goods as a stall on market day, so that what you don't trip over on the floor you bump your head against hanging from the ceiling; all of which makes it seem smaller and darker than it probably really is. We arrange to meet again at 7.30 and I go exploring. There are one or two stationers that sell a few books but, as we had guessed, W. H. Smith is the only genuine bookshop: so that's all right. I wander through the narrow streets and then down to the sea and feel very happy. I like it all: town, river, sea, hills, woods, position of shop and its price. Strolling along a narrow lane I notice a blackbird's nest and then a hedge sparrow's: a good omen?

Supper, booked for 7 o'clock, doesn't arrive until 7.15. I bolt it but even so am ten minutes late for my appointment; and in those ten minutes another prospective buyer has slipped in before me. So Newton and I have to stand outside in the road, I in an agony of suspense and cursing myself that this is the second appointment I have made and missed. At last the door opens and a man comes out. We hurry in. What is the position? He likes it, we are told, and he is prepared to buy freehold, goodwill and stock for £5000 ... but. ... And it is this 'but' that makes my firm offer of £3500 for freehold alone acceptable. No time to consult my solicitor. No time to arrange a survey. No time even to bring Lesley down to see it. I must decide *now* – or risk losing it. Help! So I ring her up. 'I've got to give an answer straight away.' And two hundred miles away a faint voice answers: 'I leave it to you. If you like it, we'd better have it.' Half an hour later Montague has summoned his solicitor and the three of us are in the kitchen signing documents while Mrs Montague is at the sink and younger Montagues come and go with a great shouting and banging of doors. . . . What a way to buy a bookshop! I go to bed with my head in a whirl.

May 18th. A hectic day, beginning at 9.45 with my BBC talk, 'My Ascent of Mont Blanc'[1] and followed at 12 o'clock by our journey to Dartmouth. This time we both go. The train takes us to Kingswear and then we cross the river by boat to Dartmouth station on the other side. It is not quite Lesley's first visit. She came once in her father's boat on a sailing holiday many years ago. All the same I am nervous she might not approve of the shop. Luckily she does. We call on the Montagues, look round and ask a hundred questions. At the back of the shop is a dark and curious room which we can use as an office. Next-door, and belonging to us, is a separate lock-up shop, rented to an electrician. On the first floor and reached by a *very* narrow staircase are two rooms. On the right a diningroom/kitchen, a pleasant room with a glimpse of the river at the end of the road from one window, and from another a view up a hill towards distant woods. This is really their living-room. Next-door to it, on the left, is what I suppose would be called their front parlour, respectably furnished with a three piece suite but clearly never used – not even for the signing of contracts! Upstairs are two bedrooms and a bathroom; and, at a bend on the stairs, no bigger than a cupboard, and obviously put in as an afterthought, is the lavatory. Decoration is dreadful: dark green paint, dados and jazzy wallpaper. Altogether there's masses to be done and we decide to get builders to tackle the outside. I'll

[1] It was not of course the famous Mont Blanc but a Petit Mont Blanc in Haute Savoie, one that we had discovered on our honeymoon.

do the inside. Shop first, of course: the awful wallpaper and paint upstairs will have to wait their turn. I call on Michelmores, the builder I had been recommended, and arrange for them to send us an estimate.

May 24th. Visit Longhurst's bookshop in High Holborn and ask them if they would like an unpaid assistant for a few days. They wouldn't, and suggested I try the great Mr Wilson of Bumpus. So I call there a little nervously, but he is nice and allows me to look around and take notes – provided I don't tell anybody who I am or what I'm doing.

May 25th. List-making at Bumpus's.

May 31st. In reply to our letters several publishers have now sent us catalogues; one or two have written; Blackie have refused to open an account with us; Customs and Excise have given helpful advice about Purchase Tax. A letter from Richard Bell says: 'I think it is very brave of you at the present time . . .' and I suppose that by 'brave' he really means 'rash' or possibly even 'foolish'. The other day I called on Alan White of Methuen. He was pleasant and friendly, of course, but he too talked about 'these difficult times'. On the whole, however, people are enthusiastic, almost envious. And certainly the idea of a little shop by the sea does sound very attractive. It will be hard work – but who cares?

We have now examined many bookshops both for their stock and for the way they display it. I have made what I think is a good list of basic stock; and I have designed some display stands and have ideas about shelving. Today I made a model of our window fitting, which was useful as it showed up one or two faults.

June 15th. We have continued our listing. Going round bookshops and trying not to look too suspicious we have completed our subject lists. These we have now rearranged, under publishers, giving us a fair idea of what we will be wanting to buy from each. I have also planned our shelves, calculated total length and thus reached an approximate figure for the total value of books we can stock. Including window display it comes to £725. Lesley and I then independently divided this up into the money to be allocated to each subject – and reached almost exactly the same answers. The actual shelves are a problem. I went to a timber-merchant in the Euston Road and learned that for most wood you need to have a permit. Would I be able to get one in Dartmouth? I decided not to take the risk and bought 230 feet of off-permit French poplar. This cost me £10 and will be travelling down to Devon with us. Add it to the existing shelving I'm buying off Montague for £5 and we'll have enough.

It seems to be generally agreed that one can't survive on books alone. So we have decided to sell a few 'fancy goods' (awful expression) as well – some of which I hope to make myself. Book ends, for instance. Today I made a cigarette box. It took about six hours, but should eventually take much less – say four. Materials cost three shillings. I'd like to sell it for £1. But can I charge less than five shillings an hour for labour?

Lesley stops work today – I mean resigns from her job – and we celebrate with a bottle of wine.

July 15th. We have now finished our tour of publishers. From some we just collected catalogues; at others we talked to Sales Managers. All were kind and helpful. One or two gave advice, urging us not just to sit in our shop waiting for customers to-come to us, but to go out and find them. Terms vary. Most publishers only give you 33⅓% discount if you order two copies of a book; a few, like Collins, allow 33⅓% on single copies; while a few want you to order three or even *six* copies. Some asked for references, others didn't bother. Some had showrooms, others not. Top marks so far go to Collins.

After two rather exhausting weeks of this, we visited the Paxtons again for a few days, learning a bit more about all the paperwork we are going to have to grapple with; learning also something about secondhand books, which we might decide to sell. Then we went to France for a quick holiday: probably our last for many years.

July 30th. Lesley has departed for Dartmouth and I am alone with our packing. Our stock orders have now all been sent off. Mysteriously we left out Churchill's *The Hinge of Fate* and – of all books – one published by Batsford called *Dartmouth*. However, this has now been put right. Michelmores for all their friendliness never sent us our estimate, so we have written to another builder called Watts. We have at last been officially 'recognized' by the book trade. (Without recognition we couldn't have got trade terms.) We have met the Secretary of the Booksellers Association, who happened to be a friend of our neighbour Felix Barker. And with Wilson[2] and Christina Foyle agreeing to be our sponsors, we found ourselves members of the Booksellers Association by return of post.

August 15th. We have now been here two weeks – though it doesn't seem like it. The move was successful though exhausting. Lesley left two days ahead of me and found poor Mrs Montague waist deep in chaos. The chaos at Chancery Lane was only ankle deep; and I threw away a lot of it to the accompaniment of comments from Mrs Roberts, our caretaker. The removal men were very good. The foreman's brother-in-law kept tropical fish and this established an immediate bond between us. At 3.30 I and our own fish caught the Paddington train.

The furniture arrived the following day and virtually none of it could get up our staircase. So after some discussion it was decided to remove the dining-room window, park the van beneath it, haul the stuff up on to the roof of the van, and then pass it through the window. This, the foreman explained to me, would be *very heavy work*, and it would have been much easier if they had gone to get a block and tackle. But this would have cost me *a lot extra*. I got the message.

The shop has vast windows, and, working inside, one feels terribly naked and exposed. So my first task was to whitewash them over.

---

[2] John Wilson of Bumpus. If it is wondered how we were able to enlist as sponsors two of the most eminent booksellers in the country, the explanation is that my father wrote to them. These were the last two letters he was to write on my behalf. For the past twelve years he had been watching, helping where help was wanted, occasionally very gently urging, and on the whole, I think approving. And I was conscious of his presence in the background, not always willing to take him into my confidence, but grateful for his help when it came. When we left for Devon the last frail tie that bound me to him was broken. My pilot had turned back and I was on my own.

'What are they doing that for?' a small child asks its mother; and two boys pressed their faces to the glass while I painted smaller and smaller circles round their noses. Privacy at last! My second task was to get rid of all Montague's drawing pins and crepe paper. Never was a shop so full of both, so that in a little while what had seemed emptiness was knee deep in the stuff and the soles of our shoes were studded all over. After that, soap and water. Then grey distemper. The grey goes quite nicely with the existing not-too-bad yellow ceiling. Then shelves and stands. Lesley and I slave away inside. Watts has sent an estimate for the outside but has not yet started work.

August 24th. Today Lesley removes our protective whitewash and, though still closed, we are visible to the outside world in all our glory. Faces peer in. Mostly children and old ladies. Two boys ask: 'Is this going to be a library?' 'No,' says Lesley. 'A bookshop.' And she almost adds, 'I'm afraid.' 'We can *buy* books?' 'Yes.' 'Oo – oo – oo!' and they hug each other and dance a jig. An old man enquires of the world 'Is this a free lending library?' and gets no reply. We put on our window lights after dark and go out to inspect ourselves. What a nice looking shop! Pity it is still nameless, however. Watts has managed to finish our painting in time but has not yet produced our fascia board.

The other day came a letter from Enid Blyton saying she had heard we were opening a bookshop and enclosing her catalogue. It lists over 200 of her books, coming from twenty different publishers. What a woman!

I wrote back to remind her that very many years ago she had presented me with a copy of *The Enid Blyton Book of Bunnies*, which in the end I almost knew by heart; and I asked if she would care to send a photograph of herself to go in our window. In reply I received three photographs, the latest version of her *Book of Bunnies*, two letters and a postcard.

Over the street is a newsagent, stationer and – yes – *bookseller*! with a small stock of children's books and paperbacks to prove it. Inside it is dark and gloomy and, behind a counter, scarcely visible in the twilight, stand two elderly, gloomy men. They never smile at me. They never even speak. Just hand me my *News Chronicle* and take my money. Oh, dear! Are they bitter about our arrival here? Are we going to be *enemies*? Will there be war between us? Thus were we imagining it; and then yesterday one of them came up to me and said: 'I want to wish you the best of luck.' And he really meant it. How easy it is to misjudge people.

How easy too to misjudge buildings. Ours, because it looked so smooth and square, I imagined to have been built between the wars, built of brick and plastered over. Inside, Montague's decorations somehow reinforced this impression. How wrong I was I discovered when attempting to peel off some of his wallpaper. Underneath was more wallpaper, and underneath yet more, layer under layer going back through the decades. I peeled away expecting eventually to reach solid brick – and instead came to the outside world. Help! I hurriedly replaced it all and resolved never again to probe too deeply. We are in fact a very old building. Our front wall is 'half-timbered', wooden frame with lath and plaster on either side. Where the plaster is soft and crumbling you can put a knife right through.

Percy Russell brought us a letter today. He is the author of *Dartmouth*, the Batsford book we so nearly didn't buy. He wrote to wish us luck, implying that we would need it, for Dartmouth, he said, was not an easy town to make money in. This letter coupled with a long article in our local paper about the town's declining population and prosperity left us momentarily depressed. But soon we cheered up, for now we can imagine ourselves as Dartmouth's saviours. The worse things are, the greater is the challenge, the greater the scope for improvement. Can the Milnes bring new life to a decaying town? No harm in dreaming so.

August 25th. At 9 o'clock, without ceremony though with trousers newly pressed, the Harbour Bookshop opens its doors. We had sent letters to several of Dartmouth's leading citizens (though not necessarily their most enthusiastic book-buyers); we had put an advertisement in the local paper (and their reporter had come round for an interview); and that was about it. At 9:15 we have our first customer, who buys a couple of 'Thrift' books. Then nothing until around 10.30 when there is a sudden influx of shoppers, mostly locals, and business is brisk. 'How nice to see a really good bookshop,' they say. 'What a wonderful collection of books.' And the children say 'Oo Mummy, aren't they lovely!' Two little girls spend hours looking at everything, occasionally glancing at us and then telling each other 'not to spoil the nice books' – to show how well behaved they are being. Several people introduce themselves. Will we remember their names when next we see them? They are all complimentary and kind and make us feel welcome to their town. Our sales include three copies of *The River Dart*, two Mazo de la Roches, several Zodiac Books and lots of Swiss flower cards. At 5.30 tired but happy we close our doors and count our takings. Twelve guineas. Not bad for a start?

6. Not Just Books

In the early 1950s you could walk round almost any small town and, if you kept your eyes above shop window level, you would have no difficulty in finding a bookseller. Lower your eyes and you would most probably discover that he was selling not books but stationery or toys or tobacco or fancy goods. No doubt he had started off with books on his shelves and good intentions in his heart; but over the years the 'other goods' had crept in, proved more popular, proved more profitable, and gradually elbowed their way along, until in the end all that remained of the bookshop was a revolving stand of paperback thrillers and romances or (at Christmas-time) a pile of children's annuals: that – and a fascia board which for one reason or another ignored the changing scene within.

We knew that we too would have to sell 'other goods', but we were determined that – when eventually Mr Watts produced it – *our* fascia board would announce not only what we were but what we would always be: booksellers. So if this chapter is about all the other things that from time to time we sold or did, it is just to get them out of the way, so that bookselling can then have an uninterrupted chapter all to itself.

The obvious accompaniments to new books were of course second-hand books. Indeed many people, hearing that we were to become booksellers, assumed that by this we meant second-hand booksellers. Also it gave our parents a chance to help us on our way with various unwanted volumes from their own shelves. These gleanings – our opening stock – travelled down with us in the furniture van. However, it was not until the end of September that we made our first and most important purchase and felt justified in adding the words 'and Second-hand Booksellers' to our visiting card. At a local auction and for an outlay of two-and-six we acquired three sackloads of books, bore them home, tipped them out onto the dining-room floor and crouched down to inspect them.

They were all old. To our inexperienced eye most of them seemed to have little but their age to recommend them, and so we gave them prices ranging from 2d to 5/–. Among them were some Bibles, very large and heavy, and these were our first problem; for it seemed as wrong to price them at 6d each – which we thought was all we were likely to get for them – as it was to put them out with the salvage; and so in the end we offered them to the vicar. Then there were half a dozen rather more attractive-looking volumes published between 1750 and 1850, and for these we chose prices between 5/– and £1; and finally there was an atlas of the world published in 1815 and a book of Victorian fashion plates. It was Lesley who recognized this last as our winner. And here we met our second problem: how could we discover its value? Was it worth £5 or £20? We sought in vain for advice. In the end we just made a guess, advertised it in the appropriate trade paper, and from the number of booksellers who wrote to us (one of them even sending a cable from America) realized that we had guessed too low.

Nevertheless our half-crown investment had shown us a very good profit and with such beginner's luck we were encouraged to continue. So we went to auctions and we were invited to private houses, and it was exciting, because you never knew what you might find. But always there remained this problem that with the better books we had no means of knowing how much we ought to offer or how much hope to get. Another difficulty was that as we had no car we had to rely on bus and muscle to get our purchases home. So that a complete set of Waverley Novels from a house at the top of the town or a miscellaneous collection of rather battered and smelly children's books from an isolated cottage on the other side of the river really did earn the modest price we sold them for when the effort of transport had been taken into account. However, in those days we were young and strong and the buses ran more frequently than they do today. And in fact it was the people who brought books to us that were the greater trial: the frail old ladies who had struggled across the ferry bearing treasures that were surely worth a fortune, for they had been in the family so long and the esses were like effs. Could I bring myself to say that they were worth practically nothing? Did they really have to cart them all the way home again – with the day's shopping too, *and* in the rain? So in the end I usually paid a price which, though very much less than had been hoped for, was also very much more than I reckoned they were worth.

But what finally turned us against second-hand books was not the buying but the selling. It was the discovery – totally unexpected – that those who came into our shop to look at them bore no resemblance at all to those who came in to look at our new books. Our new book customers, from the very first, surprised and delighted us by their obvious enthusiasm for the shop and its wares. They enjoyed coming in, they enjoyed looking around, they enjoyed making their purchases, and they were clearly going home to enjoy reading whatever it was they had bought. And naturally their pleasure was our pleasure too. How very different was the attitude of those who came in to look at our second-hand books. In fairness I must admit that in one sense of the word this attitude was not their fault. For it was we who had chosen to keep these books in the narrow passageway that separated the rest of the shop from our office and till. This meant that every time we served a customer with a card or a new book we had to squeeze our way past the second-hand browsers, and do so twice, with two sets of apologies, one on the inward journey, once again on the outward. The fault was ours, yet, because we so disliked their attitude in the other sense, we found ourselves most unjustly disliking it in this sense as well; and more and more did we resent their crouched, unyielding forms, less and less apologetic did we become as we pushed our way by.

I recorded an early encounter with a typical second-hand book customer in my journal.

'The man came in with a brisk, business-like air and carrying a briefcase. He positioned himself in the gangway, ran his eye quickly over our shelves, picked out three books, flipped through them, put them on one side, picked them up, glanced at them again, handed them to me and said: Three-and-six? I did the addition and got the answer to five shillings. Four shillings, then? said the man. I said, Sorry, five. He said that wasn't the way to do business and if I wanted his continued custom I must be more accommodating. He then looked at the books again, rejected one, tried to get the other two for three shillings, and finally, grudgingly, paid the full three and six. No doubt if I had priced the books up to seven-and-six in the first place and then allowed him to beat me down to five, he would have left the shop delighted with his bargain. But I hate doing business in that way.'

It was customers such as this – collectors, I suppose, or possibly dealers, whose measure of a book lay in how much they had paid for it and what they thought it was worth, rather than in the pleasure it might give anybody to read it – that made it such a happy day for us when we finally stopped being second-hand booksellers.

By that time, however, we were already well established in another line of business: we were selling greetings cards.

CARDS

I have already mentioned the Swiss flower cards that we sold so briskly on our opening day. This was how it started and they came to us out of the blue, a bundle of specimens sent to us by an enterprising Miss Channing who looked after the sales of a small firm of importers. Up to then cards had entered little into the lives of either of us. We knew about Christmas cards, of course, and sent them to our friends. We knew about view cards, occasionally bought them on holiday, and inherited hundreds of extremely drab Dartmouth ones from Montague. But that was all. Birthday cards,

'Best wishes' cards, 'Get well' cards, 'New Home' cards, 'Congratulations' cards: all these were quite unknown to us. And so our delight at seeing these Swiss flower cards arose not only from their beauty but also from their novelty. We fell in love with them at once, ordered them and decorated our window with them. And at once they caught the eye of passers-by and brought them into our shop. 'I just want that card ...' they would begin, then see that we had others, and hunt through them, and start making a collection ... then go on to look at the books. ... And when they had assembled all their purchases and were handing them over to us, they would say, almost apologetically: 'You know I really only came in to buy that one card.'

Thus very early on we learned that cards were worth much more to us than the profit from their sales. They gave people an excuse to come in and browse. Holding their card they could then go on to look at the books – and it didn't matter in the least if they couldn't find one they wanted to buy.

We started with Swiss flowers and they remained our favourites and the favourites of our customers for many years. Indeed you could say that they were the foundation stone on which our card reputation was established. And of course they pointed the way forward. But in what direction? We needed a guide; we needed advice; and very luckily for us there entered Mr and Mrs Worth able and willing to help. Our luck was not just that they had themselves run a card business in another town before coming to Dartmouth, it was that their taste was the same as ours. The suppliers they introduced us to had just the cards we wanted.

The cards we wanted? I might almost say 'the cards we loved'. For another discovery we made was that there were two distinct categories, those we loved and those we hated. Our reactions really were as strong and as different as this and there was very little in between. But it was many years before we hit on a definition of those in the second category that did not seem to be an insult either to the customer who preferred them or to the salesman who was offering them; and at first much time was wasted, to our growing misery and the growing exasperation of the salesman, as he turned the pages of his album of samples and we shook our heads. The phrase that saved us in the end was 'stationer's cards'. And all that then became necessary was a quick glance at the album while his opening questions were being rehearsed ('How's trade?' and 'Been on holiday yet?') and then we could interrupt with 'Sorry but these are stationer's cards', and direct him across the road.

By confining ourselves firmly to those in the first category – we never bothered to find a generic name for them: they didn't need one – we very quickly established a reputation that was, in one respect at least, quite undeserved. 'I've never seen such lovely cards anywhere else before,' customers would say. But of course they had. It was just that they had seen them mixed in with all the others, and in such company – flamboyant, tinselly, ostentatious – they appeared small and drab. Only when they were among their fellows did they shine. It is the same with people.

As we chose our books, so we chose our cards: slowly, thoughtfully, pleasurably, one by one; never if we could help it accepting a 'mixed assortment' always preferring to make our own selection, a dozen of this, a dozen of that and then perhaps, greatly daring, four dozen of something that specially took our fancy; influenced very much by our own tastes, but realizing, naturally, that we were buying for others. I used to love these buying sessions, eager to see what was new, eager to discover a publisher or importer who could offer us something entirely original. Each season brought fresh delights. Each card gave us a double pleasure: the pleasure of finding it and buying it, and then the pleasure of displaying it and selling it. 'What *lovely* cards you do have!'

Were they extra attractive in those days I wonder, or were they like the first spring flowers after the long winter of War and Austerity? As I look at our cards today and remember those cards of twenty years ago, it is like looking at a hedge-bank in high summer heavy with vegetation and remembering the starry-eyed celandines that first pricked it into colour. It is like remembering spring gentians on a hillside in Italy.

A single incident, happening out of the blue, starts one off on a new course. It was Miss Channing and her Swiss flowers who had introduced us to greetings cards. It was Harold Finlinson who now introduced us to old prints and thence to picture framing. If Miss Channing had never written her letter, if Finlinson, visiting Dartmouth, had called elsewhere, or if in either case I had said 'No' instead of 'Yes', would the fortunes of the Harbour Bookshop have been very different?

They were small steel engravings and they had come from topographical books published in the early nineteenth century. In their original state they had been black-and-white, and perhaps over the years they had become blotched with brown. But this didn't matter. They were torn out, bleached, washed, sized (to make the paper non-absorbent), tinted with watercolours and then mounted. This was how Finlinson offered them to us, and since they were all of South Devon scenes and many of them were of Dartmouth itself and since they were modestly priced at 3/– to 5/–, I was able to assure him very quickly that he had come to the right place.

Dartmouth in the 1830s was not so very different from Dartmouth in the 1950s. The Butterwalk, Bayard's Cove, Dartmouth Castle, the views up and down the river: these had changed little in those hundred-odd years. This gave the prints an added charm: they showed not just what had been but what very recognizably still was. We put them on display and were delighted to find that our customers shared our enthusiasm. And at once the question arose: what about frames? I asked Finlinson and he recommended a black-and-gold Hogarth moulding and suggested that I arranged this with a local framer. So I went to Skinner.

I had discovered Skinner the previous year, for I was already thinking of framed pictures as a possible addition to our books. One or two of our greetings card suppliers also sold prints and it seemed natural that we should, too. There was a framer in Dartmouth but he was unwilling to help us; so I had to go further afield. Skinner was in Torquay and this meant catching first a boat, then a train, then a bus. But the bus landed me almost at his door, and then came half an hour with just the sort of man whose company I so specially enjoyed – that of an elderly, Devonian craftsman – and after I had shown him my prints (they were mostly pictures of sailing ships and coastal scenes) and discussed mounts and mouldings, I could listen to his stories and laugh at his jokes and store them up for passing on to Lesley when I got home.

So now I took him my old engravings. But, alas, he could offer me only narrow oak or plain black; he didn't have Hogarth. It was too expensive, he said.

In the end, therefore – for there seemed no alternative – I became my own picture framer. I started in a very modest way with a hundred feet of half-inch Hogarth, some sheets of cardboard, glass from old pictures picked up for next to nothing at auctions, and a table in our dimly lit office behind the shop – which made it difficult, when I was working, for Lesley to get to the till. Then, as our business expanded and my skill grew, I acquired a larger, lighter workshop, added more and ever more mouldings to my range, and tackled larger and larger pictures in an increasing variety of ways. 'I expect you need lots of special tools,' people would say; but in fact I didn't. I think the only tool I had to buy straight away to add to my existing collection was a very fine nail punch. The devices I needed for cutting the angles at the corners I designed and made for myself. Today there are books telling you how to do it, but I don't think there were then; at any rate I never found – or needed – one. I was a self-taught frame maker. Only when it came to mount cutting did I need Skinner's advice. He showed me how he did it, using a chisel and a home-made ruler, and I copied him: I don't think I would have discovered so simple and effective a way on my own. The only luxury I ever allowed myself was a machine for shooting metal tacks into the backs of frames to hold everything in place. This was so much quicker than hammering in panel pins that I felt the expense was justified. When you make things for yourself, it doesn't matter how long you take over it, but when you make for resale, speed is important.

One might be excused for thinking that framing picture after picture is dull, monotonous work; but this was rarely so, even if I were putting six more Finlinson prints into Hogarth frames or six more Redouté roses into pink mounts and white box frames. It depended on what I was framing, and how: very much it depended on this.

What and how: the picture in the middle and the mount and frame that surround it: these are the two components of the completed whole; and both were able to arouse in me the strongest feelings. If I liked what I was framing and if I could frame it the way I wanted to, then the work gave me intense pleasure. I never got tired of old engravings, nor did my customers; and fortunately – Dartmouth being a more famous town at the beginning of last century than it was when Mr Webster gave me his opinion of it – many artists (including Turner) had come here and a great variety of steel engravings, copper engravings, mezzotints, aquatints and lithographs had survived to record their industry. Finlinson was able to keep me supplied with a very considerable number, but not enough, and I had to go hunting elsewhere. I searched in Dartmouth, I searched in London, and on the way I came upon other delights: old maps of Devon, old road maps, old charts, prints of old ships, flower prints. . . . Sometimes, too, my prints would come in their original state, dirty and uncoloured, and so I had to learn how to smarten them up. I had to find out how to bleach and clean them, and I have memories (and Lesley has too) of prints in the kitchen sink, prints in bowls on the kitchen table, prints floating in the bath, and throughout the house the smell of chlorine.

Parallel with this we were building up our stock of modern reproductions, becoming members of the Fine Arts Trade Guild and so being allowed to buy the larger, more expensive colour prints. Here was almost my first encounter with Art, for it had never entered much into my life before. Now, handling these luscious collotypes, I learned something of the artists who painted them, something of what they were trying to express, and felt the first prickles of the thrill that art can give its devotees.

Much depended, then, on what I was framing. And much, too,

depended on how. One might be tempted to think that, of the two components, the frame was of relatively minor importance. 'I just want a very simple frame,' customers would say to me: and sometimes even: 'It really hardly needs a frame at all, just something to hold the glass.' So, to restore the balance, may I mention those many customers who, seeing one of our completed pictures, fell in love with it and bought it scarcely even noticing the print in the middle, choosing it *solely* for its frame.

Buying mouldings was like buying cards. Once again I discovered that it could be as painful to look through the range offered by one supplier as it could be a pleasure to look through that of another. I bought from two suppliers and their salesmen called once a year to show me their latest patterns. You could say that they were just sticks of coloured wood, but, oh, how I loved them and how I loved choosing them! How hard they were to resist, and (in consequence) how hard it became to squeeze our way through the ever-growing forest of them that – because of their length – I used to keep on the stairs!

Mouldings and mounting boards; wood and paper and canvas; their colour, pattern and shape; their look and their feel: what materials these were to work with! You start with the print. How shall it be treated? You choose the ingredients, decide the proportions, blend them together, admire the result, put it on display. . . . I never made book ends. I never made another cigarette box. But I framed many hundred pictures, and, oh, what pleasure it gave.

Yet within the bud there lurked the worm; and just as it was one of our happiest days when we closed down our second-hand book department, so it was with our picture gallery. There were, in fact, two reasons, two worms, you might say, one attacking our prints, the other our framing.

I have already said that I never got tired of framing our old engravings, even though the treatment was always the same. Nor did our customers ever get tired of buying them, even though they grew progressively more expensive. The trouble came with our modern prints. Here the range was very considerable, stretching from the sort of pictures you might find in the National Gallery to the sort you might find at the Royal Academy. My own preference was for the former, but I was prepared to accept the public's preference for the latter. What I wasn't prepared for was their addiction to a tiny range of bestsellers. I could frame ten Peter Scotts with some degree of pleasure, but not fifty. And it was the same with Tretchikoff and David Shepherd, with moonlit seas and galloping horses, with sunny Spain and clipper ships. A bestselling print is so very different from a bestselling book. How nice it is if we like the book, for then each sale gives added pleasure; but if we don't, it doesn't greatly matter, for books do not press their attention on those who do not wish it. They keep themselves to themselves within their covers, and the customer who chooses and the bookseller who wraps need exchange no more than a 'please' and a 'thank you'. But it is not like that with pictures. Pictures do not lurk in shelves; they hang on walls for all to see, staring you in the face, hiding nothing. And there is another difference too. A book becomes a bestseller because it is talked about and its name becomes known: people buy it *because* it is a bestseller; *knowingly* they follow the herd. Prints are not bought in this way: they are seldom asked for by name, rarely chosen because everyone else is choosing them. Yet the bestsellers emerge, for all that; and unconsciously the public are drawn towards them; *unknowingly* they follow the herd.

So the process of choosing is different. With books it takes place at home, inspired perhaps by a review or a television programme. With the picture it takes place in the shop, rather as women choose hats.

So what happened was this.

I would look through publishers' samples, seeing them all, liking some, disliking others, buying those I liked and hoped might be saleable, buying also those I knew would be saleable but liked rather less. From this selection of loose prints I then, later, picked out those I wanted to frame for stock. Framed prints always sold better than unframed: they looked better, you could display them better, and there they were, all ready for hanging on the wall. Which ones did I choose? How could I not include some of my favourites? After all they were going to decorate our showroom before they decorated some private living-room: *we* were going to have to live with them first. And how could I not, when customers came in to look around, point them out with special affection put in a friendly word on their behalf, and hope that my feelings might be shared? Alas, they weren't. Once again it was a Tretchikoff or a moonlit sea that took their fancy. Once again I had to listen to words which, though they no doubt came fresh and spontaneous to their lips, were words that I had heard before. In the end I could bear it no longer. We took our unsold pictures home and hung them on our own walls. The rest of the stuff we sold off cheap to be rid of it.

Such was the fate of our modern reproductions. Now for the picture framing.

If you set up as a picture framer a thing you must quickly decide is whether or not you will accept customers' own pictures. It is what might be called a wedge-shaped decision. For if at first you say 'Yes, choose one of our prints and we will frame it for you', you are led on to accept similar prints that had been acquired elsewhere, to accept awful prints that *could* only have been acquired elsewhere, to accept family photographs and amateur oils. And the curious thing I found was that my own distaste was so often matched by that of my customers. They didn't like the picture any more than I did; and so they would want me to frame it as cheaply as possible. And then, to save themselves even that expense, they would fail to call back for it. Picture framers are often used as dumping grounds in this way. It eases the conscience of the dumper that he's 'done something about it'. Understandably he wants to do as little as possible.

From making frames it is a short step to repairing them: to replacing broken glass, refixing corners that are falling apart; remounting and rebacking where the mildew has got in. This was depressing work and I would spend weeks not doing it and Lesley would spend weeks apologizing on my behalf: so our dislike of it was shared.

As our business grew, I tried various ways of relieving the pressure;

for I was, after all, a bookseller. First I tried sending some of the work to London; later I got someone in to help me here. But in the end the worm triumphed. A friend of mine, an artist who also framed pictures, closed his own business down at about the same time. We compared experiences and found much in common. On his last day he had assembled all the pictures that, over the years, his customers had brought in for framing, brought and never returned to collect – the smirking children, the alderman in his robes, the certificates. ... I knew them all – and he had carried them out and lined them up at one end of his backyard, and at the other end he had assembled a pile of stones. ...

Our own uncollecteds met a less violent end: one at a time, and with a decent interval between them, they were slipped into a tea chest and put out with the rubbish.

REASONS

So for a while we were picture framers and print dealers. Then we gave it up. In the same way we ran a lending library, starting when Smiths and Boots closed down, getting our books from a man who supplied a chain of West Country shops, ran it for a while, enjoyed it for a while, then closed it down. Dilettantism? Did we simply flit from one thing to another like a butterfly, unable to do anything properly, giving up as soon as the going became hard and the first flame of enthusiasm had burnt itself out? You could say this. You could also say that we only ran a line while it was profitable, dropping it as soon as profits fell. Neither alone is the whole truth.

Whatever one does, whatever one sells, affects a number of different people and it affects them in different ways. It affects us personally; it affects our staff; it affects our shop, its profitability, its reputation and its prospects; it affects the local population; and it affects or may affect our suppliers and other traders. All this should be taken into account when deciding what or what not to sell. One may say, 'To hell with Mr So-and-so up the road', but at least one says it: the decision to compete against him is a conscious one and his possible reactions are anticipated. One may consider net profit more important than customer satisfaction: that is a personal matter. But both have to be considered.

In describing some of the 'other goods' that we sold and then stopped selling I have made no attempt to justify our decisions, no attempt to draw up a balance sheet of arguments in favour and against. For this is not a manual on retailing; it is the self-portrait of an individual. All the same, I feel I ought to add that there were reasons other than my own personal taste in Art that turned us against pictures. Nor did we altogether abandon our customers when we closed down our library and our framing. We handed them on, together with our books and our mouldings, to those who took over when we left off.

And now to turn to a question that is surely pressing for an answer: where, in a shop that I have described as small, did we find room for all these varied activities?

ROOM UPSTAIRS

With cards, with pictures and with our library the choice was a simple one: do we or don't we. But in 1956 an event occurred that called for a much harder decision. In 1956 Clare was born.

So now we had not just an extra mouth to feed, but for a time at least only one of us at work to feed it. There was thus an immediate need to increase our earnings, to expand our business. The question was how, and the answer clearly lay upstairs. We were living over the shop and this was fine while there were only two of us. Indeed we would not have wished to live anywhere else. How nice that Lesley could go upstairs and get something ready for lunch while I was still serving down below. How nice that we could linger together over our meal, with the bell on the shop door (it was a home-made device, of course) set to ring when anybody came in. What fun it was, sitting at our table by the window, to be able to look down on Dartmouth life going about its everyday business. Dartmouth was that sort of town: we were all by turns either actors or spectators; and so probably ours were not the only eyes to watch the young man from the yacht courting Sylvia from the ironmonger's. Nor did it matter that we hadn't got a garden – or even a backyard for drying the washing. We had a washing line in the attic, and the country was so close that we didn't need a garden – not yet at any rate. On a sunny day we could take our lunch and eat it sitting on a grassy hillside looking down over the rooftops to the river. In the evenings we could stroll down to Sugary Cove or find a pleasant spot among the rocks below the footpath that leads to Compass Cove, or cross the river by the Lower Ferry and walk along the railway line to the Higher Ferry, so getting the last of the evening sun. It was a new experience for us to live, to work and to find our recreation all in the same place; and for five years we enjoyed it.

With Clare's impending arrival, however, we had to think again; and there could be no doubt that the time had now come to look for a separate house, one moreover with the garden that we were both now beginning to long for. If we moved out from the shop, this would leave us with four vacant rooms. Here, clearly – though in a way yet to be decided – was the source of our extra income.

I seem to remember that our first thought was to let the rooms as offices, but the problem would then have been to provide separate access. In the end we decided to turn the first floor – our old dining-room, kitchen and sitting-room – into a showroom. Selling what? Not books or cards or Dartmouth prints. For the extra sales we might hope to make would not be in proportion to the considerable amount of extra space we would have available. It would have to be something quite different.

The answer can be given in a single word. It was a word we disliked, but we searched in vain for another and in the end we had to accept it. It was 'gifts'; and so the Harbour Bookshop became the Harbour Bookshop and Gift Gallery. Having decided on our new name we then had to decide exactly what it would encompass. Things made of wood, obviously; perhaps also things made of pottery. What else?

The advantage of being a gift shop is that you can sell almost anything as the fancy takes you – and as the fancy seems to be taking your customers. You can sell it one year and you can stop selling it the next: you are not committed. You can sell china, and it won't make you a china shop. You can sell tables and chairs, and it won't make you a furniture shop. You can sell bedspreads and tea cloths without becoming a draper, fire-irons and frying pans without becoming an ironmonger, jewellery without becoming a jeweller, dried herbs and dried flowers without becoming a grocer or a florist. Indeed over the years we have sold all these things. Moreover (and not surprisingly) what we had found with cards and pictures we now found with gifts: there were those we liked very much and those we liked very little. Once again we chose only what we liked; and in order to avoid being influenced by over-persuasive salesmen, for our first few years we did almost all our choosing through the Design Centre in London.

Gradually we established our contacts and built up our stock. Gradually our bookshop customers discovered that we now had an upstairs department. 'But we've had it for *years!*' The holidaymakers knew all about it, of course; it was our regulars who failed to notice, seeing only what they had always seen. Odd how familiarity blunts observation.

Today Lesley does all the buying, and I don't envy her. She does most of it at the annual Gift Trade Fair in Torquay, placing enormous orders in January for what she hopes to sell in July and August. How can she know? What instinct tells her that the pottery cruets that were so popular one year will not sell at all the next? Pokers with coloured knobs, teak mice, gaily decorated tin trays and egg prickers: each in turn had its year and was then forgotten, abandoned by the public in their search for the latest novelty. What will it be this year? Spoon rests? Today half our showroom – the old sitting-room half – sells kitchenware. The other half sells pottery and glass and table mats and ... and ... Yes, Lesley is quite right: I really do hardly know. How soon one loses touch. Once I did all the buying. Now I'm scarcely even aware of what is bought.

Not long ago I met Kathleen in the street. She said she had been to Newton Abbot to get a picture framed, and the man there had told her that a lot of people came to him from Dartmouth. 'Surely

Dartmouth could support its own framer,' he had said; and she had passed this observation on to me. Might I be interested? 'Oh, no. Not now,' I said. 'We used to do picture framing, as I expect you remember. I did it myself, in fact, and enjoyed it. But that was twenty years ago. Then for various reasons we gave it up.' 'You wouldn't think of starting up again?' 'No. I couldn't go back to it. . . . Anyway I'm too busy doing other things.' 'It was just a thought.' She smiled and went in to the baker's, and I went on towards the bookshop. I could have told her exactly why I had enjoyed it so much and exactly why I had given it up and exactly why there was no going back. For I had been thinking about just these things: I was in the middle of writing this chapter.

7. Books

For twenty-one years Lesley and I lived on the profits of our shop and the bulk of this came from bookselling. We had no other source of income. I say this loudly and proudly. Loudly, because a number of people seem to have suspected that all the while Pooh's earnings were keeping my pockets comfortably lined. Proudly, because it is not easy to survive as a bookseller – in fact as well as in name – in a town whose population is under seven thousand.

I have already described how we started, going round other bookshops, studying their stock, going round publishers to see what they had to offer, then making our choice and sending in our orders. And at once there will be seen a similarity to gift buying – and a difference. The similarity is that booksellers do in fact choose what they had to offer, then making our choice and sending in our because we have chosen it and ordered it. No book arrives uninvited. 'Don't they send them down to you automatically?' we are asked. Indeed they don't. Nor can we automatically send them back to their publishers if we fail to sell them; and so there may well be books on our shelves whose continued presence we are beginning to regret. But at least we have no one to blame but ourselves. That is the similarity.

The difference is that our choice is made from the *entire* range of books published. In theory (if not quite in practice) the books that we stock on, for instance, wild flowers have been chosen as being the most suitable for our needs of *all* that are available: the others for one reason or another we have rejected. This is not so with gifts. With gifts we stock what takes our fancy and it does not bother us that there might be something a little better that we don't know about. With gifts our customers choose from what they see: if they like what they see they buy it, if not they walk out. With books this is only partly what happens. For in addition there are those customers who come in asking for a particular book. And our stock must aim to satisfy them as well.

So the question that everybody asks us is: 'How do you know what books people are going to want? How do you know what to buy?'

First let me say that, although we are influenced by reviews, we do not wait until they appear before deciding; for this would be leaving it far too late. Every book has a publication date. On this date – but not before – it may be reviewed. On this date – but not before – it should be available in bookshops. It is launched with a fanfare of trumpets, a fanfare that would be incomplete without the bookseller's participation. Sometimes customers say to us: 'I've seen it in London, but probably it hasn't got down here yet.' This infuriates us. If we haven't got the book in stock when it is in stock in London, it is because we have decided against stocking it, not because Dartmouth is a small provincial town two hundred miles away and we have to wait our turn.

So most of our choosing is done before the book is published. We may do it from a publisher's catalogue or we may do it as a result of advance publicity, but most often and most satisfactorily we do it with the help and advice of the publisher's representative. Books come flooding in on two great annual tides, the spring tide and the autumn tide, and so ideally a representative will call twice a year, showing us spring books in March and autumn books in September.

What does he carry with him? Sometimes the book itself and this can be helpful; but it is not always either necessary or possible. We may not need to see it to know whether or not we want it; or it may not be possible to see it because completed copies are not yet available, or because the representative's bag is not big enough or his arm is not strong enough to carry all the seasonal offerings of his firm. If we are shown the book it is not so that we can sit down and read it before deciding whether or not we want it. Only if it is very short – a book of cartoons or a children's picture book – might we have time for that. In any case reading a book does not always make it easier to arrive at a wise decision. We are not after all buying for ourselves. We are buying for our customers, trying to anticipate their reactions, their demand. Is this a book they will hear about and come in and ask for? Is it a book that will catch their eye and arouse their interest? These are the questions we must ask ourselves; not: 'Did I myself enjoy it?' One book in a hundred we may be able to sell by communicating our own personal enthusiasm – and doing this is one of the supreme pleasures of bookselling – but the other ninety-nine must be able to sell themselves. So we must know our customers, know their book-buying tastes (not their book-reading tastes, for this is quite another matter), and be able to put ourselves in their position as they watch a television interview with the author, or read a review, or see the book in our shop. What are the factors that influence their choice? The subject? The author's name? The price? The book's appearance? Its jacket design? The general excitement or controversy that will surround its publication? Sometimes the one, sometimes the other. I have met books whose success depended almost wholly on choice of title, and I have met others whose title alone condemned them to failure. These are all things the representative can tell us about. 'Macramé? What on earth is that?' I asked – as everybody must have asked, meeting the word for the first time. So he told me about this little known craft and advised me that it might soon become very popular. He was right – and I was ready with my copies when the demand came.

A book to us, then, is very much more than a piece of writing. It is the joint product of author, typographer, paper-maker, printer, binder, jacket designer and publisher's publicity department. It is a rectangular object possessing certain qualities; and one of its most important qualities is that alone, all by itself, it is quite useless. To achieve fulfilment it must find a buyer. So if we keep only one eye on our stock, it is so that we can keep our other eye on our customers. In fact, of the two, the eye that studies the customer is almost the more important.

Lesley and I are conscious of this when engaging a new assistant. A girl who likes people – who is friendly and helpful and makes them feel welcome – is far more use to us than one who likes books. Books don't need to be liked: people do. Books don't mind if you are rude to them or offhand in your manner: people do. A bookshop is like a marriage bureau: it arranges meetings between likely partners – likely book and likely buyer. The introduction may be a formal one. 'Mr Smith, I would like you to meet this book: I think you might enjoy it.' Or it might be more casual – so placing the book that Mr Smith's eye will fall on it and his hand will reach out towards it. ... This is the art of bookbuying and bookselling: knowing your customers, knowing their tastes, realizing that their tastes are constantly changing, anticipating what they will be next season, choosing your stock accordingly and then so displaying it that you achieve the maximum number of introductions leading to the maximum number of happy marriages.

Consequently when people say to us: 'What lovely, lovely books. If I had a bookshop I would just read and read all day: I'd never want to sell a thing,' we smile politely – and change the subject. There is immense pleasure in book reading, but it has nothing to do with bookselling.

So what sort of books do we sell? This question is usually accompanied by an amazement that we sell anything at all. '*Do* people buy books these days? They are so expensive, aren't they'. Yes, luckily for us they do; and perhaps it would be helpful if I first tried to show why.

I was once – a very long time ago – invited to give a talk entitled 'Why buy books?' I remember it vividly because the clergyman who introduced me thought I was going to talk about the ten books I would take with me to a desert island, and began his introduction by telling the audience which ten books he would take to his desert island. So when my turn came I had to start by apologizing that this wasn't what I had been asked to talk about at all. .... As I have already said, one mustn't confuse a desire to buy books with a desire to read them. Booksellers are not in competition with librarians: the two serve different needs.

People buy books for one of several possible reasons. They may buy them to give away as presents; they may buy them because they need them to refer to; they may buy them because they are collecting books on a particular subject; they may buy a book because, having enjoyed reading it, they now wish to possess it; they may buy it for its decorative qualities; or they may simply buy it because everyone else is buying it. These (with one more to follow) are the main reasons; and there will be a host of minor reasons – because the copy borrowed from a friend has just been eaten by the dog, and so on. ... In all these cases the book is intended to last, and it may very well physically outlast the purpose for which it was originally bought. This is a pity, for it then merely clutters up its owner's shelves, providing a bad excuse for not buying any more books.

People will go to all sorts of extremes to avoid putting their dead books on the bonfire or out with the rubbish, and astonishingly – they are proudly convinced that this shows them to be true book lovers. On the contrary, they are the enemies of literature! For it is this attitude that discourages the buying of books solely for the pleasure of reading them. In particular it discourages the buying of novels.

Fortunately it is an attitude that does not seem to extend to paperbacks. Paperbacks are in the magazine class: expendable; read, then thrown away (or more usually left for someone else to throw away). So this gives us our final category: people buy books to read *provided they are in paperback*.

Having seen why we can now consider what.

If we had chosen a larger town we could, perhaps, have afforded to specialize. We could have stocked only those books that we liked or books on those subjects that interested us. But in a town the size of Dartmouth, though our stock may betray certain prejudices, we must be general booksellers, aiming to satisfy all tastes, not just our own, selling all – or virtually all – that we find saleable, and consequently selling a great many books on subjects about which we know very little.

Thus we sell hardcover books on yachting and fishing, on Devon, on natural history, on cookery and gardening, on a great variety of crafts, on old things (boats, trains, antiques, etc.), on the instruments of destruction (tanks, aeroplanes, warships, etc.). We sell the obvious reference books and the sort of safe classics that get chosen as school prizes. We sell 'best-sellers' (the more popular novels and biographies). We sell paperbacks on all subjects. And lastly – and I'll have more to say about this later – we sell children's books. Add it all up and – to the surprise of those who equate books with culture – you will find that we sell relatively little that can be said to possess literary merit. Poetry, novels, biographies, belles lettres, history: these in hardcover do badly and their authors, with few exceptions, must survive on their sales to public libraries – and then hope to get into paperback.

'Lovely, lovely books,' says our customer, looking around her and trying again. 'If I had a fortune, I would buy them *all*!' A very catholic book buyer she must be, with a remarkably wide range of interests. . . . For our part we might perhaps contemplate inviting one book in a hundred into our house. I doubt if it would be more than that. Yet this doesn't mean that we dislike the other ninety-nine. Very far from it.

Books are like people. You may like a person without necessarily wanting to ask him home for supper. You may like a book without necessarily wanting either to read or to possess it. So it is with the books in our shop. We know them all, we like them all, we enjoy their companionship, because to a bookseller a book is not something to read; it is something to handle, something to sell. To a bookseller a good book is one that is well designed and well made, and the handling of it – holding it, feeling it, opening it, turning the pages, letting the eye fall upon the printed word – gives him immense pleasure. I know little and care nothing about – for instance – armoured fighting vehicles, yet I know that in Dartmouth there are many people with a passion for tanks. I can recognize a well-designed, well-produced tank book when I am shown one, and it gives me great pleasure to order it, stock it, display it and even introduce it to a customer with my personal recommendation. Does it seem wrong that I am prepared to say 'Here is a good book,' when I have done no more than glance at it? How can I judge a book I have never read on a subject about which I know nothing? The answer is that I can because I enlist the help of others – the publisher, reviewers, other customers. My personal judgement is confined to the book's production, its look and feel. I leave it to the expert to judge its contents.

I have said that though we are a general bookshop our stock may display prejudices; and of course it does. It displays the prejudices of Dartmouth – so many books on sailing, so few on cricket; novels about the sea rather than sex; biographies of Tories rather than Socialists. It also displays our own. To a large extent we must follow the tastes and interests of our customers. To some small extent, however, we can attempt to lead them; and one of the most fascinating and exciting sides to bookselling is to see how far ahead we can go and how many of our customers we can carry with us. It may be a single book, one that we feel to have some special merit, not an obvious bestseller but one surely deserving our support, deserving to be read. All right, let us take a chance. Let us buy not just our usual cautious one or two copies; let us take a dozen and then really try to sell it. Or it may be a particular subject or attitude for which we have an especial sympathy or feel the stirrings of a crusading zeal. The vicar might have made it the theme of a sermon; or the editor of the local paper might have devoted an editorial to it. We, when the representative comes to it, say 'Yes. That's one I'd like.' And we add it to our order. Or perhaps we may be not for it but against it, and then we say, 'No. Not that book.' And the representative is surprised, perhaps even a little indignant, struggling to hide his anger or his scorn, trying to remain polite. 'But it is selling fantastically well. You're the first shop to refuse it.' Can anybody be so perverse, turning away good money like this? 'I'm sorry but this is my shop and you must allow me to run it my way.'

So we choose our books, influenced by the likes and dislikes of our customers and also of ourselves, seeing each book (or rather trying to visualize each book) as a rectangular object to be handled and looked at as well as read. How many copies? One? Two? Four? Ten? We tend to play safe. Better too few than too many. We can always reorder. It is not so easy to return unsold copies.

And then the books arrive and we have to sell them. Yes, it's one thing to picture a bookseller as a person who lives and moves in a world of books – even if it is not quite such a cultured, 'Eng. Lit.' sort of world as one had perhaps imagined. But it is quite another thing to put the accent on the second half of his name; for isn't there something not quite nice about selling? Isn't it all a bit *commercial*? And the librarian, sitting at his desk in the Public Library, feels smugly superior. *He* is not involved with money in this rather sordid way. *His* success is measured in 'issues', not 'net profit'. This is the difference between us: the one is a member of a learned profession; the other is engaged in trade.

Anybody with this sort of attitude towards selling should not become – and in any case would not long remain – a bookseller. For bookselling most emphatically involves both books and selling; and so, having said something about the one, I must now turn to the other.

SELLING

The man who, encouraged perhaps by a remark of Emerson's, made a mousetrap and then waited for the world to beat a path through the woods to his door, would have waited in vain unless he had first done something, however hesitantly, however reluctantly to inform the world of his existence. Everyone of us who earns a living is earning it by selling something he has – a product, a skill – to someone who wants it. Everyone with something to sell must first promote it, advertise it, look for likely buyers.

He may find that this does not take up much of his time, so that having once nailed up his sign board or found his employer, he can then get on with his trade. Or he may find that it takes up a lot of his time; and he may well enjoy it.

Thus you have two extremes of attitude towards selling. At the one extreme are the makers who, if they are also their own salesmen, see their job as *finding* people who want what they have to offer; and at the other extreme are the salesmen who see it as *persuading* people to want what they have to offer. To the maker what matters most is what he has to sell; to the salesman what matters is success. What he is selling is almost irrelevant.

Where between these extremes does the bookseller stand? The answer is that he can stand where he likes. He can see himself as a professional salesman, his job simply to get books moving out of his shop as fast as possible in exchange for money moving in. Such a bookseller once horrified the book trade by suggesting, loudly and publicly, that books could and should be sold like soap. Or he can see himself as a sort of maker, not making the books, of course, but making his shop and then, as it were, making marriages between book and customer. So for him books matter, and the final wrapping up, handing over, taking of money and giving of change is only a very small part of his work.

Where did we stand? Does the question need to be asked? For you have only to start listing the qualities required in a professional salesman to see at once how few of them I possess. Hedda saw this well enough. They saw it at John Lewis. Probably the Sales Manager of the Encyclopaedia Publisher saw it when I presented myself for interview. And certainly I see it myself in the bookshop when I meet the professional on his rounds. In he comes, instantly recognizable, smartly dressed, highly polished all over, radiating self confidence and after-shave, all set to make his killing. Poor shabby, shambling, provincial bookseller! He seizes him by the hand and wishes him a very good morning, flicks open his briefcase and starts doing conjuring tricks with its contents. Does it make any difference what he is selling? Advertising space, insurance, it's all the same. 'Just sign here, Sir. They'll invoice you from the office.'

But if I recoil from the professional, it is because I cannot buy from this sort of person in this sort of way, not because I dislike buying things. And if I cannot myself adopt his techniques, it is because I am not myself a salesman by nature, not because I dislike or disapprove of selling or feel it in some way undignified.

In fact I enjoy both buying and selling, particularly when what is being bought or sold is books. Books – new books, that is – have two things in their favour. In the first place they are introduced to us not by a 'salesman', thank goodness, but by a 'representative' – a word which implies, usually correctly, someone who shares my attitude towards doing business. So we meet as equals and sit down together and discuss his books. We do not manoeuvre for position in order to do battle with each other. The books are allowed to sell themselves; there is no pushing. That is the first thing; and there is no further problem with buying. You have only to announce that you have become a bookseller and representatives will soon be queueing up to see you, undaunted in our case by the fact that they first had to queue up to cross the river on our ferry. The second thing in favour of new books is that they all have fixed selling prices. So at least we are spared the arguing, the haggling, the trying to get for three-and-six what is clearly priced at five shillings, that so blighted our venture into secondhand bookselling.

However, books have one great disadvantage compared with gifts. With gifts we usually hope to establish what are called 'sole agencies' which ensure that the manufacturers who supply us do not also supply our nearby competitors. With books this cannot happen since every bookshop is free to buy from every publisher. So although to some extent individual shops will show individual characteristics, the universally popular books – the 'bestsellers' – will usually be stocked by them all. Why then, since the book will be the same and cost the same in each, should a customer favour one shop rather than another? It can only be because one shop in some way gives better service. So although we could promote our books, saying: 'These are good books,' at the same time we had to promote our shop – and indeed (like it or not) ourselves – saying: 'Ours is a good shop and we are good booksellers.' And this we found less easy.

First we chose a town in which there was no other private bookseller. Naturally, had he been a good bookseller this would have made the task of establishing ourselves very much harder and our excuse for trying to do so very much smaller. But whether he had been good or not it would have meant our setting up in opposition to someone else, trying to persuade the public to come to us rather than go to him: and this we would not have enjoyed. Admittedly there was in Dartmouth a branch of W. H. Smith: we could hardly expect to have the field entirely to ourselves. But the difference between a private bookshop and the branch of a well established chain was, we felt, great enough for there to be no animosity between us. Then we chose a name that we could shelter behind. Not Milne & Milne but The Harbour Bookshop – which allowed us to boast about the shop without giving the impression that we were boasting about ourselves. And initially our self-promotion amounted to little more than saying: 'Here we are'. Fortunately this was fairly obvious since our site was a good one. (Our attempts to say *who* we were were less successful; our fascia board didn't appear until three weeks after we had opened and was then virtually illegible.) After that we could turn our attention to promoting our books.

The simplest way to promote books is to put them on display and the best place to display them is the shop window. And it was when arranging our window that we became conscious of another characteristic that books possess: they have voices; and our job as window dresser was to see that they were saying the right thing to the right people in the most effective way.

So we were like the puppeteer who, standing unseen, pulls unseen strings; or like the conductor of the orchestra who, silent himself, gets the best from each instrumentalist. Each book has its own individual voice, saying 'I am me: buy me!' Some books say this very loudly, clearly and persuasively. You put them in the window and people at once know all about them and come hurrying in for them. These are our soloists, and probably our best soloist when we opened was *The Cruel Sea*. Other books are better in chorus. 'We are cookery books. We are gardening books. There are lots more of us inside.' Some books speak for themselves. Books with titles like *Devon* or *Sea Fishing for Beginners* need no help from us: they say exactly what they are. But *Jim Davis* needs a little notice pointing out that it is an exciting smuggling story with a Dartmouth setting. Only those with the best voices qualify for the window or for display face forwards inside the shop, and each must be carefully chosen not just for what it has to say but to whom we want it said. For this is important, too. Who are the people we are addressing? Who are the people walking along the pavement outside? Are they holiday-makers visiting the town for the first time and so needing to be told what a wide range of books we stock? Or are they our residents who (we trust) know this already and so can be told something else?

Thus gradually we began to understand what it is that makes books saleable and learned how to make the most of their saleability. And parallel with this we began to understand what makes people come in and buy them.

Before you can get someone to come into your shop – assuming he hadn't all along intended to do so – indeed before you can get him to look at your window, you have to attract his attention. You have to say 'Stop!' In our early days, when we lived over the shop, we had a cat who lived with us, and every now and then, because it was warm and sunny there, he climbed into our window. He sat very still. He made no noise. But he was saying 'Stop!' and he was saying it very well. We have to use other devices now, but I doubt if any can do it better.

Having stopped the passer-by, you then have to hold his attention. We found that the best way to do this was to give him something to read. People seem to like reading things, and they particularly like reading things aloud to each other. I learned this when a notice was nailed to the wall below my office window. The notice gave information about a nearby building. I never read it myself, but I heard it read aloud so many times that I almost knew it by heart.

First 'Stop' then 'Look' and finally 'Come in', and this is best said by the books themselves – with perhaps a helping word or two from us. The difficulty is that you never know how well they are doing it. It is obvious enough if someone, handing over a pile of purchases, says: 'And I only came in for that card I saw in your window'. But much more often you have no idea what brings people in; and more important than that, you don't know what has kept the others out.

People don't always find it easy to walk into a strange shop. They are frightened: frightened perhaps that they will find themselves buying something they don't really want, frightened they might make a fool of themselves. It is very easy to make a fool of yourself. I once went into a bank I found inside Victoria Station. I was on my way home from school and wanted to let my parents know which train I was catching. I suppose I should really have been looking for a telephone booth, but I was, if anything, even more frightened of telephones. So I found this bank instead and went in and said to the man behind the counter 'I want to send a telegram'. And he looked startled and said 'But this is a *bank*.' Well, I knew it was. What I didn't know was the difference between a bank and a post office. It is the fear of making this sort of mistake that keeps so many people out of bookshops: they are frightened of being told by a superior person in a superior voice: 'Oh, *no*. We don't sell *that* sort of book *here*, madam!'

This is why it is helpful if you can sell something else other than books – newspapers or cigarettes, for instance. It gets the nervous outsider into your shop. We used greetings cards for this purpose. We now use a revolving stand of paperbacks. We hated this stand when we were first given it and complained bitterly to the representative of the paperback publisher who provided it. 'We like to keep your books in a proper order so that customers can see exactly what we've got, and so that if we are asked for a title we can quickly find it. In this stand nearly half the books are invisible.' He said that this didn't matter in the least. Customers mostly just wanted a good book, not a particular book. Grudgingly we accepted it, and as soon as we could we replaced it, and since he didn't want it back, we were on the point of throwing it away. But suddenly Lesley had a bright idea. 'Let's put it just inside the doorway and fill it with all our most popular books.' So we did, and it provides a sort of stepping stone for those who are too timid to come straight in.

Once someone is properly inside, it is reasonable to assume that, if he has not just come in to escape the rain or to while away half an hour until his wife is finished at the hairdresser up the road, he does genuinely want to buy a book and will be disappointed if he has to go out empty-handed. It is also reasonable to assume that somewhere in the shop is a book that will suit him. It is therefore up to us to bring the two together. And gradually we learned the best way to do it, how best to approach each type of customer, how best to arrange our books in their shelves (though there is always room for improvement, always room for argument here), how best to introduce book and customer, giving the customer a choice but not too baffling a choice, helping him to make up his mind, and finally how best to ensure that he is happy with what he has bought and so will come back another day.

So we are indeed professional salesmen after all with an armoury of techniques every bit as subtle and elaborate and carefully perfected as those taught to smooth young men in smart grey suits; and bookselling to us is not just *book*selling but also book*selling*, the one every bit as fascinating as the other. It is, I suspect, a little like the fascination of angling. The angler must learn his river and his equipment, his fish and their habits. He may well ask his wife to cook what he has caught, because after all fish is food and man must eat; but the pleasure he finds by the river lies not so much in thoughts of supper but rather in the exercise of his knowledge and of his skill. And with us there is a further bonus. Our fish, we like to think, are the happier for being caught.

AUTHORS

On September 6th, a fortnight after we had opened, Eric Williams came into the shop and introduced himself; and from this encounter sprang that wariness towards authors that I have felt ever since. It is akin to the feeling I get when approached by a salesman, for this is indeed what the author so often becomes in a bookshop. Do I have his book in stock? Why not? Publisher not doing his job! Will write to him and get him to send me a dozen copies . . . and so on. Of course I have my answers. 'I've not got your book because I decided against it: it's not the sort of book my customers buy. Please don't write to your publisher, who knows this as well as I do. In any case what I stock is my own affair.' I can say this sort of thing to the professional salesman to whom accepting a 'No' is as much a part of his job as welcoming a 'Yes'. But an author is different. However aggressive he may be (and he can be surprisingly aggressive) and however tough his armour may seem, my rejection of his book will penetrate it and will wound him. So partly there is a feeling of 'Don't you try and teach me my job' and partly there may be a feeling of 'I don't want to be unkind'; and then there is the peculiarity of the author-bookseller relationship in which each sees himself at the top of a pyramid with the other at the bottom. For to the author the bookseller is one of thousands engaged in distributing his book, while to the bookseller the author is one of thousands whose books he distributes. 'Oh why,' I wrote in my journal that evening, 'don't Great Authors realize that there are other authors, and that if we are not selling Williams it might possibly be that we are busy selling Chaucer instead.'

Yet I ought to have been selling Williams as well as Chaucer: indeed I ought to have been selling him a great deal better. *The Wooden Horse* published in 1949 had been a staggering success. Its sequel, *The Tunnel*, had come out in the spring. Collins had told us all about it, told us too that Eric Williams and his wife were coming to live in our area. We had been forewarned. It was just that, thoroughly inexperienced, we lacked confidence. Was *The Wooden Horse* still selling? Would its sequel sell at all? What difference would it make that the author was living six miles away? Undoubtedly if we had been bolder we could have sold both books a lot better than we did. And indeed we might have done so if Williams hadn't been so pressing. As I wrote in my Journal, 'He wanted me to put on a show for him. His idea of a show is streamers all over the town, invitations to all the gentry, town-crier out with his bell and finally a Civic Reception in the Guildhall.' A two-week-old bookseller naturally recoiled from that sort of thing; and fortunately for all of us the idea was quietly dropped. 'On his way out he said he would fetch me some display material from his car to enable me to start a little advance publicity. Then, pausing at the door, he said casually, "How's *The Tunnel* doing?" I told him I had sold one copy so far; and I saw his eye fixing on the single copy of *The Wooden Horse* that now sat all alone on its shelf. At that point I should have said "Oh, good. I see we've just sold another." But I didn't because we hadn't. He looked thoughtful, and I guessed what he was thinking; and I wasn't surprised that he didn't come back with his posters.'

But a year later we had greater self confidence. Peter Churchill's book, *Of Their Own Choice*, had just been published and the author was to visit the Royal Naval College to talk about it and his experiences with the French Resistance during the War. Would we like him, asked his publisher, to call on us while he was in Dartmouth and sign copies in our shop?

This seemed a great compliment at the time, and perhaps it was. Now however the Grand Tour with its visits to bookshops alternating between lectures, television appearances, radio and press interviews and the like has become a normal way of promoting a new book. And I have become a little cynical. The signing session! How nice, of course, if it succeeds; but if it doesn't, never mind. No harm is done. No harm, that is, to the publisher. No matter to him if now and again the author seats himself at a table, walled in by copies of his works, sits and waits – and waits in vain while customers come and go and occasionally stop to stare or ask him where the birthday cards are kept – and then, his stint over, creeps off to his next appointment. True, the author may feel a little sad. True, the bookseller may feel a little embarrassed. But equally he might never have been very enthusiastic in the first place.

'Yes, all right,' he might have replied to the publisher. 'If you'll do all the publicity for us – posters and adverts – we can provide him with a table and a chair.'

This may be possible in a large and busy bookshop, where the manager, having greeted the author, can then drift off and occupy himself with more important matters. In a small shop, however, it is not so easy. The seated author, the hovering proprietors, the total lack of any customers at all: no this was not to be contemplated.

So if we were to do it at all, we must do it properly. Shall we or shan't we? Come on, let's try!

'Certainly,' we replied, 'provided you allow us to arrange a Literary Lunch so that the town as well as the College can hear his story.'

This was the first of our Literary Lunches, and we held two more the two following years. They were all successful, and we sold a lot of books at each. We found them nerve-racking, yes, but exciting and exhilarating beyond belief. We held them in late autumn and the impetus they gave to our sales and the esteem they brought to our shop lasted through to Christmas, while the exhilaration and the pleasure they brought to Lesley and to me lasts, warmly remembered, to this day. In 1953 the book we chose was *Bandoola* by J. H. Williams (*Elephant Bill*) and in 1954 it was *The Bafut Beagles* by Gerald Durrell. I say 'we chose', not 'we were offered and accepted', because this was how it was. We were not part of any publisher's publicity campaign. This was a private arrangement between ourselves and the author. And so ideally it should always be, and if any young bookseller cares for my advice, it is this. First, choose a book you know you can sell; secondly, choose a time of year when you know you can sell it; thirdly, thank the publisher for his kind offer but say you would prefer to fix up all your own publicity; and fourthly, try to arrange for the signing session to be preceded by some sort of a function – a lunch or a lecture, for instance – that will ensure a good crowd of people waiting to welcome the author, eager – afterwards – to queue for his book. For it is easier by far to be one of a jostling crowd saying 'I'd like one too' than it is to approach the solitary seated figure across an empty shop if you're not quite sure what the book is about or whether you really want it or not.

Yes, exciting and exhilarating these occasions most certainly were – but also, as I have said, nerve-racking; and it was for this reason that we never made them a regular feature of our bookshop life. For although all was well in the end, the fear of failure would haunt us right up to the last hour. In the end we managed to sell enough tickets – the dining-room looked comfortably full, the seats in the lecture hall were mostly occupied – but, oh, my beloved

Dartmouth customers, why did you always leave it to the last agonizing hour before you made up your minds? Today I look along our bookshelves at home and count those books with their special inscriptions. There are ten of them. Ten visits in twenty-five years, not many, but all the more memorable for that. Ten authors, hand-picked, well-chosen, charmers every one of them. We are proud to have met them. We bask still in the memory of the brief hours we spent in their company.

BOOKS FOR SCHOOLS

'Don't just wait for customers to come to you,' we had been told. 'Go out and find them.' So in October, 1951, I loaded my briefcase and caught the bus up the hill to Thurlestone College; and that evening in my journal I recorded my first experience as a travelling salesman.

'I had a little difficulty finding the way in and possibly I chose the wrong door. Inside it was very dark. There were stairs in front of me and I felt my way cautiously down them, and at the bottom came upon the dim figure of a man, who, to my slight surprise, seemed to be expecting me. Without asking me who I was, he led me into his study, and when we were seated, told me all about the school. From this I decided that he was not, as at first I had thought, the caretaker, but the headmaster. I learned that he trained boys for entry into the Royal Naval College and similar establishments, that he did this with considerable success and at a very modest fee. All this he explained in some detail and at some length, and then, slipping easily from one subject to another, he asked me why I had called, and while I was explaining, went on to tell me about some of his more remarkable former pupils. Eventually his eye fell on my briefcase and he asked if I had anything in it I would like to show him. I said, "Yes" and while I was getting it open he told me all about himself. ... We parted most cordially and with his assurance that if he ever needed a book he would most certainly get it from me, as he was keen to support local traders.

'All the same I thought it best not to be too optimistic. Doubting if the prospects of business that I had opened up justified the expense of a second bus fare, I walked home.'

This was my first attempt to get what is known as 'institutional business', and it was, of course, a failure. There were two other very small private schools in Dartmouth and I tried them both with equal lack of success; small private schools just don't have the money to buy books. I tried the Naval College and their librarian called, was most charming and polite, said he had practically no money, chose three books from our shelves (one of which I remember to my surprise was *Dracula*) and promised to return another day. Dartmouth State Schools were equally polite but explained that they had to order their books from the County Contractor. Finally we called on the County Librarian in Exeter and at last found someone who was both able and willing to spend money with us. He never in fact spent much, but his occasional orders were always welcome.

And there things stuck throughout the fifties. We might perhaps have gone further afield, offered our services to other richer private schools. But presumably they were already buying their books from someone, and if they were happy what right had we to try and persuade them to come to us instead? What special advantages could we offer? None, really. And that was why in 1956 when we needed to expand we expanded upwards into our Gift Gallery: at that time there seemed little hope of any great increase in our book sales.

Then in 1960 everything changed and changed most dramatically. I can give both the place and the exact date: it was at Dartington Hall and the date was May 28th.

At this point, in order that what follows should make sense, I must break off and say a little more about the book trade.

I have said already that our books have fixed retail prices and that this was one of the advantages of selling new books. I could have gone further and said that this is the one thing that makes it possible to be a proper bookseller at all.

Not all books sell equally well. There are the popular books that sell in their hundreds of thousands and there are the less popular books that sell only in thousands. Yet judged by almost any standard other than popularity the latter are often the better. So it is perhaps not unreasonable that we should ask the popular to help sustain the good. This help is needed by both the publisher and the bookseller. Each needs the high sales and high profits from the one to offset the low sales and low profits from the other. Of course we could easily wash our hands of the unpopular. We could say, 'To Hell with quality: quantity is all we care about. Money is everything.' And of course there are people who do say this; and since in a free fight they would almost certainly win, the law offers protection to the others. The publisher is protected against piracy by the Law of Copyright, the bookseller is protected against undercutting by the Net Book Agreement.[1] The Net Book Agreement allows publishers to fix the selling price of any book they wish and to take legal action against anyone who sells it to the public at less than this price. Since the Net Book Agreement is designed to protect the bookseller, it is obvious that publishers will only 'net' those books which need the services of the bookseller for their promotion and distribution. These are known as 'general books' to distinguish them from those books which the bookseller may well handle but which normally he neither stocks nor promotes, namely 'school textbooks'. School textbooks have a price but it is not a fixed or 'net' price, and so they are called 'non-net' books, and schools buying them can hope to buy them at a discount off this price if their order is large enough. The bookseller also naturally buys at a discount from the publisher. The discount he gets on a net book is about a third, and this is to finance not just the wrapping up and handing over but also the cost of stocking and displaying and the risk that this involves. On non-net books he gets a lower discount, about a sixth, and this is because he does less work: he simply handles the orders that the schools send him.

Now although schools buy a lot of textbooks, they may also

[1] An explanation of the workings of the Book Trade that included every exception to every statement made would require a whole book to itself. What follows is only the briefest summary.

buy general books; indeed they may sometimes use general books as textbooks; and in fact on average a school will spend 65% of its money on textbooks and 35% on general books. On the former it can hope for a discount but on the latter, no matter how many copies of any particular book it may order, no discount is allowed. Hence there is an illogicality: where the bookseller gets the larger discount from the publisher he keeps it all, where he gets the smaller discount he is allowed to give part of it away, thus lowering his profit even further. This causes difficulties, for it means that when a bookseller offers a discount on non-net books, part at least of this discount is in consideration of the net books that he hopes the school will also want to buy from him. Indeed competition between booksellers can be such that non-net books are often supplied at a loss where the net book order is big enough.

So now we come to the 'contract'. With a private school this will be between school and bookseller. With a state school it will be between Local Education Authority and 'Contractor'. The contractor may be an ordinary bookseller like me or he may specialize as a 'school supplier', possibly supplying stationery as well. He may be small and local or large and distant. It is for the Local Authority to decide not only who gets it but what form the contract is to take. It can go to a single supplier or it can be divided among several. Schools may be compelled to order all their books from the contractor or they may be free to buy some where they please. There are endless variations but whatever is decided on, the Authority will probably start by inviting tenders and almost the only way in which tenders can be judged is by the amount of discount offered. The supplier who offers the highest discount on non-net books will probably win the contract. Since good service costs money, the higher the discount, the worse the service. However, since bad service is expected and accepted, and since nobody knows who is to blame (for everyone blames someone else) or how much better the service might be if the discount were less, everyone is more or less happy – until a contractor optimistically offers and an Authority gleefully accepts a rather over-generous discount. And then the contractor can't pay his bills, publishers refuse to supply him and children sit at their desks with nothing to study. This happens from time to time.

In Devon during the fifties the contractor was a large Exeter bookseller, and the terms of the contract allowed schools a certain freedom to buy from other sources. I say a certain freedom, but I really mean an uncertain freedom. It is obviously convenient to a teacher if, seeing exactly the book he wants in a shop, he can go in and buy it, rather than order it from the contractor, wait six months, learn that it is reprinting and finally receive it a year later at twice the price when he no longer needs it.

If the book is a net one – as it probably will be if it is seen in a bookshop – then as far as the school is concerned there is not even a discount to be lost. But the Contractor will be less happy, for he depends upon his net book sales to subsidize his non-net sales. That was the reason for leaving it all a little uncertain. Schools were not forbidden to buy their general books where they pleased, but equally they were not encouraged to. Some head teachers knew they could, others thought they couldn't. And since practically no teacher knew the difference between 'net' and 'non-net', a rather vaguer term was used, thus increasing the uncertainty: schools were allowed to buy their 'library books' where they pleased. In those days only secondary schools had libraries; so this freedom didn't really affect primary schools – not in the fifties, that is.

Then came 1960.

Thinking back those seventeen years I find myself thinking back still further, to the day in September, 1943, when I was ordered to take my bridging lorries to a certain map reference on the road to Salerno and report to an officer from 221 Field Company whom I would find there, I had had the same sort of order a few days previously and I had been away for as long as it took to get my lorries unloaded and the bridge built – a matter of hours. So away I went this time, excited and happy to be doing something, and leaving instructions with the cook to have a good hot meal waiting for us when we got back. . . . But we didn't come back. It was not a bridge; it was the Great Advance that was to carry us through the ring of mountains and across the Plain of Naples to the banks of the Volturno. And here was I caught up in it, swept along with it; and although I did nothing very gallant or exciting or even very difficult, I could at least feel that in my Division I held a unique post. I was the Division's one and only Bridging Officer, and bridges were going to be needed now as never before and as never again.

So when in the autumn of 1959 we were invited by the South Western Branch of the School Library Association to put on an exhibition of school library books at a Conference of Primary School teachers to be held at Dartington Hall the following May, I saw it as not more than just that. I never guessed, never realized until months afterwards what it really was: that I was lining up for another Great Advance, joining the Devonshire army of teachers, librarians, school inspectors and educationists who were to advance towards the New Education. Never mind whether my role was to be gallant, exciting or difficult: as in 1943 so in 1960 it was to be unique. I was the only bookseller in the convoy.

Why had they invited us? There were other booksellers in Devon. There was indeed the contractor. Dartington Hall was only twelve miles away, it is true: but that would have been only part of the reason, for the Conference was an important one, to be attended by teachers from all over Devon and indeed from Cornwall and Somerset. So I doubt if there had been any special feeling that the invitation ought to go to a local shop. . . . Perhaps already we had begun to make a name for ourselves outside our home town.

What sort of books did they want us to bring? I was no expert when it came to schools. At that time our children's department occupied a single bookcase along one wall – the bookcase I had made nine years previously from the French poplar we had brought down with us from London. Mostly it contained story books about ponies, ballet dancers and adventurous children. Blyton and Biggies featured prominently. They talked about 'information books'. Luckily I knew what they meant. These were something new and I had ventured to stock one or two. They were thin books, about ten inches high, and each dealt with a single subject: 'travel by road', 'ports and harbours', 'coal mining' – that sort of thing. Usually they came in a series, all looking more or less alike. I could think of three such series, but perhaps there were others. We had a letter printed and we sent it to eighty Sales Managers to find out.

The figure eighty sticks in my mind, but I cannot now recall how many replies we had or how many parcels of books were sent. We took them home in our recently acquired second-hand van (for we now lived on the edge of the town) unwrapped them and made piles all over the floor of our spare-room. Two teachers would be coming to vet them. We invited them to supper and after supper they set to work, sitting on the floor, reading, reading. . . . After the first hour each had made two little heaps, those books they liked, and those they didn't; but the piles all round them seemed scarcely touched. During the next hour they went a little faster, not reading now, just glancing, but thousands of books still remained. And now we had to look at our watches for there was the last ferry to catch. Well, they had made a start; they had given us an idea of what they wanted. Perhaps we could carry on along those lines? Until May 28th, then. . . .

On May 29th I sat down with a piece of paper to work out our profit-and-loss. On the credit side were the books I had sold and the orders I had taken. I added them up and took 30% of the total: that was our profit. On the debit side was the cost of the wood I had bought to make the special stands I needed so that the books could be elegantly displayed, the cost of petrol, the cost of printing our eighty letters and the probable cost of returning the unwanted books to their publishers. Deduct the one from the other and I was left with a small credit balance. So financially it had paid off. Good.

I never bothered to do such sums again. If I counted my profit after Dartington in pounds, by the end of the year I was counting it in hundreds and soon after that in thousands. And if occasionally I travelled a hundred miles to sell a dozen books, I told myself that I owed it to Devon and to all those schools who, unsolicited, had now started sending me their orders. How many hundred mile journeys can one set against a school that takes two or three hundred pounds of 'net' books off one's shelves? For this was how it became in the end.

Thus began the Big Advance towards the New Education; and I was in it, right up at the front. For me the Dartington Conference and all that followed from it forms one of the most important episodes in my life. Through it I got to know (and do business with) the Head Teachers of over sixty schools, primary and secondary, in all parts of Devon. Visiting these schools with my books I must have met and talked to many hundreds of other teachers. Meeting them, talking to them, seeing them in the presence of my books was to be conscious of a zeal that was almost fanatical. No revolutionaries bearing aloft the banner of their newfound faith could have matched the enthusiasm, the determination, the sense of comradeship, the devotion to their cause with which these teachers greeted the Revolution in Primary School Education and marched towards the El Dorado that it appeared to offer.

For it was a revolution, almost literally. And in the end I was to become not just one of the converted, but a preacher, finding pulpits open to me in school hall after school hall. For the New Education did not come as an edict from above but rather as a forest fire that is spread by the wind and sets light only to what is combustible. Here it was welcomed, there rejected. It was revolutionary in another sense too, turning old ideas inside out, upside down. Where once children sat in silent rows all working at the same task, now they moved about each working at different tasks. Where once they learned with tears now they learned with pleasure. Where once schools were inward-looking, isolating themselves from the outside world, now they looked outwards, a part of that world; high windows with a view only of the sky were replaced by low windows with a view of the neighbourhood; walls and fences were lowered. Subject after subject fell to the conqueror. The elements of physics, chemistry and mechanics, previously taught only as specialist subjects to older children, were now introduced to infant schools. Arithmetic became the New Mathematics. Multiplication tables were replaced by coloured rods. Foreign languages were spoken, not written. Spelling and grammar took second place to poems and stories. History was how people lived, not dates of kings and Acts of Parliament. Geography, too, was how people lived, not exports and imports and principal rivers. Even religious education, though it put up a stiff resistance, eventually submitted and put on new clothes. And the life-blood that permeated all these subjects was the New Books.

No more did children in primary schools, sitting in their rows, turn obediently to page twenty-five of the well-worn textbook. Textbooks were out. Textbooks, unique among books, published by 'educational publishers', distributed by 'school suppliers', read only in schools, had no place in a school that was a part of its community. The books the children found in school must resemble as nearly as possible the books they were to find outside school. For if home and school were to be integrated what better place to start, what better link between the two, than the book that the child could read and read with pleasure in both places. Thus the 'school library book' was born, and born too was the school library book publisher and the school library bookseller. A faint aura of seriousness hung over all three, but the barriers were down. The school library book and the children's book could sit side by side on the same shelf in the same shop and each would have a beneficial influence on the other.

What did I know about it all? What does a seller of books know about education? I would have known nothing if they hadn't taken me and converted me and welcomed me as one of themselves, a fellow revolutionary, and then trusted me and sent me out, a missionary, to convert others.

They welcomed me because their Bible was the Book and the Book was mine. They needed a Bookseller to distribute their Bibles. And I was easily converted. How could I not be when I saw what it meant to them and to the children under them? Have you ever been surrounded by a playground-full of children and seen your heavy boxes of books moving across that playground like giant spiders, their great bodies carried on eight tottering, spindly legs?

'Miss! He's brought us some books. Miss! When can we have them? Oh, Miss!'

What did I know? What I saw, what I learned by talking to others, what I myself found in books. There were plenty of books being written at that time, books like Sybil Marshall's *An Experiment in Education*. I bought them all, read them all, urged others to read them. How many copies of David Holbrook's *English for the Rejected* did I force Secondary School librarians to buy?

Then there were the teachers. I never saw a class being taught; I never saw my books being used. But I talked to the teachers who used them. Earlier in this chapter I said that the way a bookseller judges the contents of a book is by enlisting the help of an expert. And so among my teachers I sought my experts: here the expert in mathematics, here the expert in I.T.A., here the expert in religious education, and so on. From each I learned which books were best and these I stocked and recommended with confidence to others.

Finally I read reviews, two publications being particularly helpful: there was the School Library Association's own quarterly publication, *The School Librarian*, which contained articles by teachers on the use of books as well as hundreds of individual book reviews; and then there was that extraordinary one-man-band of an almost-monthly, Margery Fisher's *Growing Point*.

But I couldn't have done any of this if I hadn't had three pieces of good fortune.

The first lay in the terms of the Devon contract which (as I have already said) allowed schools to buy their library books where they pleased. In the past this freedom was more in the nature of a door left unlocked than one thrown open and signposted, and not many-schools had bothered to use it, or even knew of its existence. However, it was a freedom most strongly championed and defended by the School Library Association; and now that Primary Schools were being urged to set up their own libraries, it had become one that mattered. For the question head teachers were asking was: 'Where do we find these books?' They could go to the contractor, of course. They could look through catalogues and send him an order. Or perhaps they could even visit Exeter to see what he had in stock. But if there was a better, easier way. . . . There was. 'Get in touch with the Harbour Bookshop' they were told.

They did, and they came to us in such numbers that the door was now left wide open, and even the County's advisers and inspectors were directing teachers towards it. Indeed the pressure soon became so great that yet another door had to be opened. This allowed Secondary Schools freedom to buy *all* their books where they pleased. An immense volume of school business came our way and coping with it would have been quite impossible but for our second piece of good fortune.

At the back of our shop, part of the building but not belonging to us, were two dark, damp, dilapidated flats. Even thus qualified, the word 'flats' seems too good for them conjuring up the wrong sort of picture altogether. To begin with they weren't flat: they were each on two floors. They were like two bits of a jigsaw puzzle: try and work out the shape of each one separately and you were at once lost in an incomprehensible jumble of rooms, passages and staircases. But fitted together and added to the bookshop they made a neat rectangular whole. The flat nearer to us seemed at times exceedingly near. From outside you could see a window the bottom half of which was occupied by books, the top half by a baby, and publisher's representatives could be excused for thinking that both belonged to us and for asking after the health of the latter. While from inside such alarming sounds would penetrate from the other side of the thin partition wall that Lesley and I found ourselves asking even more anxiously after the baby's health. Our second piece of good fortune, then, (and the baby's too) came when this flat was officially condemned and the two of them were offered to us for £1000. This happened in the summer of 1960, a perfect bit of timing.

The uncondemned flat remained occupied and was frankly a liability. But the condemned one gave us, when a hole had been knocked through to it, a large room at the back of the shop where books could be stored, and, on the first floor and when another hole had been made, an office, a small room in which the last of our picture framing was done, and – most important of all – a large, fairly pleasant, not too dark room which we at once fitted out with shelves and which became our 'schoolroom'. It was here that we housed our new school-library-type books. Here that we sorted out our school orders. Here that (piloted by someone who knew the way or they would have got hopelessly lost) teachers came to look and to choose. And it was here that Joyce was queen.

Joyce was our third piece of good fortune. Too good for a mere paragraph she must have her own chapter. All I will say now is that she blended the very best of amateurism with the very best of professionalism and gave schools a service that I'll bet they had never seen before and will probably never see again. With Joyce firmly in charge in the shop it was possible for Lesley and me to spend part of our time away. For if schools didn't always find it easy to come to us we would have to go to them.

And this is what we did.

All through term the calls came in, and – depending on the size of the school, the subjects wanted and how much money I guessed they were likely to spend – suitable books were assembled, listed, packed and delivered on approval. They kept what they liked and I called back for the remainder the following week. Or perhaps a head teacher might prefer a different arrangement, and we might put on a one-day exhibition, loading dozens of boxes onto the van, Lesley coming too, and then we could enjoy together a happy day in a distant part of Devon. Many of these trips became annual events: Tavistock in May, Hatherleigh in May, Bampton in July: these were our favourites.

But whatever arrangement a school preferred, the important thing was that the teachers were seeing the actual books, not just a catalogue description of them; they were choosing from an already carefully chosen assortment; and finally there was no ordering to be done, no months of waiting. Having made their choice, they kept them.

At first we let the books speak for themselves: we were no more than their escorts. But later I was often invited to say something about them. Shoved into the drawer where I keep my socks are the notes I typed for the many talks I gave. They still survive, folded and a little crumpled. I was never told what to say, and since I never liked to say exactly the same thing twice, they were always a little different. In any case they varied with the audience I was addressing, varied, too, as the years went by and there were new things to be said. To a group of French teachers visiting Devon the subject was the history of children's books in England. To a weekend course for playgroup teachers it was story-telling. At a course for teachers of backward readers I ventured my own theories on the subject. At a conference of school librarians I talked about book selection. To parents I talked about books in school and books at home.

Mostly my talks were to parents at 'parent-teacher' meetings held in a classroom after school was over. We spread out our books on desks and tables. I talked about them, and then the parents would look and ask and buy. Often these visits were to tiny, two-teacher village schools in remote parts of Devon, and these we enjoyed most of all. The smaller and more distant, the better; for there we would find the warmest welcome and the largest audience, and there we would sell the most books. And often, not wanting a long, dark journey home after it was over, we would stay the night, making a leisurely return the following morning.

But our most exciting and inspiring occasions were always the meetings organized by the School Library Association. To be invited year after year to come with our books, to see how they all delighted in these books, to share their enthusiasm, to join their discussions, to join them in the audience listening to their guest speaker . . . and then on two occasions to be one of the speakers myself: this in my bookselling life was my hilltop, and I know I shall never find a hilltop that will bring a greater sense of pride, happiness and achievement. One can fool oneself that books are 'culture' and that booksellers are therefore purveyors of culture. But one knows that for the most part this is not true. And though one may not be selling books solely in order to earn money, one is very conscious of (and sensitive to) the fact that many people see booksellers in this light. 'Commercial', 'profit', 'money': these words are used and they hurt. They hurt so much that earlier in this chapter I felt I had to show that they were often used unfairly. This attitude towards booksellers, that we are only in it for the profit, is particularly common among teachers and librarians. So let me now say how happy and grateful I was that no teacher ever seemed to feel this way about me. Indeed, selling to schools I was spared even the occasional mercenary twinges that I get in the shop – for I could never disguise from myself that if I persuaded someone to buy a book, though he might go out spiritually the richer, he would undoubtedly be financially the poorer. With teachers, however, it was different. It was not their money; it was the County's. They had been given their allocation and it had to be used up by the end of the financial year. I knew too that my books were good, that what I was selling was worth buying, that money spent with me was money well spent. So with a clear conscience I could be as persuasive as I liked. Yes, on my hilltop I could pause and say: 'What I am doing is worth doing and I am doing it well.' And then I could remember that it all started in 1960 at Dartington Hall.

At the end of the Conference I was publicly thanked. At the end of every Conference of the School Library Association that Lesley and I attended (for on many happy occasions she was able to come with me) we were publicly thanked. So now it is my turn.

This is not the sort of autobiography that has an index to which all who knew the author at once refer, hoping to find a mention. It is too personal a story for that. In any case I find it embarrassing to write about people I know, knowing that they will later read what I have written and that others will read it too. What right have I to drag private individuals on to my stage and make them dance for me? On the other hand to mention nobody is to imply that I have gone my way and done whatever it may be I have done entirely on my own and owing nothing to the existence of others. And I owe so much to those teachers; and there were so many of them, all so different, each with his or her own special enthusiasm and so making his or her own unique contribution to our lives. Each name I recall brings to mind another . . . and another . . . and another. Where do I start? Where do I stop?

If from them all I am to choose a single name, there can be no doubt, no dispute that the name must be that of Gwen Petty. To name others would be invidious: not to name her would be unthinkable. In 1960 she was our Branch Secretary. Later she became our Chairman. Later still – since you don't let people like that slip away into honourable and well-deserved retirement – she was our President. That of all the many Branches of the School Library Association the South-Western was among the most lively was her doing, her triumph. Small, neat, hawk-like, utterly dedicated, she was the librarian of Torquay Girls Grammar School. She would, one felt, have been no less at home at Cheltenham Ladies College; and I say this to give an idea of the standards of learning and of behaviour that she upheld. Such a person might well not have welcomed the very different standards of the New Education with its lack of discipline, its abandonment of formal teaching, its preference for 'creative writing' rather than good grammar and spelling. But this was not so, and it was probably because she could see the good in both worlds that she was able so brilliantly to harness and control the enthusiasm that blazed around her. How could one not feel – as we used to feel – that any conference at which she presided, whether as secretary, chairman or president, was a very special affair. None – least of all her two devoted booksellers – could grudge the weeks of preparation that led to an event so perfectly organized so immensely enjoyable. And when it was all over, when the books had been packed back into their boxes and willing hands had borne them off to the waiting van, when the hall was empty and the caretaker had been found and thanked, when the last goodbyes had been said, everyone of us could take home the glowing embers of a happy day that would give us warmth for months to come.

END OF AN ERA

Could it last? Could it be expected that the fires of the sixties would burn as strongly in the seventies? After spring and summer come autumn and winter.

One small incident stands out. It was at the Annual General Meeting of the local branch of the National Union of Teachers. These meetings were held in Newton Abbot in March, and each year for many years I had been there with my books – though on these occasions not the only bookseller. I had been disappointed in the lack of interest the previous year and, having agreed rather reluctantly to come again this year, was watching the teachers with a more than usually critical eye. ... You can take a photograph of a leaf falling to the ground and you can call it 'Autumn'. In the same way I could have taken a photograph of my book exhibition. It would have shown ten teachers lined up in front of it, none of them looking at it, each with his back to my books, gossiping, smoking or just contemplating, using my tables merely to recline against. It would have meant as little and it would have meant as much: a trivial incident, a solitary leaf, yet marking the end of summer.

Winter was indeed on its way and there were many signs of its approach. There was a bitter wind blowing from the offices of Local Government. At first it made me feel bitter too, but in retrospect I see that I was trying to have it both ways.

I have just unearthed a letter I wrote in 1966 to the *Times Literary Supplement*. There had been some correspondence about the poor quality of bookshops in some areas and the suggestion that the remedy was for Local Authorities to set up their own shops alongside their public libraries.

I felt all the indignation of a Christian listening to an atheist. In my reply I said:

> ... To remain solvent and to display the sort of stock that would meet with the approval of your correspondent, booksellers today must secure a good slice of educational business.
>
> I am luckier than many of my colleagues. I live in Devon and my local authority allows its schools to buy their library books where they please. The result is that I do a relatively very large amount of school library business, and consequently I can carry a much larger and wider range of stock, particularly in children's books, than if I were supplying only private individuals. The two markets overlap, each benefitting from the fact that I also supply the other.

But booksellers elsewhere may be less lucky. Other authorities, seeing book-buying and bookselling as no more than a bill that ultimately has to be paid, are concerned only with securing the highest discount on textbooks and will pass their entire educational contract – textbooks and library books lumped together – to the supplier, wherever he may live, who bids the highest. Few bookshops can cope with the whole of a county contract at any price, let alone at cut price. But many booksellers could give efficient service to a few nearby schools – to the benefit of both the schools and the community generally.

So before local authorities are tempted to set up and subsidise their own bookshops, they might first consider the extent to which the malaise is of their own making and whether they might not remedy it by adopting, as customers, a slightly less discouraging attitude towards existing local bookshops.

The cure would not be immediate, but it might be cheaper and surer in the long run.

This might be described as my Booksellers Faith and I preached it to unbelievers at every opportunity. So when the County Borough of Torbay was formed, how very proper that Torbay teachers should be directed towards a Torbay bookshop. And when Plymstock and Plympton left Devon to join the County Borough of Plymouth, how very proper that they should be directed towards a Plymouth bookshop. How very proper too that a large and wealthy grammar school in Exeter should be told that it must no longer buy all its books (or indeed any of its books) from a shop thirty miles beyond the Borough boundary. But of course it was sad for me. Even in what remained of Devon there came the realization that you cannot expect a contractor to offer a high discount on non-net books if the best of his net business is going to another bookshop.

So, one by one, the doors began to close, and in the end I lost almost every school.

With regret? Not altogether, for these were not the only signs that summer was coming to an end. There were signs in the books themselves.

When they had first appeared, these school library books, they were new and exciting – and there weren't enough of them. Demand was terrific and publishers were falling over each other in the scramble to meet it. Those with children's books were offering schools their better, more serious titles; those with textbooks were picking out their gayest and dressing them up in gay jackets. Other publishers were hurrying off to America, and many and colourful were the series they brought back. Others again were commissioning authors and illustrators and producing their own information books. What a jungle of series there soon were! Look Books, Outline Books, True Books, Junior Reference Books, Study Books, Signpost Books, All-About Books – and dozens more. And my job was to know them all and stock what I thought were the best. Each year brought more and more: new series born, new titles added to existing series. Each year schools would say 'What's new?' and I would sort them out and take them along. Each year our stock grew larger and larger. Where was it to end? It had to end, of course. With the forty-seventh addition to the What's-its-name Books I could no longer stock the entire range, nor perhaps could the publisher keep the entire range in print. With the arrival on the scene of the How-D'you-Do Books (first four titles: ships, space travel, dinosaurs and baby animals) I found myself wondering what particular gap this series hoped to fill. One needs choice, one needs variety, but there comes a point when one more book on the marvels of this or the wonders of that is one book too many.

So I escaped to fiction. I had been loading up my van with factual books for quite long enough: schools knew all about them, and what was new was not necessarily better than what was old. Now I loaded it up with story books. I had said all I wanted to say about non-fiction. So now I began my campaign for fiction. Invited to talk to teachers at a Teacher's Centre (for example) I gave them a list of a dozen stories, and asked them to choose any one, read it to their class and then get the children to write or paint or make or act whatever the story inspired them to do. A Harbour Bookshop Book Token would be given to the class with the best entry. ... This sort of thing helped for a while. But the wintry weather had come. It was only partly due to over-production. Demand was falling off too. Enthusiasm was dying. The Great Advance was coming to a halt.

Today we look back on the New Education and the El Dorado that it never reached. 'Ah,' say the wise ones. 'I knew it. Life is not fun, so why pretend it is? Most children will end up having to do as they're told, so they might as well learn how to do it from the start. And if they've got to join the rat-race, the nearer the front they are, the better, and so the best thing we can teach them is self-discipline, the ability to hold their noses to the grindstone however much it hurts.'

There will always be arguments about what children should be taught – and how. It's hard enough to know what is best for one's own child, let alone the children of an entire nation. Nor is it easy, looking back, to be sure how successful or otherwise one has been. But if the Great Debate on education continues, one thing is beyond debate, one thing is certain, and let all in the book trade say it as loudly and clearly as they can. The New Education brought one great unmixed, undeniable blessing, and it brought it to children's literature.

CHILDREN'S BOOKS

Though it may be the author who writes the book it is undoubtedly the buyer who determines what sort of book is written. So if we are to understand what happened to children's books in 1960 we must see who was buying them and how they chose them.

Before 1960 those who bought children's books were either the children themselves or adults buying presents for children. Children's books, as I have said, fall into two main types: story books and factual books – or as they are more usually called, fiction and non-fiction. Let us take non-fiction first. The child, money in hand, looking around him, judges these books rather as he judges cakes, going for the large and colourful, not too concerned about the exact nature of the contents provided there is enough of it. The adult, with Christmas approaching, unsure of the child's exact age, even more unsure of his current interests, plays for safety with something fairly general. The result is 'The Jolly Bumper Book About Almost Everything', printed on thick paper (to give bulk), poorly bound (to keep price down), lots of gaudy pictures (because this is what matters), an indifferent if not actually illegible text (because who's going to read it anyway?) and finally a jacket to dazzle the eye. Such is the typical factual book.

Fiction is different. If factual books can be judged by their looks, this is certainly not true of story-books, for the words inside are what matters. So can we blame the child for here choosing not the eye-catching but the familiar – something that in some way resembles what he last read? Children are, I believe, naturally conservative, wary of the unknown. Also a story can be so real and a child can identify so closely with the hero that coming to the end of a book is like waking from a wonderful dream, and he longs to return. But even if this were not so, how, without guidance (and who was there to offer guidance in the fifties?) could we expect him to find his way among unknown titles by unknown authors? So naturally he looked for yet another adventure about the Famous Five, the Secret Seven, the Naughty Nine or whatever particular gang he favoured. And children's writers, aware of this, kept him happy with Biggies after Biggies, Bunter after Bunter, Jennings after Jennings, with gymkhana after gymkhana and ballet after ballet. If this suited the child it also suited the adult; and what a relief it was to both when the Terrible Ten had yet another wonderful escapade just in time for Christmas. But some adults aimed a little higher. They wanted a *good* book, perhaps even an *improving* book, by which they meant – for what else could they possibly mean? – a 'classic'. They knew that classics were good, for they remembered them from their own childhood, and they may even have enjoyed them. Thus fiction before 1960 could have been summed up (if you were feeling mildly cynical) as Enid Blyton and ponies on the one hand and *Coral Island* and *Water Babies* on the other. And what encouragement did *this* offer to the new author, what hope for a new *Alice* or *Wind in the Willows*?

Then came the New Education and with it the New Buyers.

They were the Public Librarians and the School Librarians, professionals whose job it was to know what was good and to choose it; and they had a lot of money to spend. So for the first time good books were worth publishing, worth writing. Merit at last was being recognized and rewarded.

I have already mentioned the new 'Information Books'. They always remained separate from the Jolly Bumper Books, as if not quite liking to rub shoulders with anything quite so vulgar. But they set certain standards which the latter, if they hoped occasionally to be bought by schools, were wise to follow: better binding; text, typography and illustrations planned as a whole; a more enterprising range of subjects.

But it was with fiction that the influence of the new buyers was most welcome. I remember in 1955 when I was doing a little reviewing for *Smith's Trade News* being sent a batch of children's books that included a book called *A Swarm in May* by a writer then unknown to me. And just as a falling leaf can symbolize the approach of winter, so here was a first green shoot that announced the approach of spring. I wrote my review, and I like to think that it put me among the first of the talent-spotters to welcome the arrival of William Mayne.

Others soon followed, unknowns all of them until their sudden emergence, following no tradition, setting entirely new standards in children's literature; and setting also entirely new problems in children's bookselling. How easy it had been to sell the latest 'Lone Piner'. How very much harder it was to sell, for instance, *Flambards*, *The Piemakers*, *Jack Holborn*, *Owl Service*, *A Dog So Small*, *The Intruder* or *A Handful of Thieves*.

The first thing to do was to make room for them on our shelves, to give them a chance. So we pruned down our classics to half a dozen or so books that were really good not merely old. And then we got rid of all our Blytons and Biggies. Yes, indeed, for fifteen years or thereabouts I have not stocked a single book by Enid Blyton and I have often been asked to explain why. One can argue that her books are immoral, encouraging contempt for the law and hostility towards outsiders. One can argue that her emotions are shallow and her language feeble. And although one must recognize that her books have given great pleasure to a great many children (myself included) one can argue that a diet of nothing but Enid Blyton like a diet of nothing but cream cakes leaves out too much that is beneficial. But I think that my real reason for saying 'No' was that I was *able* to say 'No', and having said it was then able to sell more children's books than ever before. Saying 'No' to Blyton and the rest was a little like saying 'No' to stationers' cards. Our shelves looked better without them.

That was the first step, then: to make room for the new books, to find them and to stock them. The second step was to read them and recommend them. They were good all right; but they were most certainly not easy to sell. We enjoyed reading them immensely, but so often were left wondering what sort of child would also enjoy them. Often we felt that they were written not so much *for* children as *about* children. Another difficulty – these new writers certainly weren't making things easy for us – was that a success was seldom followed by a sequel to the same pattern. Not only was the author's next book often quite different, it was often addressed to a child of a different age. So each book had to be treated on its own individual merits. It was hard work and one couldn't blame the school librarian (who had plenty of other hard work to do) if he bought only non-fiction, leaving it to the County Library to send down on loan boxes of assorted fiction. Yet this seemed to me quite fatal. For it meant that the librarian didn't know what he was getting, didn't read what he got, couldn't recommend to a child what he should try, and so the child might well pick up something quite beyond him – and perhaps be put off reading for life. . . .

In short, if anyone ever thought that selling books was merely wrapping them up and handing them over and putting the money in the till, no one could ever think this of selling children's fiction in the sixties.

So when the elderly lady doctor came in and asked me to recommend a book for a seven year old god-child, and when, after looking at the three or four books I had picked out for her (none of which, naturally, meant anything to her), she thanked me and said she would leave it for today and ask Mrs Robinson who had a seven year old child of her own what *he* was reading and then perhaps I could order a copy, what I said was:

'Very well, Dr B., and when I have a pain I too will go to Mrs Robinson for advice and no doubt you will be good enough to write me a prescription for whatever it is she recommends.'

No. I lie. That is what I *ought* to have said.

TWENTY-ONE YEARS

In 1972 we celebrated our twenty first birthday. We did it in style, for it was not just an important landmark in our bookselling lives. In one sense it was the finishing post. The Harbour Bookshop would continue, but my life as a bookseller was coming to an end.

In our Christmas catalogue that year we looked back and gave thanks, as was proper, to all those books we had sold with such pleasure – and, yes, with such profit – over those years.

First: three books that helped us right from the start. Two of them of local interest, just out and which we continued to sell happily for a number of years, first at full price, later reduced: Ruth Manning-Sanders' *The River Dart* and Percy Russell's *Dartmouth*. The third, a national bestseller whose birthday virtually coincided with our own: Nicholas Monsarrat's *The Cruel Sea*.

Then two more national bestsellers of our youth, two books that gave us immense pleasure in the reading and so a double pleasure in the selling: Laurens van der Post's *Venture To The Interior* and John Hunt's *Ascent of Everest*.

Next, two more books of exploration, but spiritual rather than geographical. They may seem odd partners at first sight, but we have always felt they had much in common: John Robinson's *Honest to God* and D. H. Lawrence's *Lady Chatterley's Lover* – both deeply serious, both tilting against the establishment, both (for better or for worse) opening the flood gates of pent-up feeling.

Then a miscellaneous collection of books with this in common: that their authors kindly helped us make a success of them by putting in a personal appearance and in most cases, too, a personal word, on their behalf for our benefit. Stanley Smith's *The Wind Calls the Tune*, Peter Churchill's *Of Their Own Choice*, Brian Fawcett's *Exploration Fawcett*, Elephant Bill's *Bandoola*, Gerald Durrell's *Bafut Beagles*, Robin Knox Johnson's *A World of my Own* and Nicolette Milnes-Walker's *When I Put Out to Sea*. How many of our customers can boast signed copies of all seven?

Then *The New English Bible*. And would you have been wiser than we were in the months before publication and guessed that the version with the Apocrypha would outsell the version without by somewhere around ten to one?

Then W. Keble Martin's *The Concise British Flora*, the book that so many publishers turned down before Michael Joseph made it the bestseller of bestsellers. Readily identifiable by us, even if described as 'that book by the clergyman' or 'that book that the Duke of Edinburgh . . .' even, on occasion, merely as 'that book'.

Then two books that television (not always our rival) turned into winners: John Galsworthy's *Forsyte Saga* and Kenneth Clark's *Civilisation*.

Finally a book that sold well everywhere but especially here: Nevil Shute's *Most Secret*. Six shillings in hardcover in 1951. Six shillings in paperback today. Of special interest, of course, not only because the story has a local setting but because we can proudly claim Nevil Shute Norway (to give him his real name) as a Dartmouth author.

Where does one stop? There are still a dozen more titles we have listed, and dozens and dozens we could well add. Most of them fairly obvious and unexciting – books about Devon, about the sea, certain children's classics. . . . So let us end by thanking that vast army of books, tens of thousands of them, of which we have sold only one solitary copy. Add them together and it is they rather than their more popular companions, that have kept us in business selling books here in Dartmouth.

There are two sorts of bookseller (this is my theory): the male and the female. The male bookseller is concerned with the territory over which he operates, defending it, enlarging it. It is the male bookseller who wants to expand his business, the male bookseller who opens new branches. The female bookseller, on the other hand, is concerned with her shop, furnishing it, making it attractive, making it not the biggest but the best shop in the area.

I am a female bookseller. Once, for about a week, I did contemplate the idea of a branch in Torquay, then wisely abandoned it. My work with schools took me to far away places, it is true. But it didn't matter too much when it began to come to an end. I was not altogether unhappy to be back home again. There was plenty to do. The condemned flat had given us the space we needed, but it still had to be used in the best possible way. With the money that was coming in and with the realization that the sun would not shine for ever, came both the opportunity and the necessity for getting our schoolroom moved downstairs and united with our children's department. It was a fearful task. A wall had to be removed, another had to be taken down and rebuilt and a third had to have a large opening cut in it. A rotting wooden floor had to be replaced by a concrete one and eventually carpeted. A crumbling ceiling had to be pulled down and replastered. Finally came shelves and fittings, some bought, but many of them designed and made by myself. That gave us our children's room, and we were very proud of it. Then came new shelves, new lighting, new heating and new flooring in the rest of the shop. There was no end to it, no end to the improvements one could make. ... And finally, of course, there was all that lost business to be replaced. Oh, yes, there was plenty to do. ...

The Harbour Bookshop is very much our home – not just a machine for making money. It is old and rambling, awkward in many ways, especially when heavy parcels have to be carried. But it has a friendly feel, a personality of its own. I like it, I wouldn't want it different. I wouldn't want a modern shop with modern fittings and an electronic till. I like just being in it, especially in the evening when we are closed and it is empty. I like making things for it. All this is part of the pleasure of being a bookseller. Other shops may have grown bigger, but I don't envy them. I don't feel jealous. I would only feel jealous if I were told they were also better.

To be a good bookseller you need three things: you need a goal (or a succession of goals) to aim for; you need the spur of necessity; and you need all your working hours. After twenty one years I was about to lose all three.

It seemed that I had done as a bookseller all the things I had aimed to do, all the things I could find to do. There was no other goal in sight.

For twenty-one years the Harbour Bookshop had been our sole source of income. We had proved to ourselves that we could do it: that we could survive as booksellers here in Dartmouth. In 1971 my mother died. From now on a part of my father's royalties would be coming to me. So the spur had gone.

For seventeen years Clare had been at school. They had taught her a lot of things in that time, though not as much as some children learn. But they had not taught her how to walk. School was now finished. Clare would be living at home, and I would be helping to look after her. So I could no longer be a full-time bookseller.

So it was time to leave my grassy plain. I had found what I had wanted to find. I had done what I had wanted to do. The cloud hung its curtain across the mountains. It was time to go.

ONE MAN'S DREAM

In 1966 a half page advertisement had appeared in *The Daily Telegraph* (and doubtless in other papers). It was headed 'The Olearchs' and underneath was a large photograph of Roy Edwin

McCoskery of the Shell-Mex and BP Group. Below that we were told that Mr McCoskery was Area Manager (Consumer Markets Division) with a territory covering Shropshire, Staffordshire, Warwickshire, Worcestershire, Gloucestershire and Northamptonshire embracing Birmingham and the Black Country and that he watched over the supply of petroleum in its various forms to a wide variety of consumers including farmers, ironmongers, workshops, offices and homes. We learned something of his early life and of his career with Shell-Mex. We learned that now, at the age of 44, after 11 years with the firm and four promotions, he was beginning to think about retirement and

> dreams (as his wife would wish) of a bookshop on the quay at Dartmouth. Men of action always dream of sloth. Ah, well, dreams (like boyhood ambitions) don't affect a man at work.

Very far be it from me to discourage Mr McCoskery from coming to live in Dartmouth when he leaves Shell-Mex. Many people come here to retire and are very happy here. But I wouldn't like him – or indeed anyone – to think that running a bookshop, even in a sleepy little place like this, is a suitable retirement job for the slothful.

In any case he would be having the Harbour Bookshop to compete with.

8. *Friends and Helpers*

We are sometimes asked: 'How do you manage about holidays? Can you ever get away?' To which we reply: 'Oh, but we have staff.'

Even in our very early days, when we had no staff, the problem was not so much leaving the books as leaving the cat; and this problem remains – though 'cat' has now become 'cats'.

In our first year the answer lay in a conveniently cat-loving aunt.

We had the idea that we might find a 'locum' for the bookshop through the Booksellers Association – a married couple like us, perhaps, who were contemplating opening their own shop and wanted a little preliminary experience and advice. We would put them up in our spare bedroom, spend a fortnight with them explaining how everything worked, then leave them on their own. We suggested this to the Association and they recommended John Martin. We exchanged letters and he seemed ideal, but as he was unmarried he solved only half our problem. So, a little fearfully, we mentioned the cat; and to our great relief he said that was quite all right. He would bring his Aunt Audrey with him.

As we had only one spare bedroom Aunt Audrey's arrival had to be delayed until we were on the point of leaving, and this meant that John had to have lessons on cats as well as on books. We had to take him out at night, just before bedtime, and teach him the particular squeak to which Hodge, who usually spent the evening with friends, would respond. We had to show him the yards, building sites and so on where the friends would meet, and instruct him in the various lures that could be used if Hodge was in no hurry to return. Happily he enjoyed this side of his work as much as the other. Perhaps today one might hesitate to ask a young man to go squeaking through the streets at 11 o'clock at night. But in those days the town was quieter. Indeed if one heard anything at all at that late hour it was probably the miscellaneous warblings and croonings of other cat owners engaged on the same business.

Hodge, Aunt Audrey, John, the books and our customers all got on excellently together. Did we feel that his canvas shoes and flowery open-necked shirt were perhaps a trifle too informal? But it was a failing in the right direction; better far than to have someone arriving with a business suit packed in his luggage, expecting to find a cash register rather than a biscuit tin for putting the money in, and calling everyone 'Sir' or 'Madam' in a solemn and respectful manner. For ours has never been that sort of shop. And John in 1952, the first of our many helpers (and the first of sixteen whose names began with a 'J') set a standard which others almost without exception have been happy to follow.

Goolie joined us in 1956, as fond of cats as she was of books and so delighted to look after both. By then we had moved to a house with a garden at the top of the town. The kitchen window was left permanently open, and Hodge's comings and goings were no longer a problem. All he needed, apart from food, was a bit of company in the evenings, and this she was happy to provide.

Her real name was Eleanor Guglielmo, but hardly anyone knew her as Eleanor and few ventured on a surname that looked as if it might sound like the last of the bath water running out. So she called herself Miss Goole and most of her friends knew her as Goolie. This left the rest of the world even more baffled, and to them she was variously 'Miss Goolie', 'Miss Gold', 'Miss Gooleemo' or 'Miss Jilliamo'. She had spent her working life as private secretary to Sir Ian Fraser, meeting, getting to know, helping and for ever after keeping in touch with the many hundreds of blinded ex-service men who passed through St Dunstan's. On her retirement she bought a cottage on the beach at Torcross, arriving in Devon shortly after us.

Many people, after an active, urban, sociable, working life, and remembering carefree holidays, look for their dream cottage in South Devon. But day after rainy day for month after wintry month with nothing to do and no one to do it with is very different from summer fortnights when all one wanted was to relax. So not everyone who seeks it finds contentment here; still fewer can live happily in an isolated cottage; and very few indeed after forty years of strenuous work enjoy being both isolated and alone. Goolie was a rare exception. She was immensely sociable; she loved people; there was hardly a town in England that didn't contain a St Dunstaner with whom she continued to correspond; she was an immense letter writer and an immense talker. Yet even after her retirement her ideal of a holiday was still a wild and lonely sea coast – Sark, it might be, or the Orkneys. No matter, then, if the winter gales sent the waves beating against her walls, flinging stones at her windows and over her roof, dumping great loads of shingle on her flower beds until they were indistinguishable from the rest of the beach; warm and snug inside, she was perfectly happy and loved it there.

But content though she was to spend most of her time in her own company, now and again she needed the company of others. So she caught the bus to Dartmouth and spent an hour or two doing duty at the Borough Museum. Then, before returning to Torcross, she might perhaps look in at the Harbour Bookshop. She was a great reader. She had been a delicate child and the games she couldn't play and the adventures she couldn't enjoy she had found instead in books. Later, working with people who were unable even to read about what they couldn't do, she had spent a lot of her time reading aloud. So, as she looked along our shelves, she must have thought that, pleasant though it was to work odd hours at the Museum, it might be even pleasanter to work odd hours in a bookshop.

To us however she was at that time no more than a friendly anonymous face, one of the many elderly female faces that we found it so hard to attach a name to.

Then in 1956 Clare was born, Lesley withdrew temporarily to become a full-time mother and our Gift Gallery was opened. There was no doubt that we would need an assistant, and Tessa joined us. But with our very much larger shop, on two floors, Tessa alone, at the height of the holiday season, was not enough. We needed a part-timer as well. 'I believe there's someone who lives at Torcross,' said Lesley . . .

The arrangement we made suited us admirably. There were two rooms and a bathroom on the second floor above the shop, now no longer wanted by us. There were dozens of Goolie's friends who would love to spend a fortnight in a cottage by the sea. So, during the summer months, Goolie moved to Dartmouth and a succession of friends moved in and out of Torcross. And since these friends paid her rent it was agreed that no further financial arrangements need be made.

Thus in 1956 Goolie made her debut at the Harbour Bookshop, and since in that same year my father died, many people immediately assumed that she must be my mother – which added yet another complication to her identity.

She stayed with us off and on for fifteen years, so much a part of the shop that it seemed to some she *was* the shop; for she was a large person and when she was in residence even Lesley and I sometimes found it a little hard to squeeze round her. In a more formally organized shop where areas of responsibility and orders of seniority are more exactly determined, Goolie's status might have been a little difficult to define. I never attempted to define it and luckily I never needed to. She was devotedly loyal and immensely hard working but she never wanted more than to be allowed to meet customers and sell books. She was warm-hearted and kind and easy to get on with, yet at times she could be very fierce; and customers who misbehaved were told off like naughty children. But I need not have been alarmed: they didn't mind; they came back; they all adored her.

I said earlier that it was more important to have a sales assistant who liked people rather than one who liked books. Goolie loved both. Watching her introduce books she loved to people she loved, one's only fear was that she might never leave the two alone together. A bookseller's job is to introduce, not to chaperone.

However, the great thing about her was that she gave the shop the personality it wanted. There she was, sitting at her table, only too happy to be helpful if her help were needed, pleasantly informal, a large, motherly figure, making you feel welcome, making you feel that if you asked her a question she would probably know the answer (even though she might take five minutes over her reply). A shop is more than just a place where you buy things. It can also be a place where you meet people, sometimes indeed the only place where you meet people and shopping your only social activity. If Dartmouth is a friendly town, welcoming visitors, it is as much as anybody the shopkeepers who have made it so. And if people return year after year, eager to revisit old haunts, for many of them one haunt in particular must have been the bookshop 'run by that nice old lady.'

Joyce Green joined us in 1963. We had known the Greens in a vague sort of way ever since we had arrived. He was a biology teacher at the grammar school and she could often be seen standing in the street with a sheaf of papers in her hand interviewing passers-by on behalf of the BBC. I knew that she was wanting a more exacting job than that and it seemed ideal that what we needed – help with our expanding school business – was term-time work that would leave her free to share school holidays with her husband. So initially a 'job description' would have been simple: to deal with school and library orders and to answer the telephone.

Thus she became the bookshop's voice, and a most admirable voice it was, too, leaving you in no doubt that you had dialled the right number, no fear that you were getting a little deaf. 'Good morning. Harbour Bookshop. Can I help you?' And it became her pride that she could, that if she were asked a question she knew the answer, whether it was a school asking about the availability of a textbook or a private customer wanting something whose title was uncertain and whose author was forgotten. 'Yes, we have a copy in stock. Shall we send it or will you call?' Or sometimes, in answer to a stranger who had been telephoning shop after shop in vain: 'I'm sorry, we haven't. It's been out of print for several years, you know. Didn't they tell you? But there's a new edition coming in the autumn. . . .'

She knew better than anybody how rare and how welcome it is, when you ring up with a problem, to be able to speak at once to someone who knows what you are talking about. For frequently she would have to ring up publishers. 'Oh!' she would say crossly afterwards. 'I spoke to a wetty!' And she would imitate the wetty's voice. But sometimes: 'I got on to *such* a nice man and he called me "dear" and he was *so* helpful. . . .' And this would make her day. What a pity, that more publishers don't invest in nice men who take a pride in knowing the answers rather than wetties who don't.

Of course it would be an exaggeration to pretend that, even after doing a little spadework (as she called it). Joyce could answer every question; for there were some that offered no clue at all, and these she would deal with in her own peculiar way. She would leave them and wait until she was looking for something quite different. Then, apparently quite by chance, she would happen on the answer. This technique worked so often that we used to rely on it. Serendipity, like water divining, is one of those mysterious gifts that you can't quite believe in but which some people undoubtedly seem to possess. Another gift she had, useful to us if perhaps a little exhausting to her, was the habit of waking up at 3 o'clock in the morning to remember things. No job description would have included night work of this type; and in fact Joyce very quickly found herself doing a great deal that it would have been hard to define, and doing it all so well that when term came to an end we were extremely reluctant to let her go on holiday.

How can I describe her? The spoonful of yeast that you add to the brew to set it fermenting? The life and soul of the party? Something along those lines – and everything that we wanted. She was gay and attractive, the sort of mother you mistake for her daughter's elder sister, the sort of grandmother that surely nobody ever had, so full of apparent health and vitality that you would never believe she was one of her doctor's more worrying patients. She never walked where she could run, never smiled where she could laugh, and her most confidential whisper could be heard half way down the road. Is it to be wondered that someone who moved twice as fast as the average person would on occasion take a flight of stairs head first, sit on chairs that weren't there or fall like a stage comedian into buckets of whitewash. Over the years she had wisely taught herself to fall gracefully and without damage, and this – thank goodness – she was nearly always able to do, so that spectators could join in her laughter, not fear for her safety. On one occasion she got stuck in the cupboard where we keep our stationery. It was a large and rather inaccessible cupboard on the stairs and she had climbed into it to reach for something at the back, and there she remained in mid air, hands clinging, legs waving, until her embarrassed cries for help brought someone to her rescue.

Naturally enough a person so individual and unusual had her own peculiar way of doing things her own techniques, indeed her own language – which was perhaps not too easy to explain to others who needed to know. 'This is the "Arabia" Book. We call it that because I sent a copy to Arabia once by mistake.' Or: 'I think there might be a copy in the "weagle"'[1] Joyce's tongue went as fast as her legs, and it too sometimes fell over itself and the most extraordinary things came out, some of them too good to lose.

So you couldn't really feel solemn or sad in her company. Or could you? Well, perhaps you could. It depended on whether you were just mildly out of sorts or whether it was something more serious.

The assistant gives her friendly smile. 'Good morning. Can I help you?' What a nice shop! What a happy atmosphere! So it may seem to the visiting customer. Yet how much may be hidden behind a smile. How many resentments, jealousies, fears, unhappinesses, domestic problems. ... If I was never aware of them all it was only because Joyce kept some to herself. For they all came to her: she was that sort of person, the sort you pour out your troubles to. I suspect that most were intended for onwards transmission,

[1] A copy where? In the window. A copy of *Darwin and the 'Beagle,'* of course.

but this was never made clear and she would have fearful battles with her conscience: should she tell me or should she not? Usually, I think, she did, for she was not good at keeping things to herself; and I was always glad when she did, and she was greatly relieved when she had.

Staff problems. Oh, yes, there have been plenty over the years, some so small you might be inclined to laugh at them, some so large you could cry. And for fifteen years Joyce was there to help us cope with them. She retired a year ago to get things ready for her husband who retires this year. It was, I suppose, as good a time to leave as any. Though there was still plenty for her to do, there were moments when she could pause and wonder what to do next. The schools that had brought her to the bookshop and kept her so busy with their daily orders and daily telephone calls had now all left us. The last to go had sent us a letter. It was addressed to me but it really belonged to her and so I readdressed it and pasted it onto a card and hung it above her desk. Perhaps now she has gone I ought to take it away, for it is quite hard enough to follow someone so good without having this perpetual reminder of just how good she was. . . .

Now and again – inevitably, I suppose – Lesley and I find ourselves thinking back nostalgically to the days when the shop was just the two of us. What fun it had been! Today it is so different. I am here and she is there; much of our time is spent doing dull things in offices and often we hardly seem to meet. How much pleasanter it was when we were both together downstairs helped only by Hodge.

True, but then what a lot of people we would never have known. They all added something to the shop, helped to make it what it is; they all left their mark before they moved on – to get married or have children or seek their fortunes elsewhere. Tessa and Sarah and Ursula and Janet and Jennie and Nick and innumerable part-timers and summer helps: thank you all for coming. We couldn't really have done without you.

Interlude. *Clare*

The one question we always used to dread – the obvious question to ask of someone in their thirties to whom you have only just been introduced – was 'And do you have any children?' And I became adept at steering the conversation on to safer ground. Today, older, less sensitive, I find it better to make the matter quite plain from the start: it saves later embarrassment. 'Yes, a daughter. She's spastic.' There follows, of course, a momentary pause; then 'Oh. . . . I'm sorry to hear that.' And then, after a few more words, we move to another subject.

Hope is like a life belt: it buoys you up and may keep you afloat until you are rescued; but if it fails you and you are forced to abandon it, you sink. So it is better if you are able to swim without it. In other words it is better if you can accept things as they are rather than live in hope that they will improve.

Once we had accepted Clare's disability and its effect on us all, there were plenty of other things we could be happy about, plenty to enjoy, plenty to be grateful for. And at the top of the list was her own very evident zest for life, her high spirits, her sense of fun, her cheerful acceptance of all she couldn't do, her delight in what little she could. She set us an example and taught us a philosophy that parents don't usually expect to learn from their children.

We tend to think that, if someone is deprived of a blessing that we ourselves possess, their life is the sadder. This is particularly so in today's Age of Equality when we are made to feel almost guilty at having what others do not have. But in fact the man who has less than his neighbour is only unhappy if he had been hoping for more and chooses to feel jealous.

Is it sad that there is so little that Clare can do? Not necessarily. There are plenty of things that even the most agile person cannot do. Happiness is not measured by agility. Most of what the average person does in his daily life – housework, office work, factory work, commuting – is fairly dull and may well seem almost unbearably dull to others. 'How can you go on day after day?' Yet we can. Much of our pleasure comes not from doing but from watching. Only twenty two men actually play football, but thousands watch – with almost equal enjoyment. So it is with Clare. She doesn't do any gardening in the accepted sense, but if Lesley is digging among her vegetables and she is watching, then she is 'helping with the gardening'. 'Helping'? Of course. It is after all the word the French use. '*Assister*' includes being a spectator.

I suppose that if Lesley or I had been ambitious, pursuing our chosen career with single-minded determination, we might have felt that we didn't want to be burdened with the various domestic tasks that needed to be done. We might have preferred others to do them for us. This, after all, was the way our parents and grandparents had ordered their lives. The Master worked, the Mistress supervised and a team of retainers scrubbed and cooked and mowed and stoked the boilers. And although it is not like this today, something of the tradition still lingers here and there. But Lesley and I have never wanted it this way. It is not that she likes housework but rather that she dislikes even more the idea of someone coming in and doing it for her. So most of what has needed to be done we have done ourselves and only reluctantly have we asked for help. We have needed help in the bookshop and Lesley had a little help with Clare when she was a baby. And if a fairly large building job has been necessary, we have called in builders to do it. But it is really much pleasanter, much more satisfying, if you can manage on your own. In our parents' day it was, in any case, economically sensible for the specialist to specialise. Today it is not even that.

So when the question arose: 'Who is going to look after Clare now she is growing up and cannot look after herself?' the answer was obvious:

'We are.' And if this meant there were other things that in consequence we couldn't do, then we didn't do them.

All children limit the freedom of their parents to some extent. And in fact Clare limited ours less than most. For at the age of five she went to school, and since this had to be a Special School it had also to be a boarding school. Very luckily there was one conveniently close, the Dame Hannah Rogers School at Ivybridge, twenty miles away on the edge of Dartmoor. So our lives fell into that pattern that Lesley and I both knew so well from our own schooldays, the alternation between termtime and holidays with all the misery that attends the approach of the one and all the bliss that heralds the other. For Clare the depths and the heights were probably no less and no more than they had been for us.

With Clare at school Lesley and I were once more free to work together in the shop. And it was a happy chance that the beginning of her schooldays coincided almost exactly with the beginning of our school library business. Lesley was thus able to accompany me on all my more exciting expeditions and make them twice as enjoyable.

During the holidays, however, one of us had to be at home, and we took it in turns, Lesley in the mornings, I in the afternoons. August was our most difficult month, the town and the bookshop crowded with holiday-makers, and even with extra help it was a struggle to do all that had to be done. For in addition to the problem of keeping our shelves adequately stocked, we had to handle the books – hundreds and hundreds of them – that our schools had ordered for delivery at the beginning of September. Checking them, sorting them, finding somewhere to put them, carrying back-breaking parcels up and down our narrow stairs and loading them on to our van – when all this had been done and the holidays were at an end and Clare was back at school – well, at least we could relax.

So, term by term, the years went by; and I have no doubt that our friends, looking at us, now and again shook their heads sadly and said to each other: 'What a pity that ...' and 'If only ...' It is always easy to see and solve the problems of others. 'If I were you . . .' But of course I am not you and this makes all the difference. Could we have done more? Should we have done differently? But we do only what by our nature we are able to do.

As a child I was shy and self conscious, awkward in company and embarrassed both by my name and by my appearance. At school I would often wish I were a John or a Peter and could join all the other lucky Johns and Peters. At school one lives the life of the herd, and in the herd there is no place for the individual who is different. It is the same in the world at large. The black man in the white community, the Catholic in the Protestant community, the Jew among Gentiles: each has known what it is to be an outsider. Each has longed to be accepted as an equal, treated as a fellow human.

Hath not a Jew eyes? hath not a Jew hands, organs, dimensions, senses, affections, passions?

Shylock's famous words have been echoed down the ages – and sadly they are sometimes still echoed by the disabled today.

Of course we are not deliberately cruel to the disabled as we have at times been deliberately cruel to Jews. It is just that we are sometimes thoughtless. Or perhaps instead, and with the best of intentions, we try too hard. The blind man waiting at the kerb does not need to be seized by the arm as if he were also lame. The deaf are not better able to hear the kind of language normally reserved for small children. Walking down the street we do not wave or smile at strangers or accost them and inquire solicitously after their health and then pat them affectionately on the head. Yet complete strangers will do this to Clare.

The disabled person may need special attention, but he doesn't welcome it. He wants to be treated, as far as possible, as if he were ordinary, his differences, as far as possible, ignored. Those who travel in wheel chairs ask only that they can go where the rest of us go, without too much fuss, without too much loss of dignity.

Happily it is not Clare who minds, who is sensitive to how others behave and to what they say. It is I. And how tempting I find it to take the easy way out: to stay at home. It is always pleasant at home and there is plenty to do. There is no need to go out, to push a wheel chair through the streets of Dartmouth and into public places. But luckily Lesley is braver – or more determined or wiser or kinder, or probably all four. It is she who plans the outing, and who then insists that I am not merely the chauffeur but come too. I go reluctantly, making an obvious effort, making my effort all too obvious. But when it is over and we are home again I can admit that I too enjoyed it; and I can feel suitably shamed by two brave girls. Lucky Clare to have such a mother!

But to compensate for what I am bad at – and have after all been bad at all my life – I have a skill which, small and unimportant in the normal way, has with Clare come into its own.

Anyone who was taking door locks to bits at the age of seven to find out how they worked, who at the age of eleven was inventing burglar alarms for a Secret Passage, and who was happily defusing German mines at the age of twenty-three, was obviously the right sort of father to have when Clare, sleeping alone in her bedroom, waking in the morning and unable to get out of bed, needed a word with her parents. An electric bell that she could work and then, to make a voice pipe, a plastic funnel and a length of garden hose.... The amateur inventor, gadget maker and general handyman was in his element.

The chair we sit on, the table we sit at, the knife and fork and plate that we use when we have a meal, all these are designed to fit the average human body and make use of the things that the human body – and in particular the human hand – can do. Thus the hand can grip and move to and fro, and a knife converts this into the cutting up of meat. So if there are certain movements we cannot manage, then certain tools become useless to us and must be redesigned to make use of different movements.

There were very many things that Clare couldn't do. In fact there were very few things she could do. When she was young she could scarcely even sit in a chair. She could certainly not have sat at a table and fed herself with a conventional spoon from a conventional plate. But she could grip and she could manage a sort of circular sweep with her arm. Could the right sort of tool convert this into an ability to collect food from the right sort of plate and then carry it to her mouth? I thought it could, and sat and watched her and then went away to work it out.

The chair, the tray, the plate and the fork that I made for her were all a little unusual. Thus the plate was made from an aluminium saucepan sawn off to leave a rim that was one inch high over three quarters of its circumference and two inches high over the remaining quarter. It fitted into a well in the tray that was one inch deep. Thus there was no fear that the approaching fork might get entangled with the near edge of the plate before it reached the food and pressed it against the far edge. The fork had a wooden head set at an angle into a wooden handle; and fortunately the angle that was best for collecting the food was also the best for delivering it.

It was all a little unusual, but it worked. For the first time in her life Clare was able to feed herself, and this was a very great triumph for her and a very great excitement for us all.

On another occasion, some years later, her school allowed me to take home an old and battered tricycle that no one specially wanted. Could I do something with it? It would need a different seat, one that gave much greater support; it would need different handlebars to give a much simpler method of steering; and it would need different pedals since the only movement Clare could manage was a straightening of both legs at once.

It was enough. And in triumph, when the new term started, she propelled herself down the long corridor and into the school hall to prove it.

But designing something that worked was only half the problem. The other half was to make it look presentable.

It is a sad fact that much of the equipment designed for the disabled is inefficient and nearly all of it is ugly. To some extent the one follows from the other. An efficient design has a natural elegance which needs little embellishment to make it attractive. Whereas the wheel chair issued to Clare was such a mechanical disaster that nothing could have redeemed it. How unfair it is that a person who most needs a chair should so often have just the one

– and one so very far from beautiful – while the rest of us, who need chairs only now and again, possess so many.

Why should Clare not have as many chairs as we have? Why should she not take the pride and pleasure in them that we take in ours? Why should they not be every bit as decorative and pleasing to look at? No reason at all. They couldn't be bought, of course; but they could be made. And so I set to work to make them.

When I first started carpentry lessons at school, the pleasure I got was the pleasure of cutting and shaping the wood. The lines were ruled for me and I sawed along them and chiselled between them. At John Lewis I began to look at furniture rather more critically. Some I liked; some I disliked. But it was not until I was puzzling over Clare's needs that I discovered another pleasure as great as the pleasure of making: the pleasure of designing.

It is in fact two pleasures and they are quite distinct. The first lies in solving the mechanical problem. This is what gives to the things I make for Clare their special fascination: they are all unique. There is no standard pattern to follow as there is if you are making, say, a kitchen table. For example, Lesley might want a device that will hold a mixing bowl and an egg whisk so that Clare can turn the handle and make a cake. Working out the best way to do this is very like working out those mathematical problems that so intrigued me at school. Merely to solve them is not enough: the satisfaction lies in finding the simplest, neatest, most *elegant* solution. The second pleasure lies in taking this, the theoretical design, and giving it a bit of style, giving it shape and proportions that are pleasing to look at.

But of course the greatest pleasure of all was to see Clare sitting comfortably where before she had been uncomfortable, doing something she had not previously been able to do. And it was a pleasant thought that this was, in a sense, a legacy from her grandparents whom she had never known – a product of the fusion of my father's fondness for mathematics with my mother's competent hands. If she had inherited neither, she could at least benefit from the fact that I had inherited both.

The wise man lives in the present. Where the future is certain he may make preparations; where it is uncertain he may take precautions. But beyond that he had best forget it. While Clare was at school our lives settled into their pattern. She was at school for twelve years, and for those twelve years there was no virtue in bothering ourselves with the question of what we were all going to do when she left. The question could wait. And its answer must wait now.

Lesley and I were booksellers, but though bookselling dominated it never monopolized our lives – nor should it monopolize these pages. When people come to see me – people who have not been here before – we usually arrange to meet at the shop. It is an easy place to find and I am usually there and so it seems the logical starting point for whatever is to follow. They come in and look around and then after a moment or two we go upstairs and find a room where we can sit and talk without being disturbed. Then, if they are not in a hurry to be on their way, I like it if we can spend a few minutes looking at Dartmouth. Lesley and I are proud of the bookshop because we made it ourselves. In a rather different way we are also proud of Dartmouth, proud to feel that we belong here, and so we like showing it off to those who do not know it.

So enough for the moment about Clare, and enough for the moment about bookselling. It is time for the conducted tour.

PART THREE

The Road less Travelled by

1. *Town Life*

There are four ways into Dartmouth. On my first visit, in 1951, I had come from the east. This is the usual direction for visitors from up-country, and whether they travel by car or bus or train their first view of the town will be from the other side of the Dart, the final lap of their journey will be made on the ferry. Lesley, on her first visit, before the war, had come in her father's boat, and her approach had been from the south, by sea, through the narrow river mouth guarded by its two castles and then up the river to look for an anchorage. Or you can approach from the north, coming down the river from Totnes. Your first view of the town may be less dramatic but this you can forgive after so magical a voyage. Lastly – in one sense the least and in another the most important of the four – you can come by road from the west.

Here you will have a choice. You will have been travelling along a ridge five hundred feet above sea level. Half a mile from the river the ridge comes to an end, the town lies beneath you and six roads lead down to it. And in these six roads much of our history can be read.

The approach to Dartmouth from overland with its final precipitous dive has always been a problem. For what was good enough for foot and hoof was not good enough – for pneumatic tyre and what was good enough for our grandfathers was not good enough for us. And so, as our means of locomotion demanded it and as our engineering techniques allowed it, new routes were found, new roads built. Thus you can date the six roads into Dartmouth by their steepness and their width.

Having made your choice, what will you find when you reach

the bottom? First and most important, you will find that you have arrived. This is not by any means true of towns generally. Most towns are not for arriving at but for passing through on the way to somewhere else; but Dartmouth is not on anybody's way to anywhere. So, having arrived, you will be ready with your first question. 'Which is the main street?' The answer is: 'The river.'

One may hesitate to call it a street but it is certainly the town's main thoroughfare, the means of communication with the rest of the world which decided the earliest settlers that here was the place to build. Take away the river and no town would ever have sprung up for so little a reason on so inaccessible a site. So the town was built on the river and the roads were added afterwards. The river remains what it has always been, Dartmouth's High Street, the only way into the town from the north and from the south, wide enough and deep enough for its purpose in medieval times, still wide enough and deep enough today. Its purposes may have changed over the years; today it carries holiday-makers rather than trade, and in some ways it is more of a barrier than a thoroughfare, discouraging communication with Torbay. But for all that it is still both our High Street and the centre of our activity, the stage where the drama of the town is performed. And what more perfect stage could there be than this deep and wide anchorage right in front of the town, its narrow entrance, guarded by Dartmouth Castle, less than a mile away. And what more perfect seating arrangements for the spectators than a steep hillside allowing each row of houses to peer over the roof tops of those below so that all can see and each has its own most prized and cherished view. What do you do when you arrive in Dartmouth? You go down to the river to see what's happening. Then, having spent an hour or so in contemplation, you are ready with your next question. 'Where is the shopping centre?'

There isn't one.

Most towns have two things; first, a historic centre, the place that decided that the town was to be here rather than there, and secondly a way of reaching it, the High Street. I have already explained why Dartmouth has always had trouble with its overland

High Streets, periodically finding them too steep and too narrow and so having to try again. It has also had trouble with its centre. To build a town centre you need an adequate area that is both firm and level. Here, on the steep banks of the Dart, what was firm had a slope of one in two and what was level was mud, and only the narrow strip of land between was suitable for houses. So Dartmouth started life strung out in a line, its back to the hills, its toes in the water. Indeed it was so extended as to be two separate settlements divided by a tidal creek: Hardness to the north of the creek, Clifton Dartmouth to the south. And it was not until the nineteenth century that this creek was filled in, the river bank was pushed forward and a sufficient area of land, level and tolerably firm, was reclaimed to provide the town with the centre it lacked. And if it never quite succeeded, having left it too late, it did at least unite the two halves.

Today there can be no doubt that we are a single town. But we still like to recall the past; and so each year at the Mayor's Banquet we pass round the Loving Cup and, taking it in turns to sip the cider, we drink a toast to 'The Unity and Prosperity of the Borough of Clifton Dartmouth Hardness.'

For five years Lesley and I lived over the shop and stared at the river. Now and again destroyers would come in and moor just opposite us, wedging themselves in the gap at the end of our road. Once a school of porpoises came surging up the river. Once, very late at night, we saw a family of otters. Then when Clare came to join us we moved to a house on the edge of the town.

On the edge of the town? Here again Dartmouth is not quite like other towns. It hasn't really got an edge – at least not the usual sort. Most towns grow outwards from the centre, adding a succession of annual rings rather as a tree does. But though Dartmouth eventually got the better of its mud, it has never got the better of its hills, and so when it had taken possession of all it could at the bottom, it jumped to the top where the ground was once again level enough, and built there. And in between, still grazed by cows, the grassy hillside remained. So when I say that our house was on the edge of the town what I mean is that below us were houses and above us the cows leaned over our wall and nibbled the tops of our pear trees. But if you climbed the wall and threaded your way past the cows you came to Townstal – and then you were back in the town again.

We lived here for ten years and though we eventually bought a van we always walked to work – down and up twice a day, for we liked having lunch at home. It was not a long walk. Measured horizontally it was only half a mile. Measured vertically it was 250 feet. And the route we took, from edge to centre, must surely have been one of the most beautiful walks from edge to centre of any town. I knew this at once, but it took me four years to discover exactly why.

You look at a town and you say 'Isn't it pretty!' You say this as soon as you see it. Lesley and I said it when first we came to Dartmouth. Almost every first-time visitor says it. But if you come to stay, then, after a while, when the first fierce flames of passion have died, you find that you marvel each day a little less – until suddenly something happens to jerk you awake. . . .

With us it was the wall at Warfleet. We had not been that way for some time and so it came as a complete surprise, the widened road, the new retaining wall, twenty feet high, with its smooth, grey, cement-rendered finish, topped with huge rectangular castellations. It could have been a prison wall it looked so stern and forbidding. Dartmouth is a town of walls, it is true, but they are warm and friendly, built – and most beautifully built – of natural stone. And there had been a natural stone wall here at Warfleet before they pulled it down and replaced it with this. We felt a surge of anger. What could we do? What powers have ordinary citizens to prevent their local council from mutilating their town? There must be an answer. Who would know it? At that time Ian Nairn was editing a column in *The Observer* called 'Outrage'. Well, here was an outrage, and I wrote to tell him so.

Our reply came not from him but from an organization then unknown to us called the Civic Trust and it urged us to form an Amenity Society – an obvious enough answer today of course, but less obvious in 1961. This we did and we called it the Dartmouth and Kingswear Society, and at various times I have been its Chairman and Lesley its Secretary. For convenience the Harbour Bookshop has always been its address and this perhaps helps to explain why over the years the bookshop has provided a quite disproportionate number of officers and committee members. I like to think that in our first sixteen years we have done a lot for the town. I like to think that in the first six years (when Lesley and I were most active) we did particularly well, though perhaps there may be Town Councillors who would have reservations about this. One thing, however, is certain: the Society did an enormous lot for me. It gave me a whole new field to explore.

You look at a town and you say 'Isn't it pretty!' This is your first and, if you are just driving through, maybe your only impression. What a pretty little town that was! But if you live here you will discover that prettiness may be in conflict with other things: with good housing, efficient services, smooth traffic flow and prosperity generally. What most impresses the newcomer comes low on the Council's agenda. Thus you have two opposing points of view, and how easy and tempting it is to ally yourself wholeheartedly and unquestioningly with one side or the other. The banners of each are to hand, ready to be seized and waved aloft. 'Progress and Prosperity' on this side, 'Our National Heritage' on that. Take your choice! No need for further argument! Into battle!

So the Dartmouth and Kingswear Society, born in a passion of anger, drawing the bulk of its membership from those people – elderly, middle-class, non-Devonian – who had come here to retire, could so easily have assembled its armoury of slogans and hurled them at the enemy, could so easily have leapt to the defence of every ancient building and fought every new development. So easily – but, it seemed to me, so fatally.

What was Dartmouth's future? What were we trying to become? That was the question; and as it turned out it was one we had to answer almost at once. The County was on the point of preparing its Development Plan. If we who lived here were to have any say in the future of our town, it would be as well to get our say in first. I wondered if it ought to be a composite opinion that took into account and tried to reconcile all points of view, but decided that this would be too difficult: it was going to be quite hard enough to build a plan around the views of our two hundred members. And in the end six of us got together and three of us did the actual writing. *A Plan for Dartmouth* it was called; and Chapter One, 'General Considerations', was my own, almost unaided, work.

Walking each day to and from the shop gave plenty of time for considering things. And as I walked, so I wondered why I loved that walk so much. I had to analyse the experience. What was it that gave Dartmouth its peculiar charm? And then I had to ask myself: to what extent was this threatened? To what extent should it be protected? I had to decide just what it was possible to do and then produce convincing arguments to show that this was also desirable.

One thing was easy to see. It was the holiday-maker and the retired who were providing and who would continue to provide the bulk of Dartmouth's income; and so it was these two who would determine our future. So the first question the town had to decide was this. Should we follow the lead of Paignton and attempt to accommodate as many holiday-makers in camps and caravans and as many retired in bungalows as we could persuade to come here? Or should we admit that Dartmouth could never compete with Torbay, having no sandy beaches to offer and poor communications with the outside world, and should we instead make the most of our other assets. In other words, were there enough people who came to Dartmouth because it was *not* Torbay to keep us all happy?

My answer was that we should specialize, even though this meant saying 'No' to more caravan sites and bungalows, 'No' to what so many saw as progress and prosperity.

These may not seem particularly revolutionary words today, but I wrote them at the time with considerable nervousness. In those days we talked a lot about progress, and progress in Dartmouth meant supermarkets, not old buildings; it meant expansion, opening our doors to all who knocked, welcoming their money no matter how they wished to spend it and their cars no matter where they wished to drive them.

To some extent this belief still survives. A town, they say, must grow or die. Everything in man's world must grow. Yet nowhere outside his world does this happen. All living creatures, plants and animals alike, reach eventually the particular size that suits them best and there they stop. Of course it is our burning ambition for better and still better, our insatiable appetite for more and yet more that has taken us to the top of the ladder. But now and again it does no harm to look down at the others and see how they manage their affairs. We may be different from them. But are we so very different?

So it seemed to me then and still seems to me now that life without growth ought to be possible, and that it was not necessarily condemning the town to death to say that Dartmouth should get no bigger.

These then were the first of my 'General Considerations'. I had tried to show that, like the pretty maid in the nursery rhyme, our face was our fortune and so was worth a little trouble. The next thing to consider was the question: 'What makes us so pretty?'

Of course the answers come tumbling out. Our setting, with the river in front and the hills rising behind. Our old buildings. Our quaint streets. True enough – but less true than one might suppose. 'What is there to see in Dartmouth?' the visitor asks us; and we list our show-pieces, the buildings that get into guide books. The Butterwalk (restored in 1954, despite those who would have preferred a supermarket), Bayard's Cove, St Saviour's Church, the medieval houses at the back of the Harbour Bookshop: there really weren't very many. I passed most of them on my daily walk – and scarcely bothered to glance at them. It wasn't until I was at the far end of Foss Street, just coming to the foot of Brown's Hill, that the magic of Dartmouth gripped me; and here the houses were neither old nor beautiful, just pleasant and ordinary. Round the corner where the steps began they weren't even that. Looked at dispassionately they were quite remarkably ugly. Yet the magic remained. Half way up the steps there were no buildings at all, only walls – and still the magic was there. And so it continued – to the top of the steps, into Clarence Hill, past the old Grammar School, past the Keep, to Mount Boone. Houses, some quite attractive but mostly not; walls topped with tufts of valerian; here a magnolia tree; there a rhododendron. And all around the strong, pure essence of Dartmouth. What was it?

I found the answer in the end, and I wish I could say that I found it on my own, for this is the way to make real discoveries. But at least I can say that on my own I found the man who told me. He was Gordon Cullen and he had written a book called *Townscape*.

What makes a town? A town being a collection of buildings, presumably buildings make a town, and fine buildings will make a fine town. So one might think, but – and this was Cullen's argument – a town is more than just the sum of its buildings. It is also their arrangement. It is not just architecture. It is also townscape. Stop and stare up at a building, study its design, and it will arouse a certain emotion. Stand in a street and look around you and this will arouse a totally different emotion. The units of which a town is composed are not houses but streets – or rather those portions of street that you can see at any one moment. So a town is a succession of street scenes, each scene enclosing you in its own small world and telling you that at the end of that world, where the street bends out of sight is a new world waiting to be discovered. So, as you walk through a town, you inhabit a succession of street worlds, and although the architecture of the buildings on either side is important, it is only one of the many components of that world – just as the design of the wallpaper is only one of the components of a fully furnished room. Other things matter: the pavements and the road surface, for instance. You notice these every bit as much as you notice the walls of the houses. Also the shop windows and the street signs. And not only what you might call the fixtures and fittings but also the things that come and go: the motor cars, whether grinding their way down the middle of the road or parked all along one side; yes, even one's fellow pedestrians – for you cannot separate a town from its inhabitants.

All these things added together make one feel the way one does about a place, made me feel as I did about Dartmouth. It was townscape, then, not just its architecture, not just its age, that gave Dartmouth its peculiar charm. Or as I put it in my General Considerations: 'the charm of small scale, compactness, giving the pedestrian a very strong sense of being *in* the town. To the left and right he can almost touch it. In front and behind he can throw a stone and hit it.'

Whether or not this came as a revelation to any of those who later read it, I don't know: but it certainly came as a revelation to me. Dartmouth is a 'historic town', and ever since we came here I have tried to become interested in its history. Chaucer's 'shipman', John Davis and Sir Humphrey Gilbert, the voyage of the *Mayflower*, the battles of the Civil War, Thomas Newcomen and his famous engine: there were plenty of good names and I could list most of them. But they have never been more than just a list of names to me; they have never stirred my blood as I felt they should. Nor has architecture. Rood screens and plaster ceilings, monumental brasses and Norman fonts: these too I can list, and I am glad we have them; but I leave them to others to enjoy. Lesley is the same. I at least have been inside Dartmouth Castle (once, when I took an American visitor to see it). She never has. Abroad we are no better. What most excites the writers of guide books leaves us cold. In Italy we skip the churches and the art galleries and linger instead in the little alleyways. We hurry away from Rome, not even sparing it a glance. Our destination is Tagliacozzo.

Art, architecture and history: Italy overflows with all three, and each year pilgrims flock there in their millions, heading for the art galleries, the cathedrals and the ruins, there to pay homage to the past. But the past is dead, and for me neither the picture on the wall nor the stone on the ground nor the paragraph in the book is enough to bring it alive. Life – whether real or imagined – is movement, purpose, things happening, a sense of the passage of time, hearts beating, blood flowing – something no guide book or conducted tour can provide. But even if I wanted to listen, even if I tried to be interested, in Italy there are too many distractions. The living present swamps the dead past. From the very moment we arrive, the pulsing, bustling, dramatic present seizes us, makes us a part of it and swirls us along with it. Even when we are no more than spectators, sitting at a café table sipping Campari and watching the world go by, we are part of that world; we are on the stage with the actors.

Do towns make people or people towns? Does their natural stage make them natural actors? Or did their sense of the dramatic inspire even the stone-mason and the road-maker? Whichever came first, we have found in almost every Italian town we have visited a combination of stage, scenery and cast that has provided us with non-stop drama so intensely absorbing and exciting that our guide book, if indeed we had ever bothered to buy one – has remained unopened. It is to seek this that we make our annual pilgrimage. Not art, not architecture, not history – and yet in a way a blend of all three, brought up to date and spiced with everyday life.

This, I think, is what Gorden Cullen meant by 'townscape'. It is certainly what townscape means to me.

Having made my discovery I continued to explore; having found one book I looked for others. There were very few. For the curious thing about townscape is that it is almost entirely a natural and unconscious art, not one that has been studied and taught. Where in the past towns have been planned, the aim has been to achieve something quite different: order, symmetry, straight lines, imposing avenues, the majestic. The picturesque jumble, really so much pleasanter, was, it seemed, something that just happened. Was it by chance or instinct? Why were the Italians – and Dartmothians – so particularly good at it? And why are we so bad at it today? The answer surely is to be found beneath our feet. If you build on a plain and the ground is firm you can put your houses where you like; but if you build on a hill with no more than hand tools to shape and level with you must use your land as economically as possible. Your streets will be narrow and they will wind with the contours. The shape of the hill determines the shape of the town:

the town is the product of its hill. In Italy you can sense this even from a distance. The distant town is not something alien placed on its hilltop by man. It is as if the hill at its summit has broken into flower and the town – after how many million years of gestation? – has been thrust up from within. And of course in a sense this is true: for the stones of the houses came from beneath the ground, and all man has done is collect and reassemble them.

This is why twentieth century man fails. He is too ambitious. He tries to do too much. He disregards the site. He brings in mechanical equipment and cuts through the earth and shapes the rock to his requirements. No need for economy now. Roads can be wide and straight – and dead. It is often said of architecture that good design is good manners – that a well-designed building will respect its neighbours. One might say of good townscape that it too is good manners, that a well-designed town will respect its site and will adapt what it builds to where it builds it – not the other way round.

So although it is the builders of the past whom we must thank for the pleasures of good townscape in general and for the charm of Dartmouth in particular, the builders of today could continue the tradition if we wanted them to. It is not the mellowing of centuries that is needed, not skill or money beyond our means, just the will to do it. And our only excuse for not doing it is that we are twentieth century man and our bulldozers and motor cars won't let us.

In July, 1963, our *Plan for Dartmouth* was published. It was, I think, a good plan and on the whole it was well received. But never mind that. This is not the story of a town or of a Society. It is the story of an individual, and a catalogue of activities and achievements is here out of place. The important thing is not what the Society did for Dartmouth but what together they did for me.

For six years I championed the Dartmouth of my dreams, waving my standard aloft, rallying others to the cause, plotting campaigns, battling against the enemy. They were glorious years and I loved them. 'Towns,' I cried, 'are for living in, not for driving through. Towns are for people.'

These six years were almost exactly concurrent with the years when our school library activity was at its height, so that I was simultaneously the champion of two causes, preaching at one moment the gospel of the New Education and at the next the gospel of the Civic Trust.

It was, I suppose, just chance that these two movements arrived in Devon at about the same time, but it was a happy chance for me; for I was, I now suspect, looking for a cause to champion, looking for a chance to speak.

'Looking' is perhaps too strong a word; for there was nothing conscious or deliberate about it. And it is only in retrospect that I can guess at the possible subconscious need that steered me in this direction. It was, in fact, two needs.

The first and most obvious one was to fill the vast hole left when Clare went away to school. The second was to find a use for my newly found self confidence and in particular for my newly found voice.

Whether what had happened within me was just a much delayed step in the slow process of growing up or whether it was caused by some event in my life – Clare's birth or my father's death, for instance – I don't know. But the effect was as if a gate had been opened and all Grandfather Milne's pent up love of teaching was surging through it on to a tongue free at last of its shackles and now able to cope with it. I might still not have achieved that *disinvoltura* that Hedda had wished to cultivate, but at least I could speak in public without stammering.

So for six years I harangued at my two pulpits; then at both fell silent. Why was this? With the New Education the reason was clear: the cause was failing. But the Amenity Society movement was not failing. Indeed it was gathering strength. Why then did I not redouble my efforts, having only the one battle to fight?

If I attempt an answer to this question it is not only to explain what happened in the late sixties but to point the way to what –

of far greater importance – was going to happen in the middle seventies.

A handful of words stick in my memory. They are from the Prayer attributed to Sir Francis Drake before his attack on Cadiz in 1587, and I heard them in the chapel at the Royal Naval College in 1951 when they were the text for a sermon.

It is not the beginning [of an enterprise] but the continuing of the same until it be thoroughly finished which yieldeth the true glory. . . .

Yes, this is true and I have always held it so. Well begun is nowhere near half done. Anyone can be an enthusiast for half an hour. Real enthusiasm is like a well constructed bonfire, not flaring up and dying out and then having to be coaxed back to life, but burning strong and steady until all is consumed.

Yet all the same one can perhaps draw a distinction between the enterprise itself and an individual's contribution to it: the two need not run concurrently. We have our entrances and our exits, and if it is wrong to go too soon, it can sometimes be worse to stay too long.

It was like this in Italy. When we landed in 1943 I was an enthusiastic Sapper officer eager for a front seat in the coming battles. My enthusiasm lasted until I was wounded just over a year later, then it burned out. This was partly loss of nerve, I admit, but not wholly. When I returned to my Company the battle was still on but things were different – different faces, different atmosphere. I didn't want to go back to my Platoon, much as I had loved it. I had finished with being a Platoon Commander. I had finished with the Company too. I had done what I had set out to do. I had proved what I had wanted to prove. It was time to go, and I was glad to accept a more peaceful and less arduous role in another Company.

It was like this now. The best of our battles, so it seemed to me, had been fought and the greatest of our victories won. Perhaps I didn't want to go on saying the same thing over and over again.

Perhaps I didn't want to listen to others saying the same thing over and over again. Whatever it was, my particular task, I felt, was finished. Once more it was time to go.

I am still a member of the Society I founded but I am now only a spectator. It was no bloody head that took me out of the battle. It was simply that we moved from our house on the edge of Dartmouth to another, four miles away. And when we stopped being town-dwellers to become country-dwellers it was perhaps natural that I should transfer my affections from townscape to landscape.

2. Country Life

For ten years we lived in a house on the edge of the town. Then, quite suddenly, one evening, we decided to go.

But before I say why we left, I must say why we came.

The house had everything we were looking for. It was within pleasant walking distance of the bookshop (for in those days we had no car), yet at the same time it was virtually in open country. It was away from the main road, approached by a narrow, rural lane, and it faced the sun. It was however a house that had come down in the world. Its roof had gone, its floors were rotting away and it was inhabited only by chickens. All it had to offer now were four thick stone walls. But this was all we needed, for it gave us the added pleasure of doing our own restoration. It had been built as the coach house for the big house below it. The coach and horse had lived on the ground floor; the coachman and his family had occupied the floor above. But the last coachman and the last horse had long since departed and all they had left behind them to record their existence were the horse's manger and the house's name. We kept the one – though it served no particular purpose – but we changed the other. Swinnerton Lodge Coach House: after all it was not so much a name as a description, and one that was bound to lead to confusion with Swinnerton Lodge itself. So we changed it to Spriggs Holly, after the little hamlet in the Chilterns where we had got engaged.

In later years, when people asked 'And did you do it all yourselves?' I was never immediately sure if they meant did we mix our own cement and hammer in our own nails, or did we merely make plans and elevations and lists of specifications, leaving the mixing and hammering to others. In fact we did neither. Both were totally beyond the capabilities of a working bookseller and a nursing mother. We called in an architect and he fixed the builder. But we did from time to time say 'Yes, that's how we would like it', and to that extent it was our own work. And when it was sufficiently nearly finished to be habitable, and when what remained to be done could be done at leisure by two amateurs when the rest of the day's work was over, the three of us moved in. And then we could start work on something else as well, on what it was that had really decided us to buy a derelict coach house: its garden.

It was a walled garden growing vegetables and fruit. If the house had decayed, the garden certainly had not, and apples, pears, plums, currants and gooseberries were all in good working order. It lay beside the house, long and thin, running parallel with the lane, parallel with the contours of the hill. The hillside here was steep, and the garden had been terraced into it to reduce the slope. So at the bottom it was six feet above the lane and at the top six feet below a field. The two retaining walls, their job done, were continued upwards a further couple of feet, thus preventing those above from tumbling down on to those below. Hence the field was hidden from the garden and we were reminded of it only when cows came down to peer over the wall and perhaps experiment with a mouthful of newly-planted pear tree. But we could see it from our bedroom window, stretching away to a line of elms, curving upwards until it curved out of sight. It was a view I specially loved, and I would stand at the window every morning, looking out, absorbing it all. It was a beautiful field, so close that I almost felt we owned it. Sometimes we would put a ladder against the wall and then we could climb up and walk in it or sit on its grass. At the near end was a cluster of hazels, and on a summer's evening we could often hear hedgehogs rustling and snuffling among them. And on hot days the cows would come and stand beneath their shade.

Here we lived for nine happy years, proud of our house and our garden, slowly improving both. The garden needed a lot of work, for we wanted flowers and lawns as well as fruit and vegetables; and so the slope had to be terraced into level areas supported by dry-stone walls. Luckily there were plenty of stones from the old house left behind by the builders, but rather less helpfully they had also left behind a lot of rubble which they had spread in a layer about a foot thick over most of the ground I intended to use. So after I had collected the stones that were worth saving I then had to move the rubble, rescue the topsoil, reshape the subsoil, build my wall, bury the rubble behind it and replace the topsoil: it was a complicated business.

Walls, steps and paths: this was my work, and so too were the lawns and fruit trees. The vegetables and soft fruit were Lesley's, and together we shared the flowers. It was a garden in which almost everything succeeded. If anybody gave us a root or a cutting, the fear was not that it would fail but that it would rampage and swamp everything else. The merest flake of snow-on-the-mountain quickly became a blizzard that threatened to engulf the entire rock garden. A sucker of jasmine planted alongside the kitchen, soon blocked up two windows and a door so that they couldn't be opened, and had to be forcibly restrained from lifting off the roof. How we cursed – but later blessed – its vigour.

I still pay an annual visit to Spriggs Holly. Each year on Christmas Eve Clare and I call on a friend who lives nearby. And I take the opportunity to open the garden gate (still fastened with the wooden latch I made for it) and climb the steps (still unfinished) and stand on the lawn (with its great hollow tree stump that we found washed ashore on a distant beach and towed home behind our dinghy). It is quite dark, of course, and I cannot see the details, but I know that it is much the same as when we left it, and I can see why we loved it so, and I can see, even in the darkness, why in the end we went.

The news that our field had been sold to a developer didn't immediately fill us with alarm. It was a large field, steep at the bottom levelling off at the top. It was at the top, below Townstal Church, that they would be building – well out of sight.

Of course we could have found out. But what good would it have done us? Literally and metaphorically we refused to look at what we dreaded to see, and we continued to enjoy our last few months of peace.

The truth came slowly. First it was no more than the distant hum of a bulldozer at work. . . . Then its appearance over the brow of the hill. Then the first row of houses, still comfortingly far away. . . . Then the bulldozer at work again below the houses, its grinding and straining louder now as it wrenched at the hillside and as penetrating as a dentist's drill on an exposed nerve. . . . Then another row of houses. . . . And still the bulldozer getting nearer. . . .

One day a man came and cut the brambles at the back of our wall, tearing away the fragile screen we had been hiding behind. Then at last we could see. We could no longer pretend. We knew.

Like the pathetic remnants of a defeated army we made a few futile attempts to stem the advance, but they were brushed aside; we offered terms, but they were treated with scorn. So we nailed a screen to the top of our wall. It was hideous and one night a gale blew half of it crashing down. And we took the jasmine away from the kitchen and drove in posts and spread it along them, as a man will spread his remaining hairs to hide his baldness; and we blessed its length and vigour as we crouched behind it.

Once it had been cows, and we had loved them. Now it was people, and we hated them. No one who has not had such an experience will know the strength of our feelings; anyone who has will understand. Shortly before we left I stood at the bedroom window, a thing I had not done for many months, and I took a photograph. It showed a wall, a screen and four houses. Because our garden was long and narrow, four plots came down to our wall, four houses surveyed us from above, four families sitting on their balconies had a bird's eye view. The very steepness of our hillside, which once we had relied upon to halt the advancing estate, now added to its horror. For each house, as if to see the better, was perched on a brick base, a white bungalow on a brown pedestal, a tooth from which the gum had shrivelled to expose its root. A row of witch's teeth. . . . Or was it perhaps a battery of television cameras?. . . .

Suddenly unable to bear it any longer, we fled.

Embridge Forge, like Spriggs Holly, had been built to serve the needs of the horse, and with the horse's departure its fortunes too had declined. However, since the cart-horse had survived the coach-horse by some twenty to thirty years this decline had here come much more recently. The last blacksmith was still very much alive and Lesley and I might well have seen him at work. By 1966 however, though the house where he had lived was still habitable, the forge itself was dead and decaying and an air of sadness hung over the place.

Embridge was like Spriggs Holly in other ways. It was built into the hillside – built properly, of course, not perched uneasily on a pedestal – built as if it belonged. And as at Spriggs Holly there was much altering, adding and repairing to be done, and it wasn't until some six months after we had bought it that we were at last able to move in.

Oh the solitariness of it! Once again there was a great hill rising above us. Once again we were overlooked only by cows. Once again in the early morning I could stand at our bedroom window and enjoy it all. Late evening, just as it was getting dark, was another of my favourite times, and I would go outside and watch the darkness come. I suppose it was because in the past, if we had spent a day in the country, the approach of darkness marked the time when we had to think about going home. Now it was others who would be going home. We would be staying. A blackbird, disturbed, flew along the hedge uttering its evening cry. A wren gave a last defiant trill, then slipped from the pear tree to its roost under the eaves. Only those of us who lived here were here now. . . . the blackbird and the wren. . . . It was our valley.

It was our valley: this sums up my feelings. It belonged to me and I belonged to it. I needed to establish my ownership, to make my mark, to rebuild Embridge; but equally I needed to feel the valley's dominance over my life. I wanted to be both benevolent lord and loyal subject, to rule and be ruled. I suspect that in each of us there are these dual feelings, an urge to create and an urge to conform, and that the point of balance between the two determines our lives. If instead of Embridge I had been offered a level plot of land and told that I could build whatever sort of house I wanted and have flower beds and lawns and paths wherever I wished, I would have hated it. I would have felt lost, the freedom too great. And I would have hated it no less if I had been offered house and garden ready-made to my taste with nothing to do but enjoy them. I needed to build but I needed the four stone walls of an old coach house as a starting point. I needed the slopes and trees to direct and give purpose to my paths. I needed the old to govern the new. Not only does this set a much more interesting problem, but somehow it seems the proper thing to do, to fit the new to the old, to respect, not to ignore, the past.

At Embridge there was a lot of past to respect. The hills had been there for a million years; the house and the oak trees for a hundred or more; the apple trees for perhaps fifty. And around the place still hung the memory of the days when saw and hammer and working men's voices could be heard. In the forge I found the old bellows. They were vast and so heavy I could scarcely drag them. The ironwork was all rusted away, the leather was black and stiff, the wood dented and stained and charred. What should we do with them? No one would ever want them as bellows again. Should we restore them? But for what purpose? Or just keep them? But where put them? or make them into something else? But into what? Or sell them? For shame! Or throw them away? But how could we when there was so much in them that was still good. I don't like a house to be a museum where things are kept for what they once were. I like my house to live in the present, and it was hard to see what use we could find in our new house for an old, broken down pair of bellows. Oh sadly familiar problem: what use are the elderly when their working days are over? For ten years they waited for an answer.

Everywhere at Embridge there is this problem. What once served a small farming community serves now only the needs of leisure. Should the tools of the past be left to rot? Should the millwheel down the valley have been left undisturbed under its canopy of brambles? Or was it better that it became a rich man's diversion to restore it and set it spinning again but spinning idly with no millstone to turn, no corn to grind? I don't know. Both seem wrong, the one sad, the other a little undignified. It is a feeling that has two separate origins: nostalgia for the past and reverence for work. The one is something that afflicts the middle-aged, the other the self-employed. Put them together and a middle-aged, self-employed man will obviously consider his valley's working past greatly superior to its leisured present. What can he do about it? Not much. Lesley is toiling away in her vegetable garden, doing things to tomatoes and runner beans. 'Who dares stand idle in the harvest field?' as I used to sing in the chapel at Stowe. Not she, evidently. Nor I, come to that. So I take my scythe – what more appropriate tool? – and climb the hill.

It is mid-August and nettles and bracken are at their height, brambles have sent out their annual tentacles of new growth, and the tall grasses have bowed their heads to the wind. Altogether there is a wildly exuberant tangle of vegetation up here that only Devon can produce. It will be good when it is all cleared away and I can once again admire the trees I planted last winter. But it is slow work, and when the sun is shining it is wearyingly hot and the flies are a curse. Yet I enjoy it. Lesley thinks it is a bit unproductive, that there are more useful things I might be doing and that it's time I found a man or a machine to lend me a hand. I did try a machine once, but it was unmanageable on our steep slope. To my delight the old fashioned scythe is still the most efficient and much the pleasantest tool to use. And as for a man: no, I'd rather be on my own.

If one makes this distinction between work and idleness, should one continue it to work that is 'useful' and work that is not, contrasting Lesley's plate of beans with my pile of grass? Perhaps one should, but happily I don't. If I can look at what I have done and say 'That looks good,' or 'That looks better,' this is enough. Good for what or good for whom are not questions I bother about.

At Embridge as at Spriggs Holly we have both a vegetable and a flower garden, the one already in existence when we arrived, the other needing to be designed and made. At Embridge we have something else as well, the bit at the top that is wild. So the labour is divided a little differently. Lesley still rules over her vegetables and soft fruit, and I still look after the fruit trees. But she does more and I do less for the flowers and the lawns. And the wilderness is all mine.

You can contrast wild with cultivated, and that is to see it from the point of view of the ground. If you think of it from the point of view of what grows there the contrast is between natives and foreigners, and a garden becomes a place where the natives – impolitely referred to as 'weeds' – have been ruthlessly exterminated to make way for an immigrant population of foreigners that arrive neatly labelled in pots and packets. As time goes by some of these foreigners make it clear that they dislike their new home and hang their heads and look sad. At the same time some of the natives fight to return. So then starts a war that never ends. It is fought initially with conventional weapons – the hoe and the fork – but later, as the battle becomes fiercer, chemical weapons are used, bottles of this and cartons of that. 'You can't win!' says the despairing gardener after an exhausting session with the snails or the hairy bittercress. And this is very true; and it is partly to escape to more peaceful surroundings that I so often retreat to my wilderness.

Up here the philosophy is different. Foreigners are brought in but only on a very limited scale, mostly trees, some being seedlings that I have dug up from elsewhere, others coming from the nurseryman, and all being specimens that will look at home among my native oaks and hazels and will be able to fend for themselves. The natives are mostly allowed to remain though naturally some are given more encouragement than others. Blackthorn and elm suckers are cut down annually. Thistles, docks, ragwort and cocksfoot grass are periodically uprooted; and in August the summer tangle is cleared away. But if anything is determined to stay, I let it and make the best of it; and if anything is unhappy, it goes. I offer water to the thirsty but nothing more.

Summer is the least pleasant season here. There are too many flies. Hemp nettle has monopolized any bare earth it can find. Hogweed towers over me; and the smell of *phallus impudicus* sours the air. So I prefer the bottom where Lesley's snapdragons and marigolds, cosmos and phlox, roses and fuchsias are now at their best. It is in the spring that the top is unrivalled. Daffodils and primroses lead on to violets, bluebells, wild arum, campions, alkanet, pennywort and foxgloves. Each year they come a little differently, now one and now another being particularly prolific. Each year too adds its own speciality: trefoil one year, common vetch another. This year it was corydalis. In the summer scythe and sickle are my tools; in the autumn saw and secateurs to remove unwanted branches; in winter and spring spade and mattock to continue the work of planting and shaping. And of course a lot of time is spent just sitting and dreaming. . . .

Here we are, natives and foreigners, living together happily on a rather steep, rather rocky, rather dry slope. It is by no means a place that would suit everybody, but it suits us. It suits the oaks and hazels that were always here. It suits the spring flowers. It suits the ashes, beeches, rowans, maples, birches and hawthorns that I have planted. And – a foreigner like them – it suits me.

So if I am asked why, it is perhaps only natural that I should give a botanical reason, explaining that Lesley and I were like seeds blown here by chance, landing lucky, finding soil, climate and situation exactly to our liking, putting down our roots and thriving. And if I were then asked for a rather more detailed explanation, I might well, continuing the analogy, see the problem as one of a particular organism in a particular environment – a problem, in other words, in ecology.

That being so, let us start with the environment.

Embridge is three miles from Dartmouth as the crow flies. Surprisingly – for there are scarcely fifty yards of road without a bend – you find on looking at the map that it is very little more as the human walks. Even so this was too far for working booksellers with much to be done in the shop after the doors were shut and much waiting to be done at home. So mostly we drove, and this was four miles, but for good measure it included a view of the sea and of Start Point. It is only now that I am no longer a bookseller that more and more often I find myself doing the journey home on foot. If it takes a little longer and means starting perhaps a little earlier I can reassure myself that it is not only a great deal cheaper but that while I am walking I am indeed working.

Dartmouth, as I have said, is backed by a steep hill. On the other side of this hill is our valley; so my route is up one side, down the other and then along the valley bottom for about a mile. It starts with a long flight of steps. Then comes a road flanked by a terrace of houses. It is steep – one in three – and narrow – eight feet: one of the oldest roads out of the town. At a certain point the houses stop and the hedges start. In an instant you have left the town and are in the country. But the road takes no notice of this: it carries on up the hill as if nothing had happened and thus provides a perfect transition from town to country, as perfect as is the transition from river to town at the Lower Ferry. I wish I could say it was as invulnerable.

Walking home this way not long ago I found myself wondering what were the essential differences between the urban I had just left and the rural I was just entering. I could think of only two: the country was greener and contained fewer people. The difference that perhaps springs to mind, that towns are man-made while country is natural, is of course mistaken. Certain tracts of Devon – much of our coastline and much of Dartmoor – are entirely wild; but what lies in between is no more wild than our garden. For it was man who cleared the primeval forests, man who laid out the fields, surrounding them by hedges and deciding what each was to grow, man who planted copses, windbreaks and woodlands, man who tramped out the tracks he needed and later widened them into roads. The beech avenue that I walk beneath is there because someone put it there. The giant oak by the gate is there because someone allowed it to grow. So if we bless our long-dead builders for their instinct for good townscape, we must also bless our long dead farmers for their instinct for good landscape. Townscape and landscape: the two have a great deal in common; and it is odd that though we in this country have consciously enjoyed, consciously studied and consciously practised the one ever since the eighteenth century, it was not until a few years ago that we even acknowledged the existence of the other. Here in this corner of Devon the two go very much hand in hand with more than a chance resemblance between them. For they spring from a common parentage: our hills.

These hills have influenced everything that has ever happened here, and they will continue to influence everything that is ever likely to happen, hack at them with bulldozers though we may. They gave us the Dart, and that was countless years ago. They gave us Dartmouth, shaping it the way it is, making it small and compact. They gave us our farmlands – small farms, small fields, woodlands along coombe sides where the ground was too steep to plough. They kept both town and country that way, so that Dartmouth is still small, and farms and fields are today little bigger than they were a hundred years ago. They gave us roads that were narrow and winding and that have remained narrow and winding ever since. They and the river have been our rampart against the assault of the holiday trade that has overwhelmed Torbay. Our hills have shaped everything we find around us. Is it surprising that they shape our lives as well? 'Stay small and go slow,' is their command, and only those who are willing to obey are happy here.

Of the others. . . . Well, I remember one in particular who tried to revolutionize the pleasure-boat business; and I remember a meeting of the Dartmouth Chamber of Trade at which his iniquities were on the agenda for discussion; and I remember the one and only comment that we felt it necessary to pass.

From the depths of a chair through a cloud of tobacco smoke it floated up. 'We seen 'em come, we seen 'em go.' Within a month he was gone.

From time to time others come, seeing perhaps an opportunity to exploit in a seemingly neglected area. But this man is too ambitious: he needs more space than he will find. He is a big man and his big car needs wider roads. And this man wants to get rich quick, but here he will find he can get nothing quick. He is a fast man and his fast car needs straighter roads. The fast car creeping behind a tractor, the big car backing clumsily to where the road is wide enough for two to pass: here they both look ridiculous.

So we are a community of small people: we run small businesses, live in small houses, drive small cars and are content with small incomes. We are in no hurry. We are like that community of small plants that grow and flourish among our rocks, thrusting fine roots deep into rocky cracks. We like it here, Lesley and I. We like living among people similar to ourselves. Though we might have grown bigger, I doubt if anywhere else we would have been happier.

3. Animal Life

In my father's words: 'To say "Yes, sir" and "No, sir" and "Please, sir" and "May I? sir" was hell itself to one who had been as spoiled by good fortune as I.'

And in my words: 'He could radiate enthusiasm, but he could never impose discipline. My father's relationships were always between equals, however old or young, distinguished or undistinguished the other person.'

This did not mean that he judged all men equal. Very far from it. He was very conscious of differences both in class and in ability. It meant rather that his contacts with others were side to side, not end to end; for it gave him no pleasure either to look up or to look down. Of his first meeting with one of his Lance Corporals during the war he wrote: 'We found that we shared a passion for Jane Austen.' This, rather than the military chain of command, was the link that joined them.

I don't know whether all humanity can be neatly divided into side-by-siders and end-to-enders. But certainly I am a side-by-sider like my father – and not only with humans but also with animals. It is this that makes me prefer cats to dogs.

Although undoubtedly dog and man can live together as equals, it is more usual for dog to worship and man to command. No man ever commanded a cat. You can shout at a cat, you can even land a wallop if you are quick enough, and the cat may vanish through the window, or it may ignore you and begin washing its tail, or it may stare at you in pained surprise. But it will never apologize, never promise not to do it again.

Some people, unable to boss their cat, try to pretend that their cat bosses them. But just as no cat ever accepted discipline, so no cat ever imposed it. A mother cat can't even keep her kittens in order. It is no argument to say that your cat always insists on the most comfortable chair. Naturally, given a choice, it prefers the good to the less good: cats aren't stupid. Our cats, as a matter of fact, prefer to sit on the various unpaid bills, unanswered letters and unfilled-in forms we so often seem to leave lying around. I'm not sure what that proves.

Hodge was our first cat – I mean the first that Lesley and I shared. 'Hodge' was his 'given' name. A cat usually has one 'given' name and then a succession of 'calling' names, which are not normally for publication or use outside the family. As I have already said, in his early days he lived over the bookshop. Having no other cats to play with, except for an hour or two every evening, and with no possibilities of hunting, except once when the bookshop suffered from a plague of rats, he was forced to devise his own entertainment. Many a less enterprising animal would have gone to sleep; but Hodge was a ginger cat. Not surprisingly he was often reluctant to come home at night. It was not that we couldn't find him. He came to within an inch or two and then, as we reached to pick him up, he would dance off, rush up a lamp post and dangle upside down from the top. In the day time he would sometimes come down to the shop – where he wasn't really allowed – and get behind the books on our shelves. They were the shelves we had inherited and not yet replaced, too deep for books but leaving just enough additional space for a cat: and browsing customers were often surprised by a ginger face popping out or a ginger paw helping them choose.

Downstairs he had to entertain himself. Upstairs we played with him. One Christmas Uncle Bob sent us a joke card. 'A Present from the Sphinx', it said on the front, and when you opened it a bat flew out. We examined it. It was made of strips of cane covered with black tissue paper, and an elastic band turned a small propeller so that it could fly from one side of the room to the other. Hodge examined it too. . . .

Bats are delicate things, and though Hodge always did his best not to damage them too severely and though I always did my best with fresh tissue paper and glue, and though we rationed him to three flights a day, we were constantly appealing to Uncle Bob – or to anyone else who might happen to be in that part of London – to send us fresh supplies.

The game, which we worked out together, went like this.

The bat was wound up and put in its card. The card was put on a chair and a book was put on top to hold it closed. Hodge, who had been watching these preparations, then jumped onto the chair and sat on the book. Then, very delicately, very slowly, to spin out the pleasure, he would pull the card from under the book, holding it shut with his paw, then slowly lift his paw, peer inside, remove the bat with his mouth, and sit back holding the bat between his paws – all this without letting the elastic unwind. Finally, for the game had to have an ending, he would release it. The bat would fly off and he would watch it go.

His other mouse-substitute was a crumpet, a fresh rubbery crumpet in a paper bag. All cats love paper bags. We were playing with him one lunch hour in our dining-room. He had been getting the crumpet out of the bag, playing with the crumpet then playing with the empty bag. It was a very small bag, nowhere near big enough to get right inside. He had got his head in it and was blundering round the room playing a sort of blind-man's-buff, and there we had left him and gone back to work. Sometime later a man came into the shop, very agitated.

'Excuse me, but did you know there was a cat sitting on top of your window?'

I reassured him. It was a sash window and we often left it open a few inches, and Hodge, wanting to see the world, would jump up and squeeze himself between top of window and top of window frame. It looked perilous but was really quite safe.

'He often sits up there,' I said. 'It's quite all right.'

'Yes,' said the man, 'but did you know that he had a paper bag over his head?'

It was the arrival of Clare and our move to Spriggs Holly that started the deluge, and quite soon our cat family had gone up to four, then six, then seven – and all this not counting kittens. Kittens of course were the explanation, for you can't not have them.

'We'll easily find homes for them,' said Lesley. And she made another of her familiar kitten notices and stuck it in the shop window. And it is true that usually we did, and only sometimes we didn't.

I can't begin to remember all our kittens. It is hard enough to remember all our cats. Their entrances were always a delight; their exits not always too great a sorrow; and each was its own unique self. After Hodge we seemed to specialize in tabbies and to the visitor they may all have looked alike. This was perhaps a good thing. If the visitor met them one at a time, he might well think that he was seeing the same cat six times over and we had no need to confess the truth. But of course to us they not only looked different, they had totally different characters. Take Cosmos for instance.

Cosmos (he is named after the purple flower, not the universe) can open doors. None of the others can do this.

Our doors are fastened by what are known as Suffolk latches. On one side is a metal lever that you lift and this in turn lifts the latch. On the other side the lever is flattened into a knob that you press and below it is a handle that you hold. The knob is four feet from the ground, and on this side the door opens away from you.

Practice makes perfect and most skills are acquired by degrees; but for a cat there are no easy steps to learning how to operate a Suffolk latch. Cautious sniffing and experiment with paw are impossible, for the thing is out of reach. You can only look at it and ponder and try to puzzle it out. And this is presumably what Cosmos had been doing in private for as long as it takes a cat to master such things. The first we knew was when the kitchen door suddenly opened and he came swinging into the dining-room still clinging to the latch handle.

Of course once he had learned how, I can understand why he is for ever doing it. Anyone who has a party trick likes to show off; and he is naturally keenest when we have visitors. So we are able to introduce him with absolute confidence. 'This is Cosmos, the cat who opens doors. Would you like him to show you?' We put him out and close the door. 'Come along, Cosmos,' we call. There is a rattle at the latch and a thump. Then a paw pushes the door open, and in he comes, tail held high and running very fast, like a circus horse entering the arena, collecting applause and clearly very pleased with himself.

If you are lucky he might even show you how he does it, crouching beneath the latch and looking up, then springing, holding on to the handle with his right paw, pressing down the knob with his left. There he hangs until the door is free, then slides down and pushes it open.

Cosmos. We have him now on our roof as a weather-cock, a weather cat pointing towards the wind in an attitude that is all his own, tail erect then curving forwards, front paw extended horizontally. He points with his tail and he points with his paw. But in reality he is not pointing at all. Cats don't point, which is why they cannot understand when humans do. In reality he is saying that he would like a cheese biscuit. His special cheese biscuits are kept in a plastic box on which Lesley had once written the words 'Stewed plums'. We didn't rub them out. I think we had a theory it might fool him. But it didn't. You can't fool cats.

As a child I lived in the country, and not having any brothers or sisters to play with it was perhaps natural that I should feel a special friendship towards animals. Indeed, inspired by Dr Dolittle, there were times when I felt I might one day learn their language.

The relationship between human and animal can at times be remarkably close, and many are the books that have been written – and many are the copies of them that we have sold – to prove it. Luckily for Lesley I have never wanted to exchange her company for that of a colony of chimpanzees in a distant jungle, nor even to turn our house and garden into a sort of Whipsnade. On the other hand, fond though I am of cats, there is something peculiarly fascinating about sharing a part of your life with a truly wild creature – even if only a caterpillar or a tadpole.

Caterpillars and tadpoles were where I started and where I still often return. A couple of years ago I was walking home from the bus stop at the end of our lane. It was late summer and the willowherb that grows beside the stream was in full flower; and here I came upon a man and a woman, both of them up to their waist in the willowherb, obviously looking for something. The man saw me and came towards me. He was carrying a jar. I didn't know him, but even before he showed me, I knew what the jar held – the caterpillar of the elephant hawk moth.

We exchanged a few words and he told me that he lived near Hampstead Heath and had the idea of taking half a dozen of these caterpillars home with him in the hope that they might hatch and breed and so establish a colony there. I told Lesley all this when I got home and a few minutes later she set off down the lane to catch her bus and met the man.

'I gather you've just been talking to my husband,' she said.

He smiled a little shyly. 'Oh, yes,' he said, and paused, and then, as if feeling that an explanation was called for:

'I thought he looked like the sort of person who would be interested in my caterpillar.'

A nice compliment. Exactly what distinguishes the caterpillar enthusiast from the rest of humanity when seen at a distance I don't know. But I am happy to think that I am recognizable as such.

However, I must not give the impression that wherever I find people looking for things I know at once what they are looking for. In this case I only knew because the previous week I had myself come upon this particular caterpillar in almost the same place. Altogether that year we found three and they were housed in Clare's bedroom.

The hope with caterpillars, of course, is that you can keep them until they finally hatch into moths. The additional hope is that you may be present at one of the more exciting moments in their otherwise rather monotonous lives. I was once holding the chrysalis of a cabbage white when quite suddenly what I can only describe as the door in its undercarriage sprang open, and so, while we were having lunch in the garden, we were able to watch the butterfly slowly emerge, climb up the back of the chair where I had put it, and hang out its two little bundles of wings to drip-dry like washing on a line until the creases had come out and they were as smart as if they had been starched and ironed. With one of our hawk moth caterpillars I was present on a different occasion. I had found this one when it was still quite small and bright green – unlike the other two, which were fully grown and brown. The little one ate and grew. Then one day I noticed it had stopped eating and I was puzzled. It was still green but somehow it seemed now to be flushed with a sort of inner brownness. That was how it looked and that was exactly how it was, for as I watched the green skin split open and folded back, and there standing in its place was a caterpillar half as big again and dark brown. It happened as quickly and as magically as the transformation scene in a pantomime. Then – because in other respects caterpillars are not like princes – it turned and ate its discarded suit.

You can keep tadpoles until they become frogs or toads, but then I think they are best left free to wander through the wet grass and seek their fortunes. When they have become fully grown they can return.

Here we have few frogs but innumerable toads. There is a toad pond a quarter of a mile away opposite the big house at the top of the hill, and this is where they breed; and in the early spring on a damp night our lane becomes thronged with them as they make their way to this pond. Sometimes they travel singly. Sometimes the smaller male rides on the female's back. Occasionally you find a trio, with two males riding one above the other. The lane follows a fold in the hills. For both toad and man it is the natural route to the pond. So perhaps it is not surprising that each chose it and that though, over the centuries, man has changed it, toad still uses it. Alas now it is a dangerous route for toads and at times it can look like a battlefield, but still the ancient instinct tells them that this is the way they must go.

Sometimes, driving home at night, I have found so many blocking the way that I have had to stop the car and get out and move them into the side of the road or lob them gently over the wall into the field where the pond is. One night I moved over a hundred.

Toads are quite prepared to spend a month or two in human company, and on several occasions they have shared Clare's bedroom. Given a comfortable box and the right sort of food they are quite content. It is always a great moment and brings an immense sense of satisfaction and pride when a wild creature first takes food from one's hand. It is – or it appears to be – the moment when it says 'I trust you'. A side-to-side relationship is established and one feels immensely flattered. This is why toads make such good companions. If you are prepared to oblige them they will quickly oblige you. All they ask of their food is that it should move, and for this reason worms and caterpillars are better than slugs. You hold one end of the worm and allow the other end to wave about, and after a minute or two the toad will emerge and amble up. The worm moves, the toad comes closer. The worm moves again, the toad comes to within an inch and peers down at it. It is now within range of its tongue. The worm moves for the last time. There is a pop and it has vanished. ... No, not quite: for there is half an inch still dangling and the toad uses its hands to cram this last bit into its mouth. There is a final gulp: it blinks its eyes: and that is that.

In this – as in many ways – the toad resembles the owl. Both are nocturnal, both a little mysterious, both a little human in appearance; and both swallow their food whole and after a last gulp and blink sit absolutely still with a look of smug innocence on their faces.

You may remember Old Brown, after he had caught the infuriating Squirrel Nutkin, 'sitting on his doorstep, quite still, with his eyes closed, as if nothing had happened. But Nutkin was in his waistcoat pocket.' Beatrix Potter clearly knew about owls.

We found ours – a tawny owl, like Old Brown – in the lane under the great plane tree just below Embridge. It was an evening in early summer. Clare was back at school. We had bought Embridge but were still living at Spriggs Holly; and we had come out after work to look around. We were sitting on a grass bank when we heard what sounded like a great cursing and swearing coming from somewhere below us. And there in the middle of the road was a small, grey, oval object that was clearly very angry.

I could see the hole where its nest was but it was impossible without a ladder to reach it. The young owl was a mere nestling, covered with fluffy down and many weeks away from being able to fly: and so it was not hard to persuade ourselves that there was only one thing to be done. I picked it up and we took it home.

I had kept an owl once before, one summer term at school when I was about twelve – I and two other boys. We had been allowed to keep it in the carpenter's shop, carpentry being a winter activity only, and there it had had the run of the benches and could sleep among the chisels and no one would mind – until next term – about the mess it was making. So I knew something about their general behaviour, and in particular I knew about their curious eating habits. Their natural diet is small mammals, small birds and the larger insects, and a sympathetic butcher will be able to provide most of their nourishment. But unfortunately nourishment is not the only thing they need. They must also have roughage – bones, fur, feathers, beetle wing cases and so on. This they form into firm, dry, neatly shaped pellets which they later cough up. Roughage is the problem. A naturalist friend recommended match sticks and cotton wool – with nearly fatal results. For though they went down all right they formed a great mass that couldn't get up again. Luckily I saw it at the back of the owl's throat and was able to reach down with my fingers and help it out. After that we used to comb our cats' fur and put it round scraps of meat. And at the same time we passed the message to other cat-owning friends that they were to let us know whenever a mouse was brought in.

With any wild animal in captivity meal-time is of course the great social occasion of the day. So that if you dislike handling its food or if you are upset by the way it eats it, or if it refuses to eat in your company or only eats in the middle of the night, then relations between you are unlikely to be very close. Owls, I am pleased to say, are as obliging as toads. Although both of them normally eat after dark, they are quite willing to adjust their timetable to suit your convenience. Luckily, unlike toads, a young owl does not insist on live food. Give it a dead mouse and it will be happy to show you how it deals with it – and Clare and I were fascinated to watch.

One of the reasons why one feels such an affection for owls – and indeed toads too – is because they look so human. One can almost imagine them as little old men. And this is partly because of the position of their eyes. Owls, unlike other birds, have their two eyes side by side in the front of their head. This gives them a much more limited field of vision – they can see only what is going on in front of them. But what they do see they see with both eyes at once. In other words they have stereoscopic vision and this enables them to judge distances.

This leads to two rather pleasing characteristics. The first is that if you walk round an owl you can pretty well unscrew its head. The second is that a young owl, when it has nothing better to do, spends its time distance-judging.

We kept our owl in the spare bedroom, a room in which there was no carpet and little furniture. The bedroom door opened into our sitting-room. When it had grown enough feathers to be able to flutter around, we sometimes left this door open and it would fly up and perch on the top. From here it could survey us and watch what we were doing. And then it could calculate how far away we were and how far away the cat was and things like that. It did this by leaning forwards and moving its head from side to side – thus, I presume, increasing the stereoscopic effect. I've not seen an adult owl do this but the young do it regularly. There were two young owls that used to come across to our plane tree every evening from their nest in a wood lower down the valley. They spent the night there while their parents went hunting, their wheezing cries going on non-stop until dawn. And if ever we stood beneath the tree and looked up, they would look down and start wagging their heads at us.

Once a wild animal has consented to take food from the hand, naturally one feels that the next step is to pick it up and stroke it. But not every animal welcomes this. Although I have fed a toad while it has been sitting on my hand, they are said to dislike the dryness of human skin. Owls will happily perch on your finger though their grip may be a little painful, or they will ride on your shoulder. I used to take ours out into the garden in this way and let it scramble among the branches of the big apple tree. But if you really want to make an owl happy you must scratch its forehead just above its beak.

Instinct of course teaches them how to fly, but I'm not sure if it teaches them how to hunt. Possibly we should have attempted some lessons, but our fortnight's holiday was approaching. By then we had had our owl for about six weeks and it could fly quite well. Clare, after her half-term holiday, was back at school again. We were off to Italy. Goolie was moving in to look after the cats. Could we ask her to look after an owl as well? Hardly. So we persuaded the Field Centre at Slapton to give it board and lodging.

After that I saw it only once more. I called at the Field Centre on our return and found it greatly changed. It was now an adult, well feathered and with a wild look in its eyes. It glared at me from the top of a bookcase and clicked its beak angrily. They had fed it while we were away but had made no attempt to handle it and it clearly had no wish to be handled again. Very soon now it would be flying away, and all I wanted was one small sign of recognition which I could take for a farewell. I climbed on to a table to get a little closer; the owl shuffled away along the bookcase still clicking. I talked to it and held out a hand and moved a little closer – and, yes, it allowed me to scratch its forehead just above the beak. . . .

A few days later and it was gone.

Though perhaps it might not seem wrong to have toads and caterpillars in residence at the same time, one could certainly not invite a vole to share a bedroom with an owl. So it was lucky that the vole came some years later.

Clare and I had been doing some shopping in Dartmouth and were driving home in the van. In the back of the van was her tricycle and when we had reached the bottom of the hill I had parked the van and then she had cycled and I had walked the last mile along the valley to Embridge. Later that afternoon I walked out alone to collect the van; and on the way I met the vole.

It was sitting on the road among some leaves. It was perfectly round, like a brown golf ball, and it took no notice of me at all. So first I wondered how near I could get before it ran away. And then I wondered if I could touch it. And then I wondered if I could pick it up. And still it took no particular notice but searched among my fingers for things to eat and tried nibbling one or two of them. At that moment a large dog came down the road followed by a car and I had to squeeze into the hedge to let them both go by, and the vole ran up my arm. The car stopped and the driver looked out and said 'What have you got there?' 'A vole,' I said, and it ran up the other arm. The driver said 'Oh', the dog mercifully said nothing, and they both went on.

As the vole was still with me, I wondered whether perhaps I could get it home to show Clare. So I picked a handful of grass and made a nest for it in my jersey and walked on until I had reached the van. Driving home was a little difficult with one hand and half my attention on the vole, but luckily we didn't meet any more cars.

The vole was still remarkably unconcerned, as if travelling in vans was an everyday occurrence. I put it in a basket and carried it upstairs, and while Clare and I were looking at it, it climbed on to the edge of the basket; and at that moment one of our cats came into the room. ... So then I found a cardboard box with a lid; and with the vole in the box and the box in the spare bedroom and the bedroom door firmly shut I felt it was safe for us to drive down to Dartmouth to collect Lesley from the shop. That evening I set to work to make a proper house.

The vole lived in Clare's bedroom and was the most delightful companion we have ever had.

Its house was a wooden box turned on its side with a glass front and an intermediate shelf. It was furnished with (among other things) a jam-jar also on its side and filled with good nesting material – dead grasses, moss and so on – and one night all this was taken out and carried up to the shelf, and here the vole made its own nest, which we seldom disturbed. On the bottom I put a layer of earth and some turves of grass dug up from the garden, and this had to be renewed two or three times a week. The vole went up to its nest while I was doing its housework but came down again as soon as I had finished, eager to explore its new surroundings. The jam-jar remained empty for a while, though the vole would often hop inside after a meal to clean its whiskers. Then, as summer turned to autumn, instinct warned it that winter was on its way, and so instead of eating all the food I gave it, it began to store it; and it stored it in its jam-jar. Each day I put a variety of things into its pot – a bean, a bit of apple, a bit of artichoke, a rose hip, a hazel nut – and when I had done this and closed the glass front, out would come the vole from its nest to see what there was. It would have a quick nibble at this and another quick nibble at that and then, bean by bean and nut by nut, carry the rest off to its larder – until in the end the jar was quite full. On one occasion there was a stick across the mouth of the jar and the vole was carrying a chestnut. Here was a problem: over or under the stick? It tried over first, standing up on its back legs, chestnut in mouth and pushing. But the stick was too high and the nut kept falling back the wrong side. So then it tried under, pushing again. But the gap was too narrow and the nut wouldn't go. So then it dropped the nut, hopped into the jar and tried pulling. Success at last, and I felt like cheering.

Often if you examine the ground under a hazel Bush, you will come upon nuts with holes in their tops and empty inside, and sometimes on a ledge in a bank you will come upon a cluster of these empty shells. This is the work of a bank-vole. It is slow work of course because the shell is very hard, but it grinds away methodically, as a carpenter chips away at his wood, shell-dust. ... falling all round it, until it is through to the kernel. It needs only a very small hole, too small one would think for the vole to get its head through to reach to the last of the kernel. But it manages, although I was never able to see exactly how.

Almost its favourite food was the bark from an apple twig. We gave it a twig in the first place to make a ladder to its shelf. But this was not really necessary, for over a short distance a vole can run up a vertical surface. Indeed it can even run upside down under a horizontal one. So instead its ladder became its lunch; and when it had been reduced to a white skeleton we renewed it.

As with owls so with the vole came the problem of our holiday. Holidays were difficult enough even with only a houseful of cats. But though we felt that Goolie might draw the line at an owl, we were hopeful that we could persuade our friend, George – who with his wife, Jessie, would be looking after Embridge in our absence – to accept additional responsibility for a vole. We made it sound very simple. We promised to have all the food ready. And George said yes, he was sure he could manage. So we left for Italy confident that all would be well.

The vole by then had been with us a year.

There was, I knew, a small gap between the top of the glass and the top of its box, but neither it nor I had paid much attention to it.

It is a pleasant thought that the vole missed me and came out to look for me. Or perhaps, less forgivably, it was deliberately trying to get George into trouble. Or perhaps it felt jealous and wanted a holiday too. But I expect it was really only chance that it chose this particular fortnight to do what it could just as easily have done at any other time. It got out, discovered a bean that George had left ready for its next meal, took possession of it and went exploring. Some time later George came in and noticed that the bean was missing.

George is a man whose thoughts move in planes far, far above the level of assistant zoo keeper and he was never the ideal person to put in charge of a vole. Yet he did now exactly the right thing. He made no attempt to look for it. He simply continued to feed it, putting its food on the floor. And to his great relief he found that it was being taken.

Where was it being taken? That was for me to discover on our return. And the answer was Clare's chest of drawers. The vole had nibbled a hole in the front of the bottom drawer and this had given it access to all the other drawers. Never has a bank vole enjoyed such luxurious accommodation. Six drawers with plenty of good storage space in each and a wonderful supply of gaily coloured nesting material. One by one I took the drawers out, starting at the bottom, and in one drawer was a nest made from Clare's woolly hat and in another was a nest made from Clare's woolly scarf, and in all of them was a little larder of nuts and things. Not until I had got out the last drawer did I find the vole, clinging to the top of the now empty chest.

Both for humans and for voles holidays come to an end and then it is time to go home. But as a reminder of those happy, carefree days and to add a little gaiety to our surroundings we bring back with us some souvenir of our holiday. With Lesley and me it is often a piece of Italian pottery. Once it was a tapestry bed cover. Fair's fair, I thought; and so the vole was allowed to keep a few fragments from Clare's hat and a few fragments from her scarf. And with these it wove itself a magnificent new rainbow-coloured nest.

In the early days of its stay with us I thought it might be nice to take the vole out from time to time, for it had seemed so willing to be handled when we first met. But it never really enjoyed these excursions; nor from our point of view were they necessary. For it was always glad to come to the front of its little theatre and perform for us there; and we would sit and watch it entranced. The owl was really mine. But the vole was Clare's and she spent more hours happily watching it during school holidays and weekends air home than ever Lesley or I did. And at night she would lie awake listening to it grinding away at its nuts. She would watch it and listen to it and talk to it, sitting in her chair in front of its house. It was the perfect companion for someone who could watch and listen and talk as well as anybody – and probably a great deal more happily – but who couldn't manage the feeding or cleaning.

And I am grateful to our little bank vole for entertaining her not only so well but – by bank vole standards if not indeed by any standards – for such a remarkably long time. It lived with us for two years and eight months.

4. *Life*

One of the differences between man and the rest of the animal world is man's ability to accumulate knowledge and pass it on. Each generation starts where the previous generation left off, and it needed only one Newton watching an apple fall for today's mathematical schoolboy to be able to calculate its speed on reaching the ground. Most of what we learn we learn from others: it is the quick and easy way. Someone shows us how, or tells us how, or we look it up in a book.

Looking things up in books is something that comes naturally to a bookseller, and in this way I have extended my knowledge of a variety of subjects. But now and again I have not wanted advice. I have wanted the answer to be my answer, not somebody else's; and I have wanted the satisfaction of finding it on my own. To some extent this has been my attitude towards bookselling itself. It has also been my attitude towards what is going to be the subject of this chapter.

In my previous book, *The Enchanted Places*, I had something to say about my religious beliefs. After all, one who possesses a name that in many people's minds is indissolubly linked with the saying of prayers could hardly avoid the subject. And it was a subject I returned to in a later chapter when, wanting to illustrate my father's view on his son's education, I told the story of my conversion from Christianity to Humanism and referred in particular to a book he had sent me during the war – Winwood Reade's *The Martyrdom of Man*.

To my surprise this little story attracted a quite disproportionate amount of attention. *The Martyrdom* enjoyed a brisk sale at the

Harbour Bookshop – until, to my sorrow, it went out of print. While to counter-balance this came a number of letters from Christians who were clearly upset by what I had written.

I am now going to say rather more. But before I do so I must make it quite plain that I no more expect the reader to share my beliefs than I have expected him to share my love of bookselling or Dartmouth or Embridge. Why should he? We are all different. I only ask that he should read patiently and with as much sympathy as he can manage.

In the second half of *The Enchanted Places* I wanted to write about my father. I had probably known him better than anybody then alive. Yet when I came to think about him I realized how much there was I didn't know; and I wondered for a time whether to consult with others and add their impressions to mine. In the end I decided against this, partly because I felt that if I was going to consult anybody I ought to do the job properly and consult as many people as possible – a mammoth task – and partly because I wasn't really writing that sort of book at all. Mine was a personal memoir, not a biography. I decided therefore to confine myself to my own memories; and this, besides being a great deal easier, had the added advantage that nobody could tell me I had got them wrong.

So then I began to sort out my raw materials. There were the things we had done together, mainly during school holidays. There were my recollections of the things he had said in the letters he had written to me when I was away from home. There were his published writings. And finally the fact that I was his son and resembled him in many ways helped me to guess many of his unspoken feelings. My intention at this point was simply to string all this together and leave it to the reader to draw what conclusions he wished. But as I wrote, so I found myself being led on to form my own conclusions. I was like an archaeologist who, not content with excavating a handful of pottery fragments, goes on to deduce how the completed vase must have looked. No one could dispute the fragments, but somebody else, holding fragments of their own, might dispute the vase.

This search for my father has, I believe, something in common with man's search for God. I could say that I 'knew' him as many say that they 'know' God. I knew him through his published words, through our personal contacts and through his reflection in myself. And this is how the Christian knows his God: through the Bible, through personal experiences and through himself. And the Christian too, whether describing God in words or pictures, fills in the gaps between the fragments.

Is it the truth? What is the truth? What do we mean by the word 'Truth' anyway?

Having suggested that a parallel exists, let me return again to my father. If the parallel continues, so much the better: but I am not forcing it.

What was the truth about my father? It seemed to me when I first asked myself this question that there were two kinds of truth. On the one hand there was factual truth – the information one finds in *Who's Who* or can obtain with a tape-measure. And on the other hand there were the opinions and impressions of those who knew him. 'He was born in 1882' may at first sight seem truer than 'He was a kindly man' because the second statement could be disputed. But if one qualifies it by adding the words 'In my view. . . . then it becomes as true as the first. These opinions and impressions might therefore be described as personal truths, for they are truths concerning a personal relationship between the observed and the observer.

So the truth about anybody consists of a collection of facts – universal truths – which provide a sort of skeletal framework but little more, and a whole mass of personal truths. And it is these personal truths that fill in the flesh and blood, add the smiles and the frowns and thus bring the skeleton to life.

Writing about my father I had relied on factual truths and my own set of personal truths. Had I been writing instead a biography, I would have needed to make a collection of other people's personal truths. Comparing them I might then have noticed certain similarities and so could have recorded a 'general opinion'. But no general opinion, however widely held, can ever invalidate a personal opinion, however contradictory. And this is an important difference between factual truth and personal truth. A factual truth makes its converse false. 'Born in 1882' implies 'not born in 1883'. But one observer's personal truth leaves another's untouched. 'He is kind' and 'He is unkind' can exist together both truthfully expressing the impressions of two different people. Many people, for example, tried to draw my father's portrait. Only one achieved what I felt was a true likeness. But this didn't make the others untrue; for a picture is not a description of the sitter alone but also of the artist, and only the artist knows what the artist sees.

Eddington once described man as 'a kind of four dimensional worm' meaning that he occupied a small volume of space but had considerable extension – seventy odd years – in time. Elaborating a little on this picture, I see man as a kind of four dimensional marine bristle-worm – the sort that can unfurl a crown of long, waving, thread-like tentacles from the top of its head. The body of the worm is the factual truth about the man. Each thread as it touches someone becomes their personal truth. The tentacles that range on either side of the worm's body are those personal truths established during the man's lifetime. Those that stretch ahead are those truths that will be established after his death as people in the years ahead are touched by his life. Every child who, at some future date, reads about Pooh – whether in the original text or in translation or even in Disney's version – will be holding a personal truth about my father. Disney's Pooh may have little resemblance to the original Pooh, but this in no way affects the matter or makes this personal truth less truthful. Should it ever happen that the supporters of Shepard went to war with the supporters of Disney, this might be regrettable. People might die. But truth would not.

What applies to man applies generally. On the one hand you have factual truths, scientific truths, truths that can be tested and checked and to which all must agree (or else prove them mistaken): the astronomer's Moon, the botanist's flower, sodium chloride. On the other hand you have personal truths, artistic truths, poetic truths, emotional truths, Keats's 'truth of imagination': the poet's Moon, the artist's flower, the taste of salt.

Today we worship our scientists and despise our poets; and so we sometimes dress up our truths as if they were scientific truths to give them an air of greater authority. I once heard it suggested that we should approach the theory of Christianity as a mathematician approaches the theory of gravitation, testing it and so proving it true. But Newton knew better.

> I do not know what I may appear to the world, but to myself I seem to have been only a boy playing on the sea-shore, and diverting myself in now and again finding a smoother pebble or a prettier shell than ordinary, whilst the great ocean of truth lay all undiscovered before me.

In this great ocean lie all the more important truths about man. And here too, never to be washed up on to the shore, never to be picked up and handled and looked at under a microscope, lies the Truth about God.

If one thinks of man as a marine bristle worm, then God is a marine bristle worm of infinite length whose body is totally beyond the range of all our recording and measuring devices. We know him only through our personal threads of contact and from what others report of their contacts. The extent to which we are influenced and helped by others depends on the similarity of their threads to ours. It is the same with music. I get great pleasure listening to Mozart but none at all listening to Debussy. I am much helped in my enjoyment of Mozart by those who, sharing my feelings, have made recordings which I can then buy. Other musicians have made recordings of Debussy. These I do not buy. I do not dispute the facts of Debussy's life nor the opinions of his admirers, but I do not see that this is any reason for submitting myself to another unhappy session with 'L'après-midi d'un faune' when I might be listening instead to the Flute and Harp Concerto.

And so it is with religious beliefs: we welcome those that harmonize with our own feelings. Those that do not we leave. This is not to imply that they are false, merely that they are not for us. To suggest that one picture of God is so complete and perfect that it makes all other pictures false is surely to diminish God to the size and simplicity of the rounded stone in Newton's hand. The Christian may argue that his picture is authenticated by the Bible which is God's Word and therefore True. But the truths one finds in the Bible are like the truths one finds in everything else: a few are factual, most are personal. The greatness of Shakespeare's plays does not lie in the historical facts one can glean from them, nor does the greatness of Genesis lie in its geological or anthropological accuracy. So each of us interprets the Bible in his own way. Some hold to the literal truth of every word and incident. For others the truth is of a different kind. The very vitality of the Bible lies in its multitude of meanings. Do you believe that Christ physically rose into the air and disappeared into the sky? This is one question. Was it believed and reported that he did? This is another question. What emotions are aroused in you by the story of the Ascension? This is a third question. And finally, what emotions are aroused indirectly through the words, paintings or music that the story has inspired in others? This is a fourth question. On Ascension Sunday at school I used to sing the solo 'Ye Men of Galilee' from Stainer's anthem, 'Leave us not, neither forsake us'. This was for me a very great and has remained a very enduring experience – in no way lessened by the fact that my answer to my first question is 'No.'

If all this seems a rather long introduction to a statement of what exactly I do believe, it is because the most important part of my belief is that my picture of God – my own personal individual thread – and all the other pictures of God held by man whenever and wherever he may have lived are all parts of a Divine Truth that is quite beyond our tiny perceptions. Though they may differ from each other there need be no conflict between them; nor need there be any conflict with science.

Although it is always possible to find something you are *not* looking for – which, it may be remembered, was Joyce Green's technique for finding things – more often it helps to look. And probably what man was looking for when – long before Christianity – he first discovered God was something to alleviate his fear of the Unknown. So much was unknown in those early days: the sun, the storm, the sea, the forest. . . . There was so much to be afraid of. And so the early gods were near at hand. But gradually, century by century, as man explored and understood, tamed and cultivated, learned to predict and to control, so the frontiers of the unknown were pushed back. Once they lay on the other side of the mountain. Today they are so distant that only the astronaut ventures beyond them and few of us are afraid of what he might find there. Yet distant though they are in space, they are still as near as ever in time, less than an hour away, less than a minute.

We are all of us explorers in time, feeling our way forward into the unknown future. Some move with confidence. Others need reassurance. They peer ahead to be certain they are on the right road. 'Is the Ruler of this Country friendly or hostile?' they ask. 'Will anyone come to our rescue if we get lost?'

But whether we are confident or afraid and however often or anxiously we peer ahead, we all of us now and again look back along the way we have come. Ahead lies the unknown and possibly frightening, the fluid and uncertain future; behind us is the known, frightening no more, solid and firm. So we look back for additional reassurance. As a tree needs strong anchor roots running deep into the ground to give it stability and enable it to withstand the winter gales, so to enable us to weather the future, we need to feel ourselves well rooted in the past.

The need is common to us all; but we satisfy it each in his own way. Most obvious is the family root, linking us to our parents: family name, family tree, family business, family possessions passed down, the home town. But another root can lie in a more general past: old customs and traditions, antiques, vintage cars, steam trains, the Queen Anne cottage, the Queen Anne-style pub, the historical biography and the historical romance. And a third root can tie us to our own past: photographs of ourselves when young, old clothes, old books, old junk. Goolie had a pile of old copies of *The Times* that reached practically to the ceiling. All these things reflect a fear of the future, of what is new and uncertain, of change and insecurity.

Nevertheless, though we are rooted in the past we are at the same time moving forward into the future.

There are two ways of navigating. You can take a bearing on something ahead of you and steer towards it. Or you can take a bearing on something behind you and steer away from it. Equally there are two methods of propulsion. You can mount your propeller at the front, as the aeroplane does, and, using the air ahead of you, pull your way forwards. Or you can mount your propeller in the stern as the boat does and push. So it is with humans. There are those who look ahead and pull and those who look behind and push.

We all of us live in this world, the world that starts now and stretches back into the past. This is Creation and all that we have experienced through our senses, all knowledge, all memory lie within it. Ahead of us lies. . . . nothing. Darkness and silence. We can guess what there might be, as a man walking in the dark guesses at the road ahead of him, though he cannot see it. But we can guess only a little way. We may be fairly sure of today, but tomorrow is more doubtful.

So naturally most of us most of the time mount our propellers in the stern and steer away from the past. But some of us sometimes turn to face the future. We may do this in disgust or despair at what we have seen behind us. Or we may do it because we have been told that it is a better way of navigating. In either case, facing the unknown and seeing nothing, we may well be afraid and will certainly need guidance. We need a mark to aim for. We need a guide to help us through the unseen dangers ahead. We need the assurance that at our journey's end we will come to a safe haven. These things we cannot immediately find on our own: we need someone to guide us to our guide. And in the Western world this is the Christian Church. The Christian Church points the way through present sorrow to future bliss, through sin to redemption, through life on earth to life eternal and so to the final triumph of good over evil. The Christian Church introduces us to Christ, our guide, to God, who is the King of the Country we are entering, and to Heaven, our ultimate destination.

It is of course only a picture that the Church shows us: it is not the reality. It is Christ-in-words that we are introduced to, not

Christ-in-person. It is a collection of the personal truths of others that we are given. Our own personal God-truths remain to be established. We can, if we like, accept it as we accept a portrait or a biography of someone long dead, and look no further. Or we can seek a personal encounter.

Thus for some the Church is a means to an end and for others it is an end in itself. Some through the Church find God. Others find only the Church. But even this is something – and may well be enough. They will find the Church's own anchor root: the building itself and its furnishings, Christian rituals and traditions, familiar words and familiar music. They will find Christian morality and a way of life. They will find human fellowship and love.

As a child I accepted what I was taught. From Monday to Saturday I learned about the Ancient Romans; on Sunday about the Ancient Hebrews. After six days of struggling with my voice in class, on the seventh I shook it free of its chains and sent it, pure and clear, soaring up into the rafters of the school chapel. In solos and descants I praised the Lord. How could I doubt the truth of what I did so well?

But alas the fluting treble became the croaking bass, and when my voice broke, my strongest link with the church broke with it. In the end I was left holding a guidebook to a Guide whom I had never really met, and a picture which, though once it had satisfied me, satisfied no longer.

Why had the picture failed? Partly because, having no particular reason to dislike the world I was living in, I had no particular desire to turn away from it. Partly because the Church as an institution held no particular attraction for me once my singing days were over. But mostly, I think, because the Christian Truth I was being shown was presented as if it were Scientific Truth and therefore having to hold its own against other scientific truths. This, in my view, it failed to do. The answer was simple. God had not made Man; it was Man who had made God.

I said this in 1944 and I said it in a way that implied, 'I am right and you are wrong. Today I still maintain the truth of the second half of the statement: Man made God. But I say it now in a way that I hope allows us both to be right.

Man has made God in the sense that our truths about God are not scientific but personal truths, mere threads from an infinite, invisible bristle worm, the tiniest fraction of a Total Truth that is utterly beyond our comprehension. Personal truths being those that link observed to observer, our personal God-truths are man-made in the sense that they are of necessity reduced and simplified to a level at which man can understand them. How can God appear to man except in a way he can understand? How can man report the encounter to his fellow men except in human words and worldly images? Did God make man God-shaped or did man make God man-shaped? The answer is 'Both'.

My discovery in 1944 was really a personal one: that I was a boat rather than an aeroplane, a pusher rather than a puller, that I went better with my propellers mounted in the stern. I turned away from the world of the future to the world of the past and speculated not about the Creator but about Creation.

The Christian may well reply that God is everywhere, in the past as well as in the future. Maybe; but it is like saying that the stars are still overhead, even in daytime. Dazzled by the sun, we do not see them. It is like telling us about the life of the composer while we are listening to his music. Or so it seems to me. Dazzled by the world, I see only the world. Everything I see, everything I hear, all experience, all thought, all emotions – *all* for me lies *within* Creation. Thus the Bible is not the Word of God. It is the Word of Man in search of God. Christ is not God but man – and so for me becomes infinitely more wonderful. His courage was human courage. The death he went towards and suffered was real death, human death. Everything he did lies within our human capabilities. This is the inspiration he offers, us: not that he was an intervention on the part of the Creator, but that, being man, he showed us the heights to which man can reach.

So my relationship with the Creator of the Universe is a little like my relationship with the Army Commander during the war. Yes, no doubt he existed. Maybe he even knew that I existed. Certainly he was benevolently disposed towards me and hoped I wouldn't get myself killed. But I never met him, never spoke to him. If there was anything I wanted I went, not to him, but to my Company Commander. If things happen within Creation that I do not understand, this does not surprise me. Why should anyone expect to be able to understand it all? Maybe we will one day find the answer, as today we know the answers to many questions that baffled earlier generations. There is no need to go outside Creation for what we cannot at the moment explain within it.

The world contains good things and bad things. Each individual is unique, living his own unique life, seeing the world in his own unique way and labelling it according to his own set of values. For the Christian the bad things may outnumber the good and so he turns his back on both and faces the Ultimate Good that lies ahead. I too see good and bad in this world, and agree with the Christian that most of the bad are man-made. Perhaps, unlike him, I feel that good cannot exist on its own. Just as you need valleys in order to have hills so you need fear to have courage, work to enjoy rest, pain to enjoy freedom from pain. You may even need war to enjoy peace (though I hope not). A flat plain is flat whether at sea level or at ten thousand feet, and after a while everlasting joy might begin to pall and everlasting life become a burden. But the main difference between us is that I must find my good not outside Creation but within it.

I find it in Nature.

I have a vision. It is of a sort of Jacob's Ladder running from earth to heaven. Its foot rests on the rocks. On its first rung are the very simplest of living organisms, the first forms of life. A little above come the plants; then the simplest of animals; then the mammals. Then Man. Above Man the rungs are empty but the ladder continues until it disappears into the clouds. The Christian and I are standing side by side. He is staring upwards, straining his eyes. Now and again, through a gap in the clouds, he catches a momentary glimpse. Something perhaps a little like himself – but more perfect. . . . Might it be an Angel? Might it be God? He and God. . . . The gap is very great, but if he climbed a little higher, and if God reached down a hand. . . .

I am looking downwards. The other creatures are very close to me. I can touch them. Look. There is Brother Ass whom St Francis knew. And those are his birds. And here is Cousin Oak. . . .

That is how I feel about Nature: that I am a part of it, a part of the great convoy that many millions of years ago climbed out of the primeval swamp.

Depressed by the ugliness of what he sees around him, the Christian refreshes himself with half an hour in church. I spend half an hour under a tree. The Christian is in communion with his God. I am in communion with. . . . what? With God's work? With the Earth Goddess? Certainly I am not in communion with my fellow man, and that is something. Certainly I am, if not in communion at least in contact with the grass and the ground and *that* is something. Also I am in contact with such generalities as Beauty, Continuity and Renewal. These, which the Christian finds within the Church calendar, I find in the changing seasons. Then too I find what I found so memorably in Italy: that feeling of an all-pervading Benevolence that dwarfs the unpleasant things that man does to man. This is perhaps the nearest I get to the Christian's God-the-Father. And finally perhaps I am in contact with something a little deeper. Perhaps I am, like the tree I am sitting under, just another sort of tree, a mobile tree with roots that can move from place to place, roots that are invisible but which are roots none the less, thrusting into the earth and drawing nourishment from deep down among the rocks. . . . Sometimes I feel this way. . . .

We say of the misfit that he is a square peg in a round hole. Every one of us is a peg of a certain shape. Our shape may change over the years but it is uniquely ours, determined at birth, part of our nature. And each of us occupies a hole in the world, a hole of approximately the same shape. Where the fit is good we are comfortable and happy. Where it is less good we are unhappy, ill at ease and under strain. The clothes we wear, the house we live in, the husband or wife we have married, our job, our friends: these are all part of our hole. And so too is the God we worship. If we are to be at peace within ourselves, then our religious beliefs – our philosophy of life – must fit us as comfortably as our shoes.

I would like to close this chapter by suggesting that there is no single Royal Road to this goal. Each must find his own best way as he pursues his lonely pilgrimage across the world. Others are moving forward with him, some on his path, some on parallel paths.

All are within shouting distance, and cries for help mingle with shouts of encouragement and exhortation.

What advice can one give that all may accept? Surely only the advice given by Polonius to Laertes. 'This above all: to thine own self be true.' This above all. Above conformity for conformity's sake. Above forcing our foot into somebody else's ill-fitting shoe for the sake of appearances. Above saying 'I believe' when in honesty we don't.

Of the path I have found I say only that it is the right path for me and I ask of others only that they should understand this and accept it.

Epilogue. *The New Path*

In 1956 my father died. In a sense, however, he was already dead; for the operation that had given him an extra year of life had made him a different person. It had made my mother a different person too. And it had made Cotchford a different place. Yes indeed, if it is sad to go too soon, it is worse to stay too long.

Selfishly I was glad that I lived in Devon and had a bookshop that I could not easily leave. Children drift away from their parents as they grow up, and it is right that they should. I had been very close to mine, especially to my father, for rather longer than is usual, and so the drifting when it came was perhaps a little further than is usual. I saw my father on two occasions during his illness, my mother and Cotchford on three. On his death I never saw Cotchford again. And although my mother survived him by fifteen years I saw her only once.

On my father's death my mother had taken over responsibility for his estate. If any decisions were to be made they were hers to make. I was two hundred miles away and only too relieved to be able to say to enquirers 'I am afraid it is nothing to do with me.'

In 1971 my mother died. My reaction was not typically that of a child who has lost a parent. There was little sadness, little sense of bereavement. How could there be? I had last seen her at my father's memorial service and we had scarcely written to each other since. When Cotchford was sold I knew only when her next letter came from a London address. No, my chief concern was that a part of my father's royalties would now be mine – and I didn't want it.

To write about one's attitude to money is almost as dangerous as to write about one's religious beliefs. Having dared the one, I must now dare the other.

It is easy to give. It is extremely hard to receive. I am bad at receiving, bad at having to be grateful. I like to be able to boast to myself that what I have done I have done without help. Hence my insistence that I was a professional bookseller and that the bookshop was the sole source of our income. Hence my anger when anyone implied that they thought I was only a dilettante, not really having to make the business pay, happily able to rely on a private income.

But in spite of my determination to earn my own living, I looked upon what I earned more as a measure of my ability to sell books than anything else. I didn't particularly welcome the money for its own sake or for the sake of what it would buy. My ambition was to be a good rather than a rich bookseller: there was something not quite nice about being rich.

Whether or not this attitude is understandable, it does, I hope, explain why a sudden, relatively large and unearned addition to our income was not at all what I wanted. Many dream of winning the football pools. For me this would be nightmare. To travel hopefully being a better thing than to arrive, I didn't welcome the offer of a lift. No, thank you, I prefer to walk. How often have I said this!

To be offered a lift by *anybody* would therefore have been bad enough and I would have been tempted to decline it. But to be offered a lift by, of all people, my fictional namesake, to have to travel the rest of my way in *his* company – this was the final insult to my injured pride.

Yet however much I might wish to be independent, standing on my own feet, I was very much aware that this, both figuratively and literally, was something Clare would never be able to do. So here was a dilemma. Fortunately it was not one that called for an immediate decision.

It would be a long while before probate had been settled, leaving my emotions plenty of time to sort themselves out inside me. Meanwhile Clare was still at school, Lesley and I were still full-time booksellers, and things could continue much as before.

And meanwhile I had another series of emotions to battle with. These arose from the discovery that of my father's personal possessions nothing had survived. All had been destroyed.

Looking back on it now I can understand why my mother did what she did. Indeed I am utterly convinced that she did the right thing and precisely what my father would have wished.

What did his possessions amount to anyway? I have already described Cotchford in *The Enchanted Places*. The house and its furnishings, the garden with its flowers, everything that the visitor was so proudly shown, all these, though bought with my father's money, in every other sense belonged to my mother. The things he needed for himself, a chair to sit on, a table to write at, a bed to sleep in and a chest of drawers for his clothes and his belongings, were just bits of furniture, not particularly his, not particularly anybody's. His golf clubs, his pipes and his books: these were more personal of course, and much loved by him. But they were never particularly loved by my mother, indeed rather the reverse. For she had never shared with him those things that were closest to his heart. So what were they to her now, when all that she had loved was gone? If you have memories, you don't need mementos.

But of course an author leaves more than his table and his pen. He leaves his unfinished manuscripts. This surely is another matter – of public rather than private concern.

Or is it?

To his many friends my father had been 'Alan' or 'Blue', the man they had talked to at the Garrick Club, the man they had played golf with at Addington or Ashdown Forest; and as they had known him so they would remember him. To many others he was known only through what he had written. He was articles in *Punch*. He was plays. He was Pooh. We never give all of ourselves to anybody. Even from those who are nearest to us there is a part of ourselves that we withhold. My father was a private person. He gave sparingly; and to the public at large during his lifetime he gave little more than his published words. Why should we expect more on his death and assume that because he is no longer there to say 'No' we may rummage without his permission through all he left behind? His feelings for his unfinished writings were precisely those of a mother for her unborn child. If the mother dies it may be kinder to let the child die with her.

This is how I feel now. But it was not how I felt at the time.

When I first learned what my mother had done I felt only a sudden surge of anger and a stab of sorrow. My poor father that she should have treated him like this! And so started the train of emotions that led in the end to my writing *The Enchanted Places*.

It was I suppose a feeling of guilt, a guilt which my mother and I had shared. We had both in our different ways failed him. And I owed it to him to make amends. Yes, if nothing had been left, I would provide something. I would write something and I would write it for his sake. This was my first thought. Later a rather more selfish reason occurred to me. I needed to write something for my own sake too.

For if I did nothing, then sooner or later someone would come to me and propose himself as my father's biographer. And of course he would hope to see what in fact didn't exist and hear what I didn't wish to tell. Could I refuse to have anything to do with him? Or could I agree to answer certain questions but not others? To say 'No' would be hard enough; but to say anything but 'No' would be in the end to open my private world to a complete stranger and allow him to trample all over it, picking from it what he pleased and interpreting it how he wished. There was only one way out. 'Yes, I will write my own account in my own time and in my own words.' I had only to say this, first to myself, then to Lesley, to become immediately and utterly safe. For here was my reply, my impregnable defence. And twice in the course of the next two years I was to shelter behind it.

It has been said that the difference between the professional and the amateur writer is that the professional writes even when he is not in the mood. I was an amateur. I knew that duty and self defence were not enough and that I was surrounded by excuses for saying 'Not today'. And I was going to need many todays before I had finished. Day after day I would have to ignore all the other things I ought to be doing. Day after day I would have to sit alone at my typewriter. Only the most intense pleasure could hold me to such a task: and at first contemplation I was filled with nothing but intense repugnance.

What exactly was I going to write? At first I visualized it as no more than an introduction to a new edition of the Pooh books, scarcely even deserving its own covers. I could say something about the real toys and the real places. But there were other questions that people would want to ask. Should I just ignore them? Perhaps I could make my essay take the form of an imaginary interview in which *all* the questions were asked but only the easy ones were answered, the others being warded off in the manner of the skilled politician. This seemed quite an ingenious idea and I began to contemplate it, letting my mind float back among its memories. I had now stopped saying to myself, 'This is something I must do,' and I had begun to consider how I might do it.

It was at this point that I began to see, not the Christopher Robin I had intended to write about, but another small boy. And as I looked at him he grew clearer and I saw to my surprise that he was beckoning to me. I took a few hesitant steps towards him and he came to meet me. He took me by the hand and he led me back. . . .

This was how in the end the book came to be written, and when I had finished it I added an introduction. 'If I have imagined an audience,' I said, 'it has been a gathering of Pooh's friends and admirers.' It seemed the polite thing to say, but of course it wasn't true. Having spent my entire adult life running away from Pooh and his friends, was it likely that I should now want them sitting round my table as I worked? No, I wasn't writing for them at all. I was writing for myself. I was back in the place that I had loved. Hand in hand with my small companion I was re-exploring the rambling old farmhouse, the garden, the meadows, the woods, the river, the lane, the forest – the enchanted places of my childhood. Day after day I returned, happily writing. And since I couldn't altogether forget my reason for writing, now and again I made myself throw in a bit about Christopher Robin so as not to disappoint the reader.

So it was a book that took me a year to think about and then another year to write. The first half of it was written in the afternoons at Embridge. Clare was at school. Lesley was at the bookshop. I was alone – except for a coming and going of cats. At the half way point I paused, partly to see if what I had written was publishable, partly because term had ended and Clare was home.

She was home not just for the holidays. She was home for good. She was seventeen and had been at her boarding school since she was six. During that time Lesley and I had both of us been full-time booksellers for three-quarters of the year. For the other quarter, the school holidays, I had worked in the mornings, she in the afternoons. What was going to happen now?

For the time being at any rate Clare would be living at home: this was what we all three wanted. She had spent little enough of her life at home and we had spent little enough of ours with her; and now we would make up for it. In any case there wasn't any very acceptable alternative.

This meant that Lesley would have to remain a permanent part-time bookseller. As for me, I still had half a book to finish; and if it had been hard enough before – hard on the others, I mean – it was going to be very much harder now. Could I for the next few months abandon the bookshop altogether? Luckily for my conscience I had no option. For I had now got what I now needed, a contract with Eyre Methuen to deliver the completed manuscript by the end of March.

So we would struggle on – but not indefinitely. Eventually we would have to reorganize our lives, and eventually we would have to decide how.

As I said in an earlier chapter, to be a good bookseller you need three things: a goal to aim for; the spur of necessity; and all your working hours. If I had been deprived of any one of these I might well have questioned whether I wanted to continue. Very happily I was deprived almost simultaneously of all three. There was no question about it: once again something had come to an end and it was time to go.

But if my personal decision that I wanted to stop being a bookseller was an inevitable one, it still left two questions unanswered. What should we do with the shop and what should I then do with myself?

The first question was the easier. Lesley wanted to go on working there. If half of every day was now to be spent at Embridge with Clare, she wanted to spend the other half in Dartmouth – and what pleasanter place than the Harbour Bookshop? So, although we did consider the idea of selling up, it was an idea we quickly abandoned. In any case we wanted the shop to continue as a small private bookshop. We wanted its customers to continue being its customers, finding the sort of books they had been accustomed to find. In other words we wanted it to remain the *same* shop. Of course there would be changes. In bookselling there are always changes and this is what gives it its fascination. No two years are alike and you must be for ever on the alert to seize opportunities as they come by. But in spite of change, something remains constant, the shop's identity, its personality. It was this we wanted to continue. And we knew from observation of the book trade, from seeing what had happened to so many small private bookshops when their proprietors had retired and newcomers had taken over, that the chances of this happening were not large.

Ideally therefore we wanted someone – or perhaps a married couple – a little like us as we had been when we started, someone who would work with us for a short while and then gradually take over. The proudest and happiest moment in a shopkeeper's life is when he adds the words '& Son' to his signboard. If we could never do this, let us at least aim for the next best thing.

Thus we planned the future of the shop. As for me, I would remain a bookseller until we had found someone to whom I could hand over. I would enjoy this: setting the shop on its course for what I could hope might be the next twenty years of its life, passing on what I had learned. This would make a good and satisfying end to my bookselling life.

But after that, what?

This, as I have said, is the story of someone who at birth was blessed – or was it cursed? – with two talents, his father's head and his mother's hands. To 'succeed in life' – if that is what you want to do – you need a single talent to command your undivided energies and steer you, dedicated and determined, to the mountain top. To have two talents is like trying to ride two horses: you don't get there any quicker. In fact you are lucky to get anywhere at all. On the other hand you may be a great deal happier, for mountain tops can be cold and lonely.

It was my mother's skill with her hands that had qualified me as a Carpenter and Joiner in the Royal Engineers, and it was my father's aptitude for mathematics that had subsequently qualified me for a commission. My mother had got me into John Lewis and – assuming one or other of my parents must take the blame – it was my father who had got me the sack. As a bookseller I could be grateful to both of them, since not only did I have to choose books for our shelves, but I first had to make shelves for our books. And all the while at odd moments I had been making things for the house.

I have already mentioned the satisfaction I had found in designing and making furniture and equipment for Clare. And it did seem to me that, financed perhaps by those royalties I was so reluctant to accept for myself, this was something I might do for others. I might almost convince myself that it was something Clare and I might do together. 'C. R. Milne & Daughter – Makers of Furniture for the Disabled.' The idea appealed to me: a pleasant dream. But it was never more than a dream.

I doubt if I could have turned it into reality. Meanwhile there was my book to be finished.

I had spent a year not writing it, a year writing it and then eight months helping it into print. It was published in November 1974. And that, I thought, was that. My venture into authorship was at an end. Back for a while to the retail side of the trade; and then perhaps on to the carpenter's bench.

But it didn't happen like that.

The first part of *The Enchanted Places* was concerned mainly with the Sussex countryside. The second part was concerned with my parents and especially with my father. In other words I was writing about a writer. Many sons follow their fathers; but mine had never wanted this and I had wanted it only at odd moments in my life. He had feared that, whatever I wrote, comparisons would be made and one of us judged less good than the other. Jealous by nature – as I was too – more than anything he hated rivalry. Yet here I was, not just writing a book but writing one which, whether I liked it or not, was going to be put alongside the Pooh books and tested by its ability to hold its own in such company. Not only that but one of my purposes was to show the extent to which the son was a product of his parents – thus tacitly inviting the all too inevitable comparison.

Clearly if the general verdict had been that, though doubtless there were many things I had inherited from my father, an ability to write was not one of them, that would have been that. 'I would have done what I had initially set out to do but not what I had later privately hoped to do. Sad, but not altogether surprising.

An autobiography is quite unlike any other form of literature. Not only is it a public *apologia pro vita sua* but during the actual writing of it each session at one's typewriter is like a session on the analyst's couch. Consequently its effect on the writer is considerable. In my case the writing and its reception combined to lift me from under the shadow of my father and of Christopher Robin, and to my surprise and pleasure I found myself standing beside them in the sunshine able to look them both in the eye.

'Why, you're only a sort of thing in his dream!' cried Tweedledee to Alice seeing the Red King asleep beneath a tree. That for so long and for so many people was what I had been. And now at last I could feel that I was myself. If I had any lingering sorrow over what had happened on my father's death it was a pleasing thought that, out of the flames of the bonfire that had destroyed what was left of him, had been born something that was in another sense his too. And at that moment, whether he liked it or not – and I hoped that he would have liked it – the words '& Son' had been nailed to *his* signboard.

I have said that a professional bookseller needs all his working hours. Happily a professional writer does not. If mornings only were all I could now manage, mornings only would be enough. So here was something I could do and here was the moment to start doing it. Here was a challenge and both the encouragement and the opportunity to accept it. The current served. The tide was at the flood. I took it.

I doubt if it leads me on to fortune and luckily it doesn't need to; for I have accepted my namesake's offer of help. I had to accept it for Clare's sake, of course. But perhaps I might need to accept it for my sake and for Lesley's as well. For although one might measure the ability of a bookseller by what he earns, this has never been the measure of a writer.

So each morning I work at the Harbour Bookshop – not on the ground floor among the books, not on the first floor in our Gift Gallery, not (thank goodness) on the second floor where the invoices are sorted and the accounts paid, but, up again, up a very narrow flight of stairs, to the attic beneath the roof.

It is still as unlovely as it was when I described it in *The Enchanted Places*, but at least it now has a proper light and an electric fire. Through the little window (which still lets in the rain) I can see the sky, and if it is blue and inviting, then, in the afternoon, I shall be happy to accept its invitation. Up again, up, up, up, carrying Clare this time, to the 'Top' that isn't a top, to where the bluebells grow and the longhorn moths fly, to where I have planted my trees and once intended to build a hut.

Of course the hut has not yet been built. In fact I am not even sure now that I want to build it. For it will mean putting a wall between me and the rocks at my back and a roof between me and the sky overhead. And who wants that on an afternoon in late autumn when there is still a bit of heat in the sun and the wind is warm and caressing?

Here we come, Clare and I. It is a tiring climb with one set of muscles having to do the work of two, and I am grateful that she is little and light. And here we sit and dream and perhaps I do this and that among my trees. There is much to be done, but there is no hurry. I can do a bit more another day. Small and slow is our world, and luckily this is how we like it.

Just below our terrace the ground drops away steeply. Here there is a patch of gorse seedlings – over a thousand, I should guess. There is much around me that I can't explain, but this I can. We had a fire here the summer before last – that very dry summer of 1976. It had been our last surviving area of original jungle, a tangle of furze and bramble and blackthorn. Then one evening it all went up in flames and we returned from an afternoon on the river to find a landscape transformed, to see a boundary wall we had never seen before and contours we had only been able to guess at, to see black stumps jutting out of black earth.

It is not only the wise bookseller who seizes his opportunities: it is all nature. Gorse seeds lie dormant in the soil waiting for the intense heat that is necessary for their germination. And so the flames of the fire that had destroyed what was left of their parents had brought life, phoenix-like, to a new generation. This was their moment – and mine too. For within hours the fire had done what had daunted me for years; and I set to work with mattock and spade to cut the path I had always been meaning to cut, another path to the top.

Up here we are now a little more exposed than we were: the bushes that had sheltered us from the south west are gone; and a chill puff of wind comes across the valley warning us that the afternoon is nearly over. The sun is only a fraction of an inch above the horizon. Sunset comes early to those who live in a valley, but the higher slopes remain aglow and sunlight shines on the herring gulls as they fly overhead.

Lesley will be walking home from the shop. Shall we go and meet her?

If she leaves at half past five and if the journey takes her fifty minutes (because she may stop to pick blackberries or look for mushrooms on the way) and if we want to meet her somewhere about the end of the beech avenue, what time should we leave? There's a mathematical problem for you! I ought to be able to solve it: I was a mathematician once, or so I boast. But I'm getting rusty: I'd need pencil and paper and no interruptions; and by the time I'd worked it out we'd be too late. So perhaps it would be wise to start now; then we needn't hurry. Which is it to be: tricycle or wheelchair?

I grip Clare round her waist and she puts her arms around my neck and I hoist her up. Comfortable? And away we go, slowly because the path is a little slippery, down through the trees.